COLORADO
4-WHEEL DRIVE
ROADS

Acknowledgements
A special thanks to the U.S. Forest Service and
its rangers whose help made this guide possible.

U.S. Geological Survey
Durango Area Chamber Resort
Vail Valley Tourism & Convention Center

DISCLAIMER
CALL A RANGER DISTRICT OFFICE BEFORE PLANNING TO
TRAVEL A 4WD ROAD DESCRIBED IN THIS GUIDE. DESCRIBED
4-WHEEL DRIVE ROADS ARE SUBJECT TO CLOSURE WITHOUT
NOTICE.

Outdoor Books and Maps compiled information for this guide from US
Forest Service data and maps. The information contained in the guide is
intended for trip planning only. Outdoor Books & Maps is not responsible
for getting lost, injury or mishap from use of this guide for other than its
intended use.

ISBN 978-0-930657-40-6

Outdoor Books & Maps
An imprint of Adler Publishing Company, Inc.
P.O. Box 519
Castle Rock, CO 80104
Phone: (800) 660-5107
Fax: (303) 688-4388

COLORADO

4-WHEEL DRIVE
ROADS

A COLORADO 4WD ATLAS

Colorado National Forests Index Map

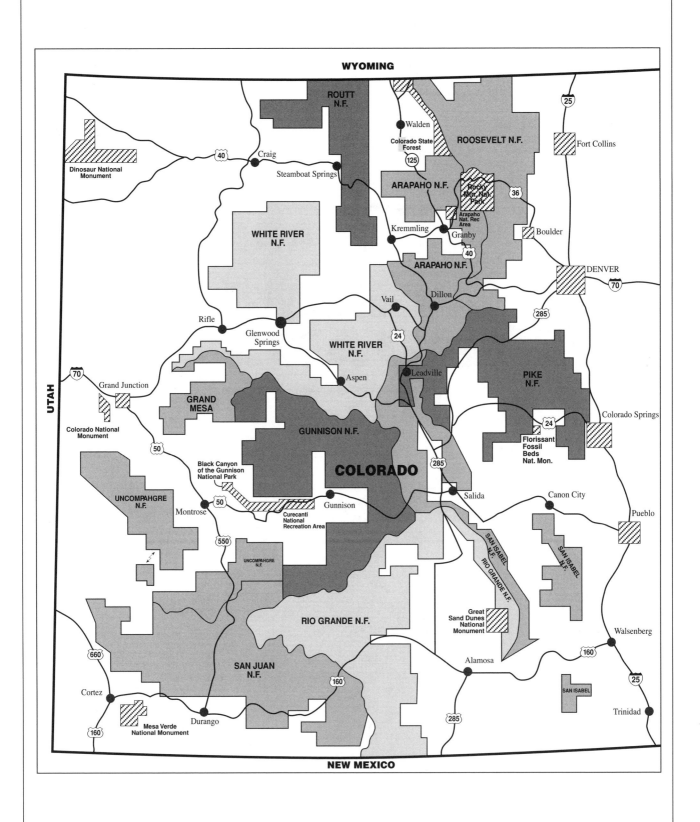

Table Of Contents

Table of Contents

THE BEST FOUR-WHEEL DRIVE ROADS IN COLORADO

A majority of Colorado's open access four-wheel roads are located within its National Forests. These roads travel to scenic and historic areas in the backcountry of the Rocky Mountains. Trails described in this guide lead to historic mining areas, abandoned town sites, mountain passes, remote valleys, and views of majestic mountain ranges.

Four-wheel drive roads described are rated for difficulty and length. Those roads rated most difficult are for the expert driver, other roads are rated down to easy for those seeking a relaxing drive in the backcountry. A map accompanies text, depicting connecting roads, trails, and campgrounds, with towns, physical features and historic sites. The maps and descriptions will guide you to your destination.

All of Colorado's National Forests are included in this guide. The information was compiled from Forest Service data and maps.

Enjoy a safe Colorado experience!

MAP SYMBOL EXPLANATION

P Parking Area	**⌂** Forest Service Facility	**(285)** U.S. Highway	National Forest Area
⊼ Picnic Area	**⬛** Fishing Area	**(126)** State Highway	Water
⚑ Trailhead	**⬛** RV Dump Station	**(9)** County Highway	Trail
⛷ Downhill Ski Area	**♛♛** Restrooms	**(200)** Trail Number	River or Stream
⛴ Boat Launch	**♿** Handicap Accessible	**358** Forest Service Road	Primary Road - Paved
🚲 Bicycle Trail	**🦌** Hunting	**▲** Mountain/Peak	Improved Road - Unpaved
4WD 4WD Road	**△** Campground	**Ⱥ** Colorado Trail	Unimproved Road - 4WD
🏍 Motorcycle Trail	**▨** Towns & Locals	**CDT** Continental Divide Trail	Forest/Wilderness Boundary

MULTIPLE USE ROADS

Mountain Bikes

ATV's and Motorcycles

Horse Back Riding

Hiking

4WD Vehicles

Most 4WD Roads are open to mountain bikes, ATVs, motorcycles, horses, and hikers. Contact a Forest Service Ranger District for travel restrictions.

MAP FEATURES

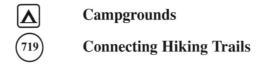

Campgrounds

Connecting Hiking Trails

Other features on the maps include: Roads, Towns, Mountain Passes, Historical Sites, Streams, and Rivers.

NOTE: Maps contained in this guide are accurate but simplified depiction of Forest Service maps. National Forests have tracts of private property within their boundaries that are not shown on the maps in this guide. Observe marked property boundaries and respect the rights of private owners.

A quick reference information bar is located above the 4-wheel drive road text and location map.

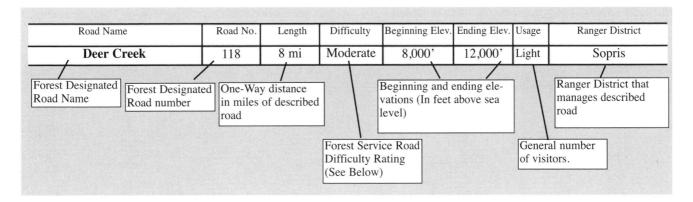

Road Name	Road No.	Length	Difficulty	Beginning Elev.	Ending Elev.	Usage	Ranger District
Deer Creek	118	8 mi	Moderate	8,000'	12,000'	Light	Sopris

Forest Designated Road Name

Forest Designated Road number

One-Way distance in miles of described road

Forest Service Road Difficulty Rating (See Below)

Beginning and ending elevations (In feet above sea level)

General number of visitors.

Ranger District that manages described road

Each 4-wheel drive road has the following information in the text:

ACCESS: Direction and distance to reach describe road.
LENGTH: Distance in miles One-Way unless noted otherwise.
ATTRACTIONS: What to expect when traveling described 4-wheel drive road. General road conditions, scenery and destination.
USE: Number of vehicles that use road during the year. Weekend and holiday traffic account for a large share of 4-wheel drive use.
USGS Maps: 7.5 minute US Geological Survey topographic maps on which road is located.

 Indicates beginning and ending of the described road.

RATING ROAD/TRAIL DIFFICULTY

Four categories for degree of difficulty are as follows:
EASY
A.   Route is mostly level with short uphill/downhill sections.
B.   Excellent to good tread surface and clearance.
C.   Absence of navigational difficulties or hazards.
MODERATE
A.   Routes level to sloping with longer uphill/downhill sections.
B.   Good to fair surface and clearance.
C.   Minimal navigational difficulties or hazards.
MORE DIFFICULT
A.   Route is level to steep with sustained uphill/downhill sections.
B.   Fair to poor surface and clearance.
C.   Short sections involving significant navigational difficulties or hazards.
MOST DIFFICULT
A.   Route is mostly steep with sustained uphill/downhill sections.
B.   Poor to nonexistent tread surface and clearance.
C.   Longer sections involving significant navigational difficulties or hazards.

Any rating (i.e., moderate trail difficulty) found in this guide is based on the above scale which has been established for Forest Service purposes. **Ratings are subjective; use good judgment.** Consider factors such as weather, vehicle, driver experience, and season of year before attempting any 4 wheel drive trip.

ARAPAHO & ROOSEVELT NATIONAL FORESTS

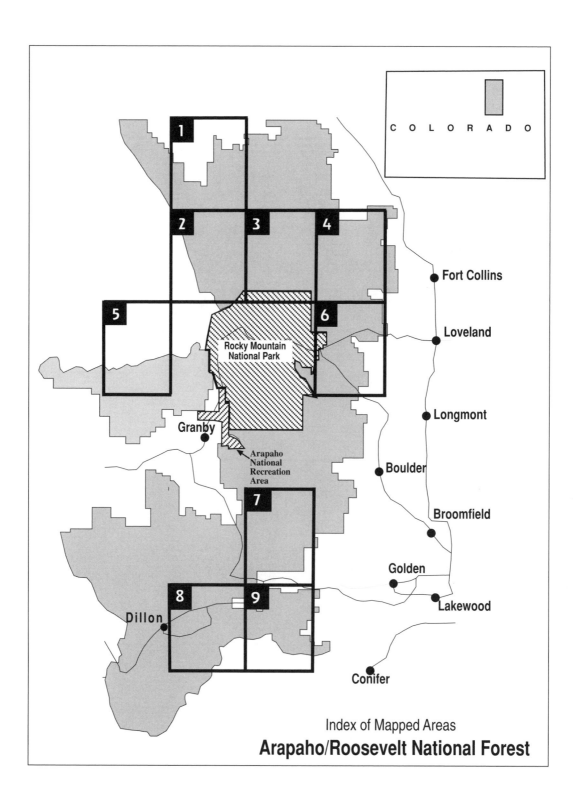

Index of Mapped Areas
Arapaho/Roosevelt National Forest

ARAPAHO & ROOSEVELT NATIONAL FORESTS

Roosevelt National Forest was originally part of the Medicine Bow Forest Reserve established in 1897. It became the Colorado National Forest in 1910. In 1932, President Herbert Hoover renamed it in honor of President Theodore Roosevelt.

Arapaho National Forest, established July 1, 1908 by President Theodore Roosevelt, is named after the plains Indian tribe which frequented the area for summer hunting. Management of the Districts of the Arapaho National Forest is now divided between two national forests; the Boulder, Canyon Lakes, Sulphur, and Clear Creek Districts are administered as part of the Arapaho and Roosevelt National Forests.

Because of their nearness to the high populations of Front Range communities, and area of nationally known significance, the Arapaho and Roosevelt rank among the top national forests for year-round recreation use. They are a major part of the scenic backdrop for tourism in Colorado. Camping, hiking, fishing, hunting, skiing, and other winter sports, as well as driving for pleasure are all popular activities.

CULTURAL HISTORY

The Arapaho and Roosevelt National Forests are rich in cultural history. The first human use probably occurred between 5,000 and 10,000 years B.C. Native tribes occupied the forests and plains up through the early 19th century. Then early day ranching, mining, and agriculture uses developed on the lands. Signs of these early uses are old mines, pack trails, wagon roads, narrow and standard gauge railroad grades, and prospector, trapper, and homestead cabins. If you discover any remnants and relics of our past, leave them in place for the next visitor to appreciate. Cultural artifacts may not be collected from federal lands; please report them to the district office.

WILDERNESS

Seven wildernesses are managed to protect their natural ecosystem. They also offer opportunities for human isolation, solitude, self-reliance, and challenge while hiking cross-country or on trails. Please practice low impact camping techniques and follow local regulations for use of these areas.

ARAPAHO NATIONAL RECREATION AREA (ANRA)

The ANRA covers over 36,000 acres and contains five major lakes, often referred as "the Great Lakes of Colorado." Boating and fishing are primary activities, with many developed campgrounds, picnic areas, and hiking trails available for public recreation and enjoyment.

DISPERSED RECREATION

Although off-road motorized travel is restricted on the Arapaho and Roosevelt National Forests, you can enjoy motorized travel challenges on unimproved roads open to primitive sites for hunting, fishing, camping, picnicking, hiking, horseback riding, and viewing wildlife and scenery. Many roads are passable only by high-clearance, and/or four-wheel-drive vehicles. Within the national forest boundary are many parcels of privately-owned land; please respect the rights of private landowners.

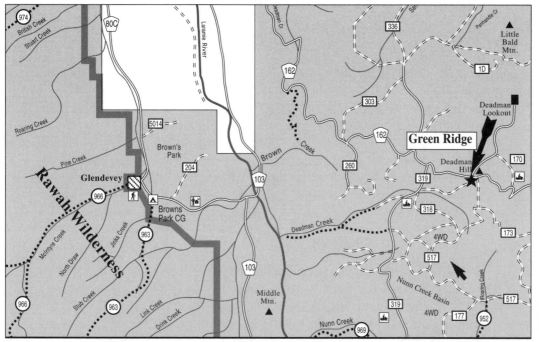

**Arap/Roosevelt
Map 1**

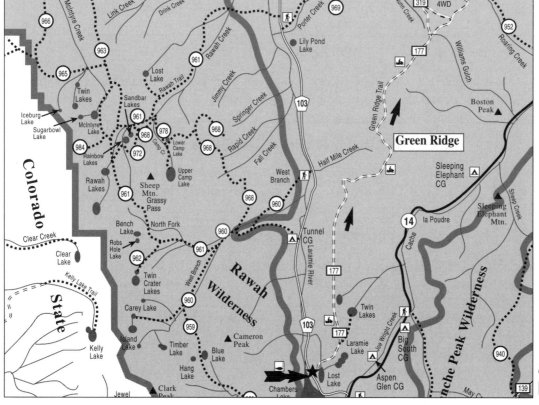

**Arap/Roosevelt
Map 2**

Road Name	Road Number	Length Miles	Difficulty	Beginning Elevation	Ending Elev.	Usage	Ranger District
Green Ridge	177	17	Mod/Diff	8,900'	10,203'	Low	Canyon Lakes

USGS Maps: Deadman, Boston Peak, Chambers Lake.

The trail runs between the Laramie River Road at Chambers Lake to the Bald Mountain Jeep Trail. The Green Ridge Trail begins near Lost Lake, passes Laramie Lake, Twin Lakes and continues north along Green Ridge. The trail travels through lodgepole pine until it reaches the Nunn Creek Basin. Here the country opens up due to past logging activity. A panoramic view of the Medicine Bow Range to the west from the basin.

The Green Ridge Trail is long but scenic off-road trail with narrow sections and numerous mud holes. It is recommended you try this drive late in the summer, when the "water hazards" are easier to navigate. At approximately 12 miles you can continue north on FDR 319 through Nunn Creek Basin to Deadman Road (County Road 162).

The trail is open to hikers, horsemen, 4WD, ATV's and bicyclist's.

Directions from Fort Collins: Travel 59 miles west on Highway 14, 2 miles north on County Road 103 (Laramie River Road). Follow road 1.5 miles to Lost Lake Parking lot. River Trail takes off from north end of parking lot.

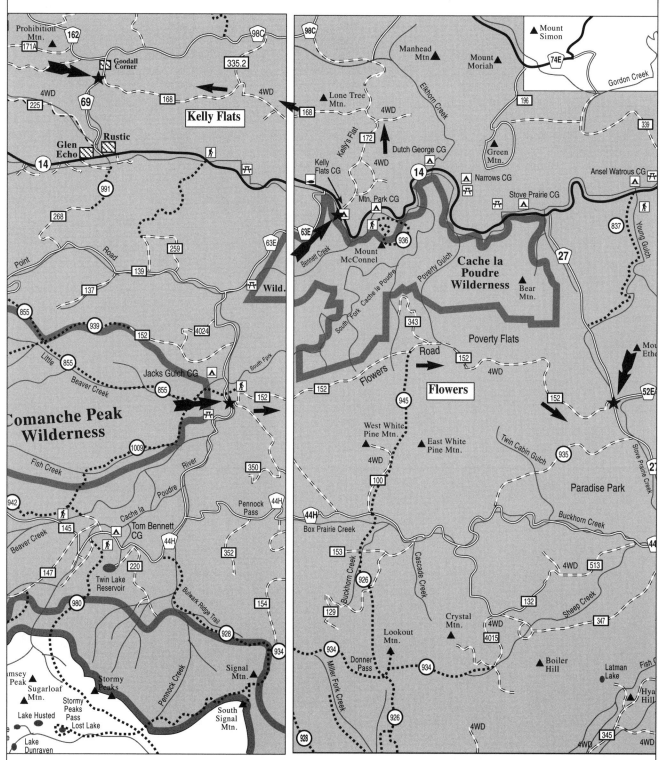

Arap/Roosevelt Map 3

Arap/Roosevelt Map 4

Road Name	Road Number	Length Miles	Difficulty	Beginning Elevation	Ending Elev.	Usage	Ranger District
Kelly Flats	168	10.5	Difficult	6,800'	8,450'	Heavy	Canyon Lakes

USGS Maps: Deadman Lookout, Sand Creek Pass, So. Bald Mtn, Eaton Reservoir.

The Kelly Flats area offers rugged trails with very steep hills and sometimes tricky stream crossings. The trail is narrow and rocky and not recommended for beginners. It does cross private land. Please respect private property. The trail is closed from December 15 to May 15 annually to protect soft roadbed and wintering wildlife. This is a very rugged and difficult trail. Good ground clearance is a must.

The Kelly Flats Trail winds its way from Poudre Canyon up the north rim to the top of Wintersteen Mesa. A panoramic view of Poudre Canyon and parts of Rocky Mountain National Park can be seen from the mesa. As the trail ascends the vegetation changes from sagebrush and grass to ponderosa pine interspersed with meadows.

The first 1.5 miles is the steepest climb. The trail ascends along a narrow rocky bench before dropping off into a drainage. It then climbs steeply up the next ridge for approximately 2 miles, it then levels off onto a grassy meadow before entering the timber. At 3 miles continue west on FDR 168 to graveled road on private property. Leaving private property you enter a stretch that leads to the "chutes". Only high clearance vehicles should attempt to travel "The Chutes", walk this section and decide for yourself if your vehicle can make it. From here it is 3 miles to County Road 69.

Directions from Fort Collins: North on Highway 287 9 miles, 25 miles west on Highway 14 to Kelly Flats Campground.

Road Name	Road Number	Length Miles	Difficulty	Beginning Elevation	Ending Elev.	Usage	Ranger District
Flowers	152	11	Moderate	7,920'	7,326'	Heavy	Canyon Lakes

USGS Maps: Pingree Park, Crystal Mountain, Buckhorn Mountain.

Flowers Road is located on the east side of the Pingree Park Road at Jacks Gulch Campground.

Directions from Fort Collins: Travel north 11 miles on Highway 287 to Highway 14. Travel west on Highway 14 approximately 22 miles to County Road 63E. Turn south (left) on County Road 63E to Jacks Gulch Campground. FDR 152 is located on the east side of Pingree Park Road (County Road 63E). Total length of the road is about 11 miles, running from County Road 63E to Stove Prairie Road.

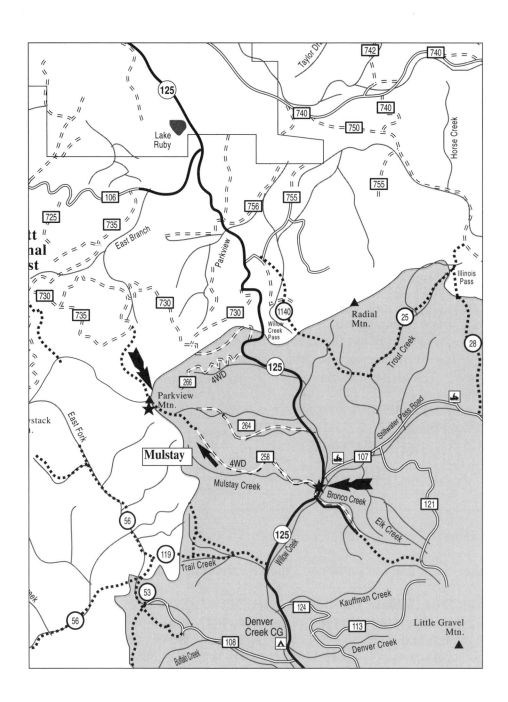

Arap/Roosevelt Map 5

Road Name	Road Number	Length Miles	Difficulty	Beginning Elevation	Ending Elev.	Usage	Ranger District
Mulstay	258	3.6	Moderate	8,800'	12,296'	Heavy	Sulphur

USGS Maps: Radial Mountain, Parkview Mountain.

This intermediate 4WD trail climbs from Highway 125 to 500 ft below the top of Parkview Mountain. It has steep grades, side hills, traverses tight turns through trees and numerous other obstacles. This 3.6 mile route passes through stands of pine, spruce, and fir until it reaches the mountain tundra where the trail ends. Please "Tread Lightly" by stopping here. You may wish to hike to the abandoned fire lookout atop 12,296 foot Parkview Mountain. This trail offers spectacular views. In addition, bighorn sheep, elk and moose are often seen. The best time to drive this route is July through September when the snow is off the road.

A good four-wheel day drive can be made by taking Colorado Hwy 34 north from Grand Lake to Country Rd 491 at the entrance to Rocky Mountain National Park. Turn west and travel to the Arapaho/Roosevelt National Forest boundary. Travel along the North Supply Creek jeep trail until you reach FDR 120, turn left, continue for approximately 6 miles to FDR 123. Turn right and stay on this road over Stillwater Pass to Highway 125. (An optional 4WD side-route to Stillwater Pass off of FDR 123 is signed and begins about 7 miles from the FDR 120/123 junction). Once you reach Highway 125, the Mulstay Road is just 100' to the south. This day trip provides intermediate 4WD and spectacular scenery. Sections of this route from Grand Lake are not open to non-street legal vehicles, due to the use of Colorado highways.

Directions from Granby: West on Highway 40 approximately 3.5 miles to Highway 125. North on Highway 125 approximately 17 miles to Mulstay Road (FDR 258), turn left to begin trip.

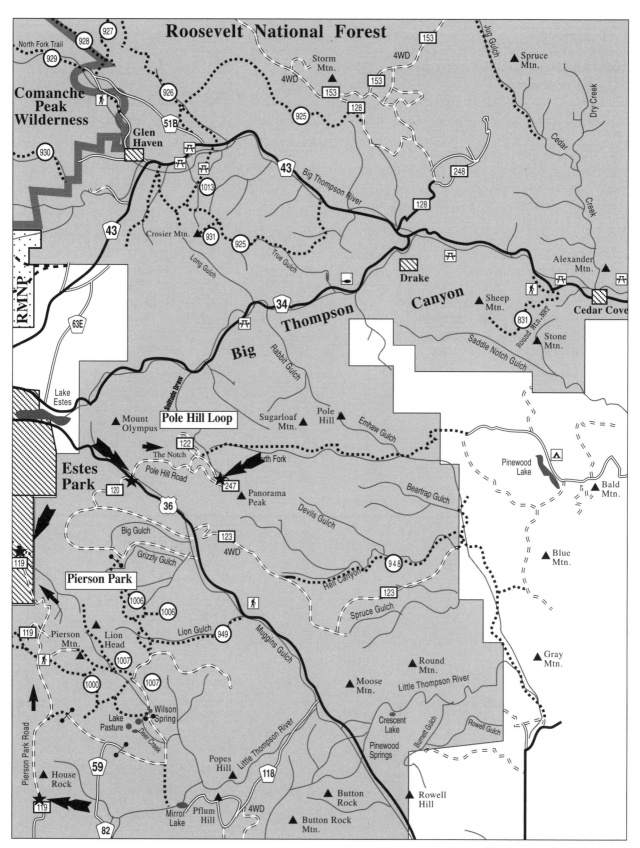

Arap/Roosevelt Map 6

Road Name	Road Number	Length Miles	Difficulty	Beginning Elevation	Ending Elev.	Usage	Ranger District
Pole Hill Loop		10	Moderate	8,000'	9,200'	Heavy	Canyon Lakes

(Panorama Peak/Solitude Creek) FDR 122/247A, B, C
USGS Maps: Panorama Peak.

Pole Hill provides a couple of loop options with a variety of views and terrain's. The Notch Loop (FDR 122A) is located 1.5 miles from the Forest boundary and travels north of the main road (FDR 122). The observation platform at the notch is an excellent point for viewing the Estes Valley, the Mummy Range to the north, Flat Top Mountain and Hallet Peak west along the Continental Divide. Continuing on the road past the observation platform you will descend to Solitude Creek. This north-south canyon receives very little light which makes it cooler, moister place than the surrounding area.

Pole Hill Road starts on private land with many side roads branching off. The National Forest boundary is .9 miles from the highway and is marked by a forest welcome sign. There is no designated parking lot on the Pole Hill road so parking is limited to the roadside. Please keep the roadways clear.

Directions from Estes Park: Travel 3 miles east on Hwy 36 to the top of Park Hill. This entrance puts you on the dirt road signed as Pole Hill Road.

Road Name	Road Number	Length Miles	Difficulty	Beginning Elevation	Ending Elev.	Usage	Ranger District
Pierson Park	119	10	Moderate	7,741'	8,800'	Moderate	Canyon Lakes

USGS Maps: Panorama Peak, Raymond.

Pierson Park Road (FDR 119) runs north and south along the valleys below and east of Twin Sisters Peaks. The road heads to the north ascending and descending several steep hills. Numerous, numbered open side routes lead off to the West. Eventually the road connects to the subdivision in Little Valley. Follow the subdivision roads down to the paved Fish Creek Road, and travel north to Estes Park. It is 10 miles back to Estes Park via Pierson Park on the Pierson Park Road.

Directions from Estes Park: Follow Highway 7 south from Estes Park to Meeker Park and turnoff east on to County Road 82. Follow County Road 82 to FDR 119 (Pierson Park Road).

Plan Your Trip

Consider:
Elevation and Season; Snow at higher elevations can make travel during the spring and early summer impossible. Spring and early summer run-off can make stream crossings difficult. Check conditions with the local Ranger District. Elevations and Ranger District information are provided with trail text.

Four-Wheel Drive Information Arapaho & Roosevelt National Forest Area 970-295-6600

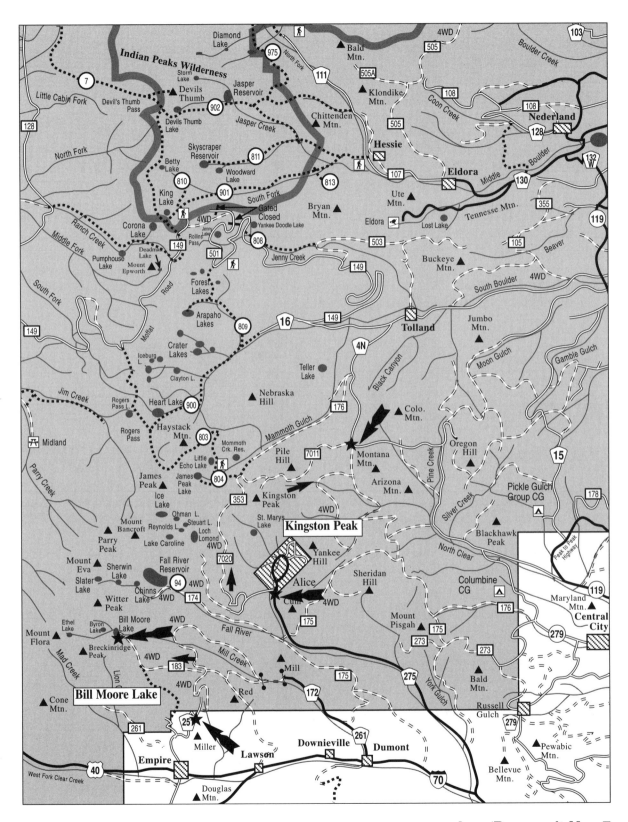

Arap/Roosevelt Map 7

Road Name	Road Number	Length Miles	Difficulty	Beginning Elevation	Ending Elev.	Usage	Ranger District
Bill Moore Lake	183	5	Difficult	10,000'	11,800'	Heavy	Clear Creek

USGS Map: Empire.

Drive north along N. Empire Creek Road (County Road 251), continue on this road to the top of the ridge and follow it to the north. Continue along the east side of the ridge on this road. Turn left at each of the three closely spaced junctions. Turn left (west) onto FDR 183 across a non-forested area, approximately 1.3 miles to where the road descends the northeast-facing slope of Breckenridge Peak to Bill Moore Lake. No motorized vehicles past this point. From Bill Moore Lake you can see the Continental Divide and hike to two lakes between Bill Moore Lake and the Divide. The upper section of this road has several steep rocky sections with poor tread. The upper section is not recommended for stock vehicles.

Directions from Empire: Exit I-70 onto Highway 40 at exit 232 and proceed west into Empire. At the center of town turn right onto Park Ave. This is the only paved road going north out-of-town and is just past the Hard Rock Café. There are many road junctions from this point so it will help if you have a topographic map.

Road Name	Road Number	Length Miles	Difficulty	Beginning Elevation	Ending Elev.	Usage	Ranger District
Kingston Peak	353	8.5	Difficult	8,550'	11,360'	Heavy	Clear Creek

FDR 353/7020/7011
USGS Maps: Empire.

The road travels above timberline with excellent views of Loch Lomond, James Peak and the Indian Peaks. A few steep rocky sections with poor tread gives this road its difficult rating. Snow can block sections of this road until late summer.

Directions from Fall River Road: Exit I-70 at Fall River Road (Exit 238). Stay on Fall River Road till you get to the town of Alice. Turn left onto Alice Road and stay to the right at the first fork in front of the old schoolhouse. Stay on this road for about 1 mile and turn right onto Harris Drive. From Harris Dr. turn left onto Glory Hole Road, then take the first right onto Nebraska, left to Hillsdale, and finally right to Lincoln. Go up Lincoln and Kingston Peak Road takes off to your left about .25 mile up Lincoln Rd. This road continues and come out in the Boulder Ranger District.

Road Name	Road Number	Length Miles	Difficulty	Beginning Elevation	Ending Elev.	Usage	Ranger District
Waldorf	248	6	Moderate	9,800'	11,594'	Moderate	Clear Lake

USGS Maps: Georgetown, Grays Peak.

The upper part of the road follows the old Argentine Central Railroad. The town of Waldorf was a mining and milling camp around 1910. When ore stopped coming in, the town just died. The mines are privately owned, so please respect the owner's property.

Directions from Idaho Springs: Follow I-70 to the Georgetown exit, (228). Follow the signs to Guanella Pass Road. Climb up Guanella Pass for about 3.5 miles. After 3.5 miles, turn right at the corner of a sharp curve onto a dirt road, that is Waldorf Road.

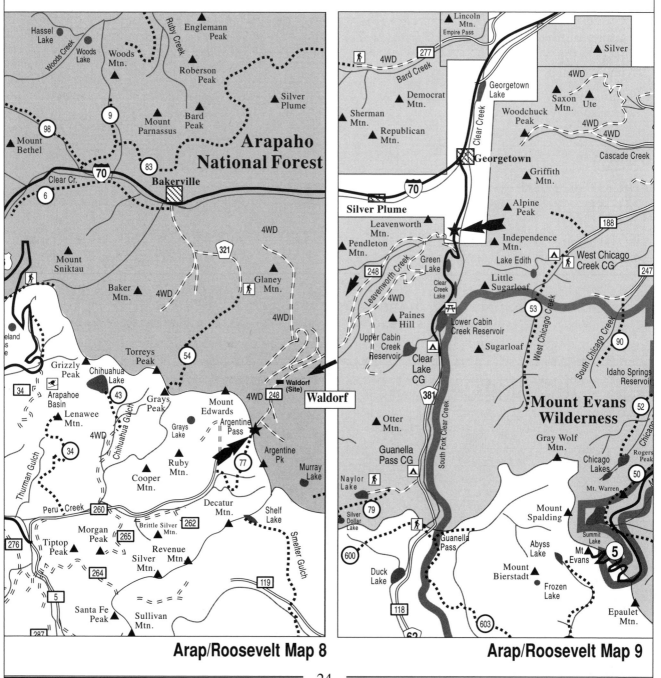

Arap/Roosevelt Map 8

Arap/Roosevelt Map 9

PIKE NATIONAL FOREST

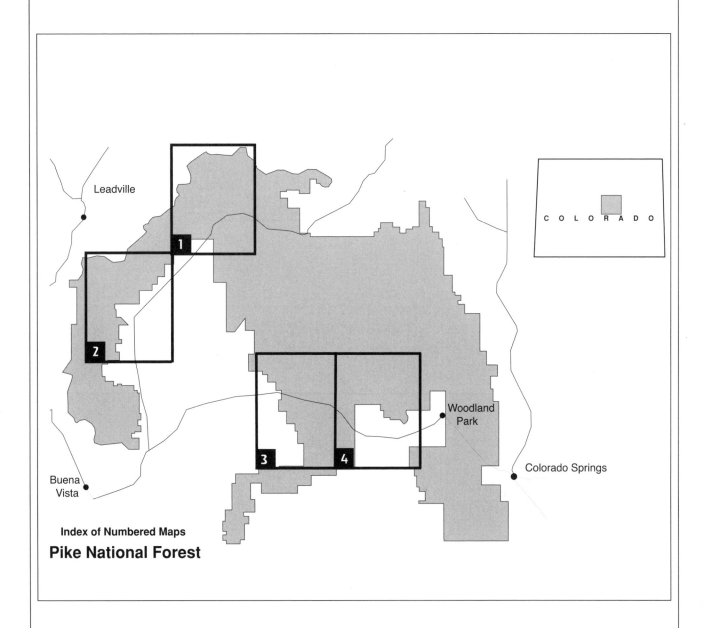

Leadville

1

2

Index of Numbered Maps

Pike National Forest

Buena
Vista

3

4

Woodland
Park

Colorado Springs

C O L O R A D O

PIKE NATIONAL FOREST

The Pike National Forest is one of eleven National Forests in Colorado and one of 154 within the National Forest System of the United States. The 1,106,604 acres of Pike National Forest falls within Clear Creek, Teller, Park, Jefferson, Douglas and El Paso counties.

The recreation resource on the Pike National Forest is widespread and varied. Marking the north end is Mount Evans at 14,264 ft. elevation surrounded by the 73,000 acre Mount Evans Wilderness. Mount Bierstadt, another of Colorado's "fourteeners" at 14,060 ft elevation is also located in the Mount Evans Wilderness. North and west of South Park in the western part of the Forest, are the high elevations of the Mosquito Range from Guanella Pass southward to the Buffalo Peaks country. Except for Geneva and Jefferson Creeks, the recreation resource in this large expanse of Park County remains primarily primitive and undeveloped, accessible mainly by four-wheel drive, horse or foot. Remains of early day mining railroads and stage routes are still easily discernible, further adding to the attraction are more "fourteeners found west of Fairplay: Mount Lincoln 14,286 ft., Mount Bross 14,172 ft., and Mount Democrat 14,148 ft.

Also located in this portion of the Forest is the Windy-Ridge Bristlecone Pine Scenic Area. This scenic area, located about four miles northwest of Alma was established in July 1967 to protect a unique grove of beautifully grotesque and deformed bristlecone pine trees.

East of South Park but still in Park County are the popular fishing and camping areas of Lost Park, Tarryall Creek, and Elevenmile Canyon. Most of the Pike National Forest in this area remains undeveloped allowing the visitor to enjoy his recreation experience in a near natural environment.

Tarryall Creek and Lost Park are jump-off points for the Lost Creek Wilderness where motorized travel is prohibited. This approximately 106,000 acre area provides a place within an hours drive of the metropolitan area of Colorado Springs where an individual can experience a wilderness setting. The Lost Creek Wilderness contains bold outcrops of Pikes Peak granite that have been carved into an infinite variety of forms and shapes by the forces of erosion. Great dome like forms, spires, turrets and arete crests characterize the landscape. Talus slopes of huge boulders are common. Stream courses are tortuous and have in places carved underground channels through the talus debris. In addition to its great scenic beauty, the area offers the geologist, professional or amateur, an outstanding opportunity to study the effects of erosion of granite in a semi-arid climate.

Manitou Park is a popular area on the Pike National Forest in Teller County. This picturesque area of ponderosa pines and grass serves mainly as a "base camp" for visitors to the Pikes Peak Region. Numerous Forest Service campgrounds and commercial campgrounds are used to capacity from the middle of June to Labor Day. Manitou Lake Picnic Ground in the area is heavily used year around for fishing and picnicking. The remainder of National Forest land in Pikes Peak rising to 14,110 ft. elevation is the most dominant and well known recreation attraction on the National Forest in El Paso County. The Gold Camp and Rampart Range Roads are popular recreation roads just west of Colorado Springs on the Front Range. They provide opportunities for camping, picnicking and sightseeing as well as circle trips connecting Colorado Springs, Cripple Creek and Woodland Park.

The Pike National Forest offers sightseeing, hiking, lake fishing, boating, picnicking and cross-country skiing at the 500 acre Rampart Reservoir, a 60 minute drive from Colorado Springs. Also, at the area is the Business and Professional Women's Club Nature Trail designed for wheelchairs and with signing in Braille.

The Devil's Head Lookout Tower in Douglas County, the last operational lookout on the Front Range, sets on the highest point on the Rampart Range. This tower is accessible by the 1.3 mile long foot Devil's Head National Recreation Trail.

Road Name Number	Road Miles	Length	Difficulty Elevation	Beginning Elev.	Ending	Usage	Ranger District
Red Cone Peak	565	10	More Diff	9,750'	12,801'	Moderate	South Platte

USGS Maps: Montezuma, Jefferson.

Special attractions include historic mine sites (not for exploration), view of Hall Valley and points east. Possible dispersed campsites. Water sources enroute include north fork of the South Platte, not for drinking.

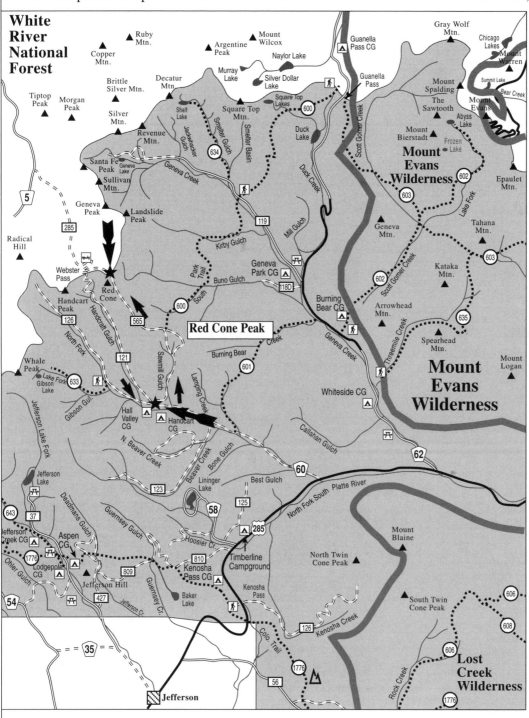

Possible hazards include rockslides at top. Vegetation includes spruce, aspen at lower elevation with tundra and boulder fields at higher elevations. Round trip is usually only possible in August and September because the snow does not melt off on Webster Pass until then. After September, new snow has accumulated. (Call the Ranger District for date of gate closing and opening) Return down to Hall Valley on rugged FDR 121.

Directions from US 285: US 285 to Hall Valley (CR 60) turn off. On County Road 60 travel .25 mile past Halls Valley Campground to Webster Pass and Red Cone Pass sign. Right-of-way conditions include crossing mine claims.

Pike Map 1

Road Name	Road Number	Length Miles	Difficulty	Beginning Elevation	Ending Elev.	Usage	Ranger District
Breakneck Pass	175	8	Moderate	9,706'	11,450'	Light	South Park

USGS Maps: Fairplay West.

Breakneck Pass Road (FDR 175) is an access point to Sheep Park and Twelve-Mile Creek areas southwest of Sheep Ridge. The road is accessible for high clearance vehicles and one steep section of road requires four-wheel drive.

The road was originally developed by miners to access the valley below the Mosquito Range. Round Hill (11,243 feet) lies west of the intersection of Weston Pass Road and Breakneck Pass Road. The road follows its northern flanks as it climbs to the pass. As the road reaches the pass it intersects with Round Hill Road which is gated on the southern side of Round Hill. On the western side of the pass Breakneck Road leads into the Sheep Creek drainage. The pass is usually open mid-May to mid-October, weather dependent.

Directions from Fairplay: From Fairplay drive south on Highway 285 for 4.4 miles. Turn right on County Road 5 and begin traveling west. Breakneck Pass can be reached by traveling on FDR 175.

Road Name	Road Number	Length Miles	Difficulty	Beginning Elevation	Ending Elev.	Usage	Ranger District
Browns Pass	176	7.5	Mod/Diff	10,000'	11,372'	Light	South Park

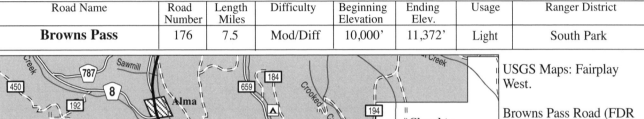

USGS Maps: Fairplay West.

Browns Pass Road (FDR 176) is a steep and narrow dirt road. Travelers should proceed at their own risk. A high-clearance four-Wheel drive vehicle is strongly recommended. This pass is usually open mid-May to mid-October.

Browns Pass Road is located north of Breakneck Pass and leads into the same drainage. The pass lies near timberline between Sheep Park and Sheep Ridge. Visitors who reach the pass can see Horseshoe Mountain (13,898 feet) directly to the west. Horseshoe Mountain is a glacial cirque, otherwise known as the birthplace of glaciers.

Directions from Fairplay: From Fairplay drive south 3.2 miles on Highway 285 to County Road 20. County Road 20 will eventually turn into FDR 176, also known as Brown Pass Road.

Pike Map 2

Road Name	Road Number	Length Miles	Difficulty	Beginning Elevation	Ending Elev.	Usage	Ranger District
China Wall	212	2.5	Easy	8,760'	8,400'	Moderate	South Park

Beginning Elevation: 8,760 Feet - Intersection with Tarryall Road.
USGS Maps: Tarryall.

Beautiful rock outcroppings dominate the scenery throughout this well known rock climbing area. You may primitive camp in the area if you wish. However, Spruce Grove Campground is just 2 miles further north on County Road 77. China Wall Road is short; approximately 2.5 miles one-way. It begins on the Tarryall Road and descends into the Tarryall Creek drainage. A high clearance 4WD vehicle is recommended.

An interesting side route is Forest Road 504, a 4WD route located east on approx. 10 miles on FDR 211. This road takes you through yet more rock formations, then down a VERY STEEP 4WD hill, and then through some rolling hills to the Tarryall Road.

Directions from Highway 24:
From US Highway 24 (west of Lake George) turn north onto County Road 77 (Tarryall Road). Follow County Road 77 about 12 miles to the China Wall turn off (FDR 212).

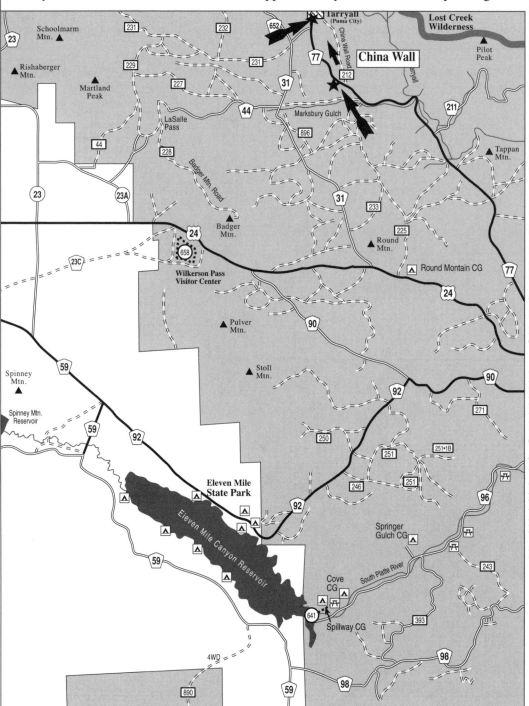

Pike Map 3

Road Name	Road Number	Length Miles	Difficulty	Beginning Elevation	Ending Elev.	Usage	Ranger District
LaSalle Pass	CR 44	6.5	Moderate	8,776'	8,907'	Light	South Park

Length: 6.5 miles, (4.4 miles to LaSalle Pass).
Ending Elevation: 8,907 Feet - Summit LaSalle Pass.
USGS Maps: Glentivar.

LaSalle Pass Road is located north of Wilkerson Pass. It leads through the Puma Hills immediately north of Badger Mountain and accesses upper Tarryall Creek from South Park. LaSalle Pass has an excellent view of South Park, the Sawatch and Mosquito Ranges. The pass is open during the summer, spring and fall months-weather dependent. High clearance vehicle. The road to Badger Mountain (FDR 228) is rough but moderate drive. Sections of road pass through private property, leave gates as you found them.

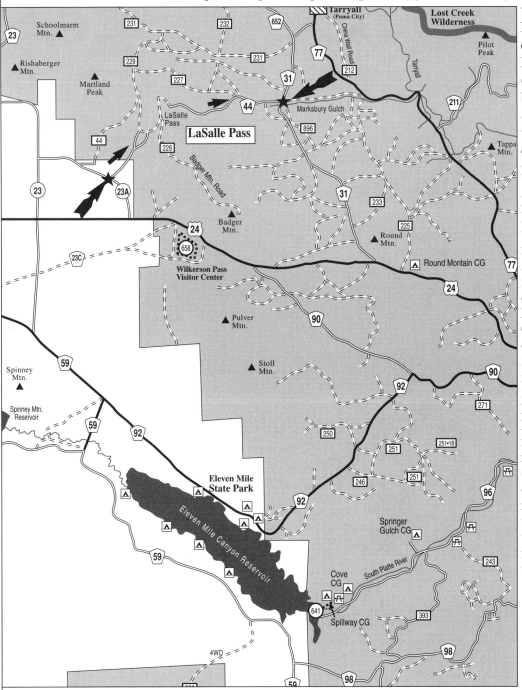

Directions from Highway 24: Drive west on Highway 24 from Lake George. Approximately .5 miles west of the entrance for Round Mountain Campground turn left on to County Road 31. Travel almost 5 miles or until Road 31 intersects County Road 44. This is LaSalle Pass Road; follow is westward to reach the pass. (County Road 31 is a dirt road that is not recommended during wet conditions, otherwise accessible by four-wheel drive vehicles.)

Pike Map 3

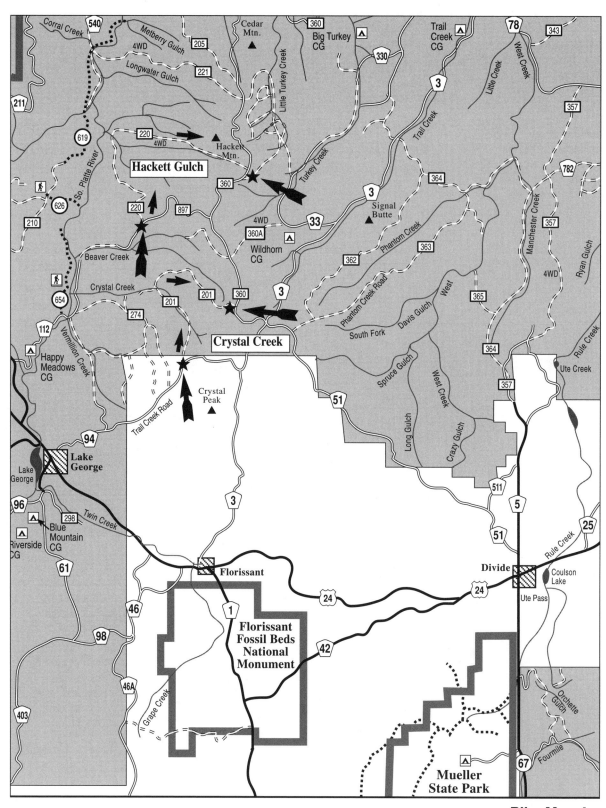

Pike Map 4

Road Name	Road Number	Length Miles	Difficulty	Beginning Elevation	Ending Elev.	Usage	Ranger District
Crystal Creek	201	5.1	Easy/More Diff	8,800'	8,400''	Moderate	South Park

USGS Maps: Hackett Mountain.

Crystal Creek Road (FDR 201) is located west of the West Creek area. A series of motorized trails are designated in this region for ATV's and motorcycles. Intermingled with the motorized trails are 4WD roads, Crystal Creek Road is one of these roads. Mining and rock hunting activities are evident throughout the area.

Directions from Highway 24: Travel west on Highway 24 from Colorado Springs. Immediately east of Lake George turn north onto Trail Creek Road, State Highway 94. Follow the Trail Creek Road to its intersection with Crystal Creek Road (FDR 201). Alternate access is past the Forest Service work center, from the Cedar Mountain Road (FDR 360).

Road Name	Road Number	Length Miles	Difficulty	Beginning Elevation	Ending Elev.	Usage	Ranger District
Hackett Gulch	220	11.2	Very Diff	8,800'	9,203'	High	South Park

Very difficult, for expert drivers only.
USGS Maps: Hackett Mountain.

The Hackett Gulch area encompasses the beautiful canyon along the South Platte River. Fishing, camping and motorized recreation are popular pastimes along this stretch of the river. Massive rock formations, heavily forested canyon walls and spectacular views dominate the area. Hackett Gulch Road in conjunction with FDR 897 forms a loop that eventually comes back to Cedar Mountain Road. The area is also used by snowmobilers in the winter.

From FDR 360 the first 1.5 miles is easy it then becomes steep hillsides with rocky loose tread conditions that make this road very difficult. At the end of this section is Hackett Mountain. It is recommended you take the bypass just before the rock. It is necessary to ford the Platte River which can be impassable in early spring or during periods of heavy rain. Vehicle Accessibility: High-clearance 4WD.

Directions from Colorado Springs: Driving west on Highway 24 you will reach an intersection in Florissant. Turn north on to Highway 31. Within .5 miles Hwy 31 intersects with County Road 3. Turn north on County Road 3 and follow it for several miles. The second left you can make from County Road 3 will be FDR 360, which is also, Cedar Mountain Road. Follow FDR 360 to the left for approximately 5.5 miles. You will see FDR 220 to the left; this is Hackett Gulch Road.

Special Note on Crystal Creek and Hackett Gulch: Currently these trails are closed due to the Hayman Fire of August 2002. Teller County has an easement from the Forest Service for the roads through the burn area, and the county has a crew of volunteers repairing the roads in order to reopen them. Unfortunately the county does not have a time frame yet for reopening they roads. They hope to have all the forest roads in the area reopened for public recreation as soon as possible. Contact Teller County Department of Transportation for details.

Rampart Reservoir near Woodland Park

ROUTT NATIONAL FOREST

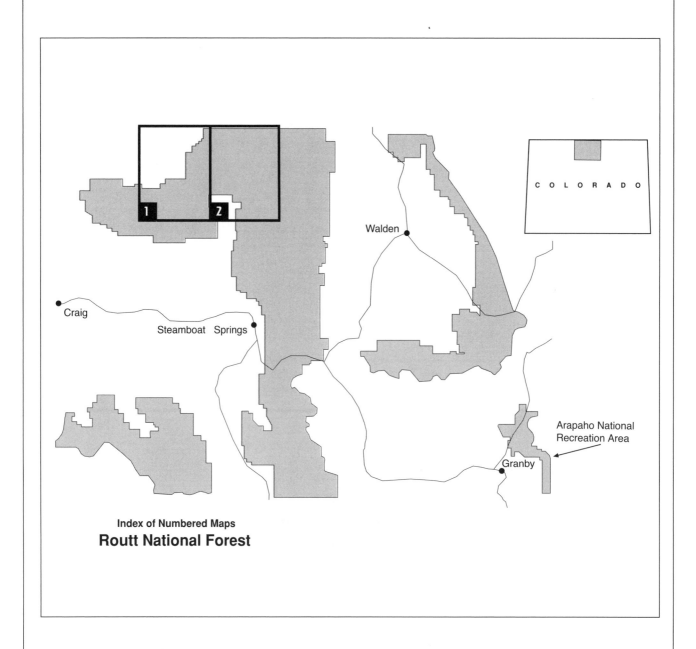

Index of Numbered Maps
Routt National Forest

ROUTT NATIONAL FOREST

Established by President Theodore Roosevelt in 1905 as the Park Range Forest Reserve, the Routt National Forest includes 1,126,346 acres of Federal lands within its boundaries. The Forest is named in memory of Col. John N. Routt, the last territorial and first State Governor of Colorado.

The Continental Divide and spectacular peaks of the 160,568 acre Mt. Zirkel Wilderness split the major watersheds of the National Forest. On the East, the North Park region is drained by the North Platte River, a tributary of the Missouri and Mississippi; and on the west, the Yampa River flows to the Green and Colorado. On the southeast corner of the Forest the 47,140 acre Sarvis Creek Wilderness Area was created in 1993. Elevations are high, ranging from 7,000 feet in the irrigated valley's to 13,000 feet along the Divide. Heavy winter snows are common, and frost may occur anytime during the short summer season.

Modern tourists and travelers enjoy the beautiful drive over Rabbit Ears Pass on U.S. Highway 40, and camping facilities are located near the highway and at other spots throughout the Forest. Years ago, the "ears" stone pinnacles near the pass were landmarks for Indians and late "mountain men", trappers, and settlers.

Elk and deer are residents of the Forest during the warmer months, and drift to the lower elevations with less snow during the winter. Bear, bighorn sheep, mountain lion, coyote, and antelope may be observed on occasion, and beaver, marmot, ptarmigan, osprey, eagle, and other smaller species are present in varying numbers. The hiker has little to fear from resident wildlife populations, Black bears, mountain lion and poisonous snakes are rarely seen. Long famous for hunting and fishing the Forest still provides this opportunity under seasons set by the Colorado Division of Wildlife. A valid Colorado license is required for hunting or fishing.

The Forest Supervisor, responsible for overall administration of the National Forest, is located at 29587 West U.S. 40, near Steamboat Springs. District Rangers are located at Steamboat Springs, Walden and Yampa. Information or assistance is available at any of these locations.

Road Name	Road Number	Length Miles	Difficulty	Beginning Elevation	Ending Elev.	Usage	Ranger District
Elkhorn Mountain	508	8	Moderate	8,400'	9,550'	Moderate	Hahns Peak/Bears Ears

USGS Maps: Elkhorn Mountain.

Westward on FDR 508 for approximately 3 miles to Elkhorn Mountain. Continue westward approximately 5 miles down to FDR 551, south on FDR 551 to FDR 129. Road has numerous areas of muddy and rocky spots with some narrow sections.

Directions from Hahns Peak Village: Northwest on FDR 129 approximately 7 miles to FDR 550, north approximately 12 miles to FDR 508.

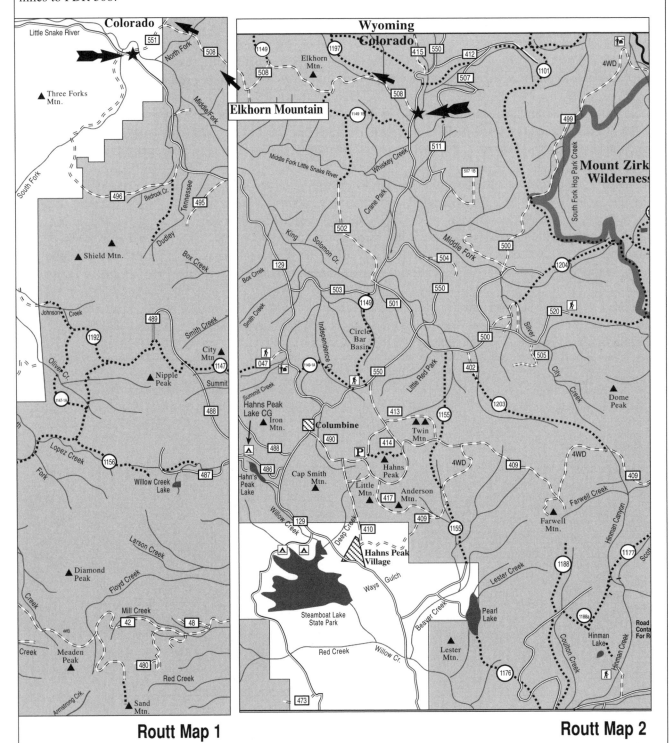

Routt Map 1

Routt Map 2

Road Name	Road Number	Length Miles	Difficulty	Beginning Elevation	Ending Elev.	Usage	Ranger District
Farwell Mountain	409	8	Moderate	8,400'	8,000'	Moderate	Hahns Peak/Bears Ears

USGS: Hahns Peak, Farwell Mountain.

Road is usually muddy through Beaver Basin area, then rough rocky road to Farwell Mountain. Then numerous areas of either rocky or muddy spots the rest of the way. The road can become slick when wet, use caution on the side hills.

Diamond Park is approximately 6 miles east. Road is subject to closure, contact the Forest Service before planning trip (Hahns Peak/ Bears Ear Ranger District 1-970-879-1870).

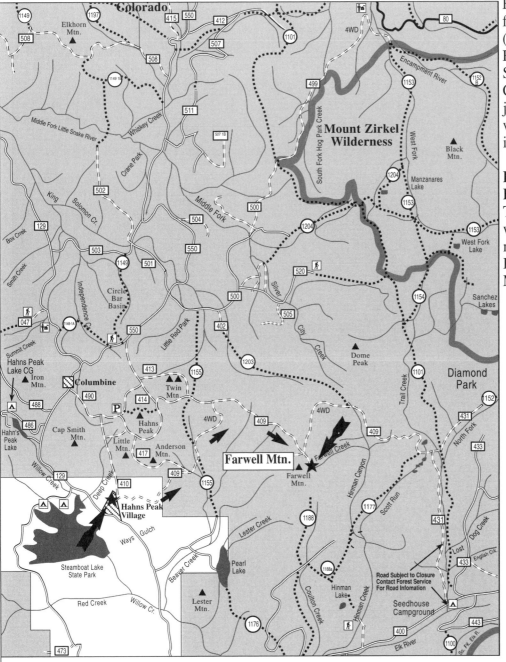

Forest Road FDR 431 from FDR 409 (Approx. 4 miles) to FDR 400 to Seedhouse Campground is subject to closure and will be reconfigured in the future.

Directions from Hahns Peak Village: Take FDR 409 eastward approximately 8 miles through Beaver Basin up to Farwell Mountain.

Routt Map 2

SAN ISABEL NATIONAL FOREST

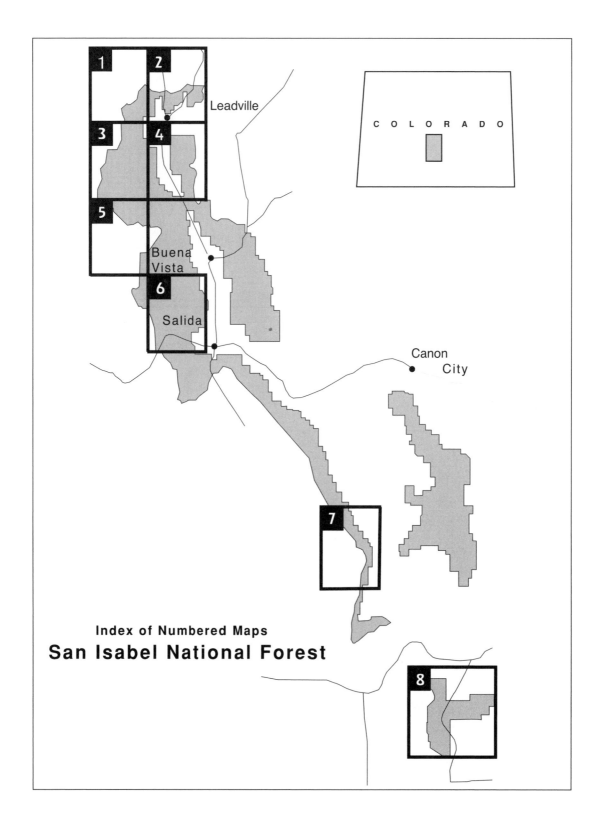

1
2
Leadville
3
4
5
Buena
Vista
6
Salida
Canon
City
7

COLORADO

Index of Numbered Maps
San Isabel National Forest

8

SAN ISABEL NATIONAL FOREST

Welcome to the San Isabel National Forest, one of eleven National Forests in Colorado. The Forest includes over one million acres of beautiful scenery with snow-capped mountains, wildflowers, autumn colors, mountain lakes, and clear blue skies to enjoy.

Prior to the establishment of the Forest, the presence of Indians, Spanish land grants, homesteading and the discovery of gold were important in shaping the land. The lands originally set aside as a Forest Reserve in 1902 were renamed San Isabel National Forest in March 1907. From 1907 until 1945 the Forest grew steadily in size, as several other Forests and additional lands were integrated into the San Isabel National Forest. Today the Forest is administered by three District Offices and the Supervisor's Office.

The Forest is bounded on the west and north by the Continental Divide and on the east by the Pike National Forest. The Wet Mountains, Collegiate Peaks, Sawatch Range, Spanish Peaks and the Sangre De Cristo provide a variety of scenery. Elevations range from a low of 5,860 feet to 14,433. The highest point is Mount Elbert, Colorado's highest peak. The high elevations account for the comfortable summer temperatures and year round snow on the higher peaks.

Another attraction is the Arkansas Headwaters Recreation Area. The Recreation Area that stretches for 148 miles along the Arkansas begins in Leadville and provides numerous opportunities for fishing, rafting, picnicking and camping. The Bureau of Land Management and the Colorado State Parks manages the Recreation Area.

Black bear, mule deer, elk, bighorn sheep, mountain goats, turkey, mountain lions are among the animals and birds that make their homes within the Forest.

Today, almost 800 miles of trails, ski areas, nineteen peaks over 14,000 feet, scenic byways, numerous roads and highways, campgrounds and picnic areas provide challenges and opportunities for everyone.

All this is yours to enjoy, but please, do so in ways that will allow others to enjoy it today and tomorrow!

Road Name	Road Number	Length Miles	Difficulty	Beginning Elevation	Ending Elev.	Usage	Ranger District
Hagerman Pass	105	22.5	Moderate	10,200'	9,000'	Heavy	Leadville

USGS Maps: Homestake Reservoir, Nast.

Visitors traveling the entire Hagerman Pass Road from Turquoise Lake Road (FDR 105) to Fryingpan Lakes Road (State Highway 4) drive 22.5 miles. The western side of the pass from Turquoise Lake Road to the summit of Hagerman Pass (FDR 104) is 7.3 miles. Hagerman Pass begins on the south side of Turquoise Lake about 4 miles west of the Sugar Loaf Dam. It continues on the western side of the pass past Ruedi Reservoir and onto State Highway 82 at Basalt.

Although not one of the more difficult passes in the area four-wheel drive vehicles are highly recommended. At the top of the pass (12,075 feet) there are great views of the Turquoise Lake area to the east and the Hunter-Fryingpan Wilderness to the southwest. It's a good scenic drive for viewing wildflowers, pikas and marmots. Just east of the pass look to the south over Hagerman Lake to see remnants of the Colorado Midland Railroad, which blazed through the wilderness to reach the silver mining town of Aspen in 1887.

Directions from Leadville: From Harrison Street turn on to West Sixth Street to County Road 4. Make a right on to County Road 4, at the "T" and drive to the Sugarloaf Dam site. From the dam drive 4 miles to Hagerman Pass Road (FDR 105). Hagerman Pass Road will be on the left or south side of County Road 9.

Directions from Carbondale: From Carbondale travel east on Highway 82 to Basalt. Turn left at the stoplight and travel through Basalt following the main street through town. This road is the Fryingpan River Road and travels out of Basalt following the Fryingpan River. From Basalt travel 27 miles until the pavement ends turn left at the fork in the road and then left again, staying on road FDR 105. Travel on the all-weather road for 11 miles and take the left fork to Hagerman Pass. Here the road becomes suitable for high clearance vehicles only.

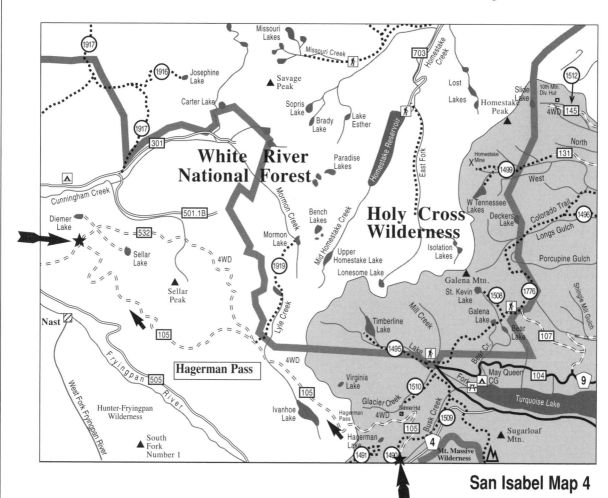

San Isabel Map 4

Road Name	Road Number	Length Miles	Difficulty	Beginning Elevation	Ending Elev.	Usage	Ranger District
Birdseye Gulch Loop		17	Mod/Diff.	10,569'	10,200'	Heavy	Leadville

Elevation Gain: 1,800 Feet.
USGS Maps: Leadville.

This 17-mile loop is usually ridden by mountain bikers, but horseback riders, hikers, ATV riders and motorcyclist's may want to try this route. Begin in Leadville at East 7th and Harrison. Follow East 7th Street past the Matchless Mine where it will turn to dirt. Stay on the main road staying left at the two forks and continue up toward Mosquito Pass. At the saddle before the high switchbacks begin you will take a left and travel north down Birdseye Gulch. You will follow this road through a major bog and past the railroad tracks to Colorado Hwy 91. At this point, take a left and travel along the highway back to Leadville. You may want to try this route from Highway 91 and ending in town.

Directions from Leadville: Begin in Leadville at East 7th and Harrison.

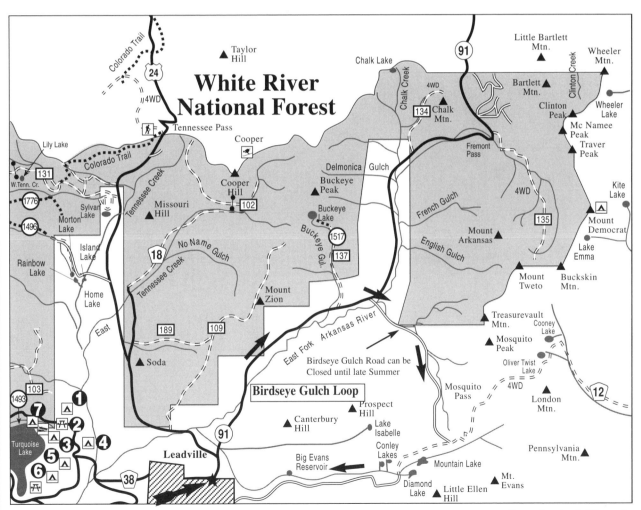

San Isabel Map 2

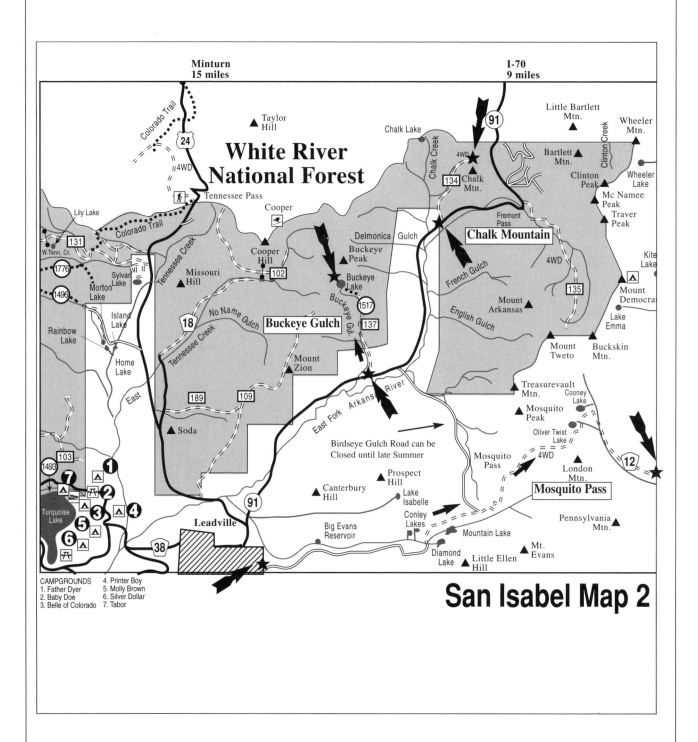

Minturn
15 miles

I-70
9 miles

Colorado Trail

4WD

24

Taylor
Hill

Chalk Lake

91

Little Bartlett
Mtn.

Wheeler
Mtn.

Clinton Creek

White River
National Forest

Chalk Creek

4WD

134

Chalk
Mtn.

Bartlett
Mtn.

Clinton
Peak

Wheeler
Lake

Mc Namee
Peak

Tennessee Pass

Cooper

Delmonica   Gulch

Fremont
Pass

Chalk Mountain

Traver
Peak

Lily Lake

131

Colorado Trail

Cooper
Hill

102

Buckeye
Peak

Buckeye
Lake

French Gulch

4WD

135

Kite
Lake

W.Tenn. Cr.

1776

1496

Sylvan
Lake

Morton
Lake

Tennessee Creek

Missouri
Hill

No Name Gulch

Buckeye Gul.

1517

137

English Gulch

Mount
Arkansas

Mount
Democra

Mount
Democrat

Island
Lake

Buckeye Gulch

Lake
Emma

Rainbow
Lake

Home
Lake

East

Tennessee Creek

18

Mount
Zion

189   109

Soda

East Fork Arkansas River

Mount
Tweto

Buckskin
Mtn.

Treasurevault
Mtn.

Cooney
Lake

103

1493

7

1

2

Birdseye Gulch Road can be
Closed until late Summer

Mosquito
Peak

Oliver Twist
Lake

4WD

London
Mtn.

12

3

4

Turquoise
Lake

5

6

Canterbury
Hill

Prospect
Hill

Lake
Isabelle

Mosquito
Pass

Mosquito Pass

Pennsylvania
Mtn.

Leadville

Conley
Lakes

38

91

Big Evans
Reservoir

Mountain Lake

Diamond
Lake

Little Ellen
Hill

Mt.
Evans

CAMPGROUNDS
1. Father Dyer
2. Baby Doe
3. Belle of Colorado
4. Printer Boy
5. Molly Brown
6. Silver Dollar
7. Tabor

San Isabel Map 2

Road Name	Road Number	Length Miles	Difficulty	Beginning Elevation	Ending Elev.	Usage	Ranger District
Mosquito Pass		15.2	More Diff.	10,600'	9,800'	Heavy	Leadville

USGS Maps: Climax, Leadville North.

Road starts at end of pavement at 7th St. east of Leadville. Come to a road junction stay left, cross Evans Creek, continue you will cross Evans Creek again. Come to road junction, stay left and the 4 WD road begins. Cross drainage of Mountain and Diamond Lakes. Watch for road junction at switchback, continue NE around switchback. Continue east-northeast on main road past junction with Birdseye Gulch road. After a series of switchbacks, stay on main road at junctions, at 6 miles you will come to the top of the pass. There is a monument to Father Dyer. Continue down road, you will come to junction with FDR 696, stay left, east, toward north side of London Mountain. Pass road junctions, stay right (ENE). Continue across Mosquito Creek at approx. 8.25 miles look for junction, turn right (SE) on FDR 12. Further ahead you will see London Mill site on west side of road. Continue on road, American Mill site will be on the southwest. Continue SE on FDR 12 to the end of 4WD road. Pass several road junctions; stay on main (graded) road. Cross the South Platte River and continue to Junction Hwy 9, which is SE of Alma. Road as described is not in a national forest. Near Oliver Twist Lake you enter Pike National Forest. Some years the pass is not passable due to snow.

One way (end of pavement on East 7th St. in Leadville to Highway 9 in Park County). This is the highest vehicular pass in North America. This road is never plowed and often opens very late in the summer. Be sure to check with the Leadville Chamber of Commerce, Leadville Ranger District or South Park Ranger District to assure that it is passable before beginning your trip.

Directions from Leadville: From the traffic light at 6th street travel north along Highway 24 for one block. Take a right (east) on East 7th St. continue up Evans Gulch to Mosquito Pass.

NOTE: West side of pass is not on National Forest Land - East side of pass is in Pike NF, South Park Ranger District.

Road Name	Road Number	Length Miles	Difficulty	Beginning Elevation	Ending Elev.	Usage	Ranger District
Chalk Mountain	134	2.9	Moderate	10,603'	12,017'	Low	Leadville

USGS Maps: Climax.

Chalk Mountain Road leads users through old growth spruce/fir forest and alpine meadows. The road provides good views of Mount of the Holy Cross, Chicago Ridge and Climax Molylbdenum Company mining operations. During the 1970's, Chalk Mountain served a site of an observatory constructed by Louisiana State University.

Directions from Leadville: Chalk Mountain Road begins 9 miles north of Leadville on Highway 91 and ends at the top of Chalk Mountain.

Road Name	Road Number	Length Miles	Difficulty	Beginning Elevation	Ending Elev.	Usage	Ranger District
Buckeye Gulch	137	2	Mod/Diff	10,150'	10,800'	Moderate	Leadville

USGS Maps: Leadville North, Climax.

The section of the road which can be driven with a four-wheel drive vehicle begins 4.5 miles north of Leadville on Colorado 91 and ends on Buckeye Trail (FDT 1517) about .25 mile before the lake. A moderate to difficult road with some rough, rocky spots. Buckeye Gulch Road follows the stream through dense, lush willows and shrubs. The first part of this road crosses private land. Please stay on the roadway and be respectful of private property.

Directions from Leadville: Drive north on Highway 91 approximately 4.5 miles turn left on to Buckeye Gulch Road.

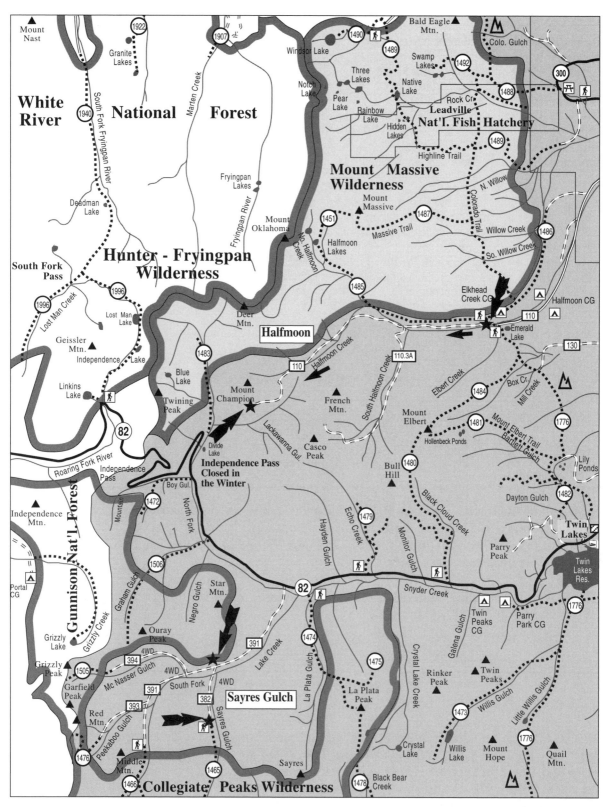

San Isabel Map 3

Road Name	Road Number	Length Miles	Difficulty	Beginning Elevation	Ending Elev.	Usage	Ranger District
Halfmoon	110	7.8	Difficult	9,547'	12,450'	Heavy	Leadville

Halfmoon Road FDR 110/South Halfmoon Road FDR 110.3A.
USGS Maps: Mt. Massive, Mt. Elbert, Independence Pass.

Halfmoon Road (FDR 110) begins approximately 1 mile west of Highway 24 on FDR 300 (Fish Hatchery Road) and ends on private land at the Champion Mine. The road is passable by passenger car for the first 7 miles to the Mt. Massive Trailhead. The remaining road is a rough, four-wheel drive road along the valley floor. The four-wheel drive section of the road is a gradual climb with a few steep pitches. South Halfmoon Road (FDR 110.3A) 2 miles west of Mt. Massive and Mt. Elbert Trailheads on FDR 110 travels south for 4.6 miles ending at Iron Mike Mine. Very rough 4WD road with a few difficult stream crossings. Experienced 4WD drivers only. Climbs into large open basin.

Directions from Leadville: Drive 3 miles southwest from Leadville on Highway 24. Make a right on to Highway 300 toward the Leadville National Fish Hatchery. Drive approximately 1 mile on Highway 300 to State Highway 11, which eventually turns into Halfmoon Road (FDR 110).

Road Name	Road Number	Length Miles	Difficulty	Beginning Elevation	Ending Elev.	Usage	Ranger District
Sayres Gulch	382	2.1	Difficult	10,560'	10,920'	Moderate	Leadville

USGS Map: Independence Pass.

Sayres Gulch Road (FDR 382) is 2.1 miles in length and begins at South Fork Lake Creek Road (FDR 391) 2.7 miles southwest of Hwy 82. The road ends near the Collegiate Peaks Wilderness boundary and FDT 1465. Sayres Gulch is a rough road with a significant stream crossing at the beginning of the route. It continues into an alpine valley filled with willow bushes and beaver ponds. Hikers gain access to the Sayres Gulch Trail FDT 1465 and the Collegiate Peaks Wilderness from Sayres Gulch Road.

Directions from Twin Lakes: Travel 8 miles west on Hwy 82 to South Fork Lake Creek Road. This is FDR 391 and will be on the left or south side of the highway. Follow this 4WD road 2.7 miles to FDR 382 on the left side of South Fork Creek Road. This is Sayres Gulch Road.

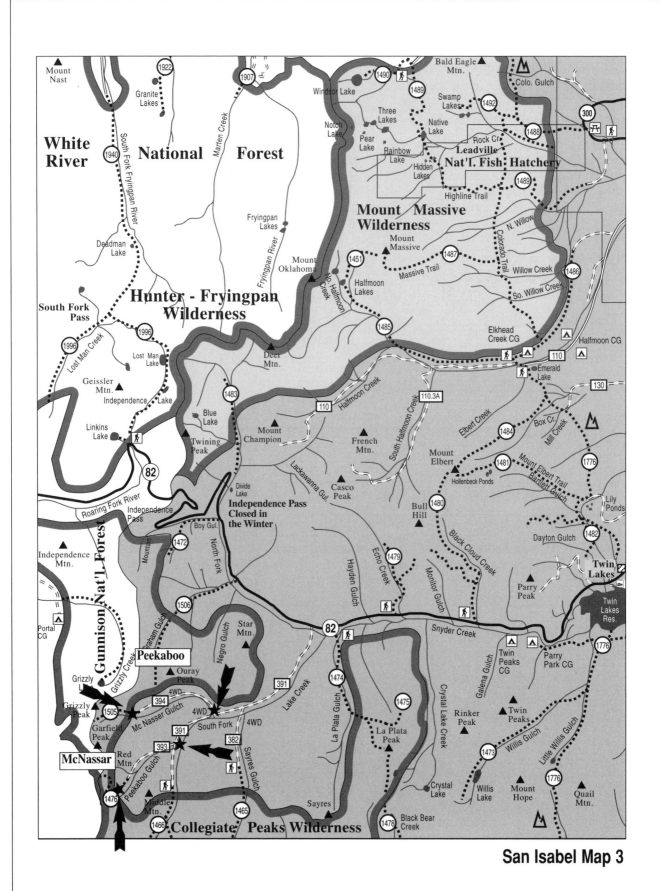

Mount Nast

Granite Lakes

White River

National   **Forest**

1922

1907

1940

South Fork Fryingpan River

Marten Creek

Deadman Lake

Windsor Lake

Notch Lake

Pear Lake

Three Lakes

Rainbow Lake

Hidden Lakes

Native Lake

Swamp Lakes

Bald Eagle Mtn.

Colo. Gulch

1490

1489

1492

1488

300

Leadville Nat'l. Fish Hatchery

Rock Cr.

1489

Fryingpan Lakes

Mount Oklahoma

Fryingpan River

Hunter - Fryingpan Wilderness

South Fork Pass

1996

1996

Lost Man Creek

Lost Man Lake

Geissler Mtn.

Independence Lake

Linkins Lake

1996

Mount Massive Wilderness

Mount Massive

Massive Trail

No. Halfmoon Creek

Halfmoon Lakes

Colorado Trail

N. Willow

Willow Creek

So. Willow Creek

1451

1487

1485

1486

Elkhead Creek CG

Halfmoon CG

Emerald Lake

110

130

82

Roaring Fork River

Independence Pass

Divide Lake

Independence Pass Closed in the Winter

Blue Lake

Twining Peak

Mount Champion

1483

110

Halfmoon Creek

South Halfmoon Creek

110.3A

French Mtn.

Lackawanna Gul.

Casco Peak

Mount Elbert

Elbert Creek

Box Cr.

Mill Creek

Mount Elbert Trail

Bartlett Gulch

Hollenbeck Ponds

1484

1481

1776

Lily Ponds

1480

Bull Hill

Dayton Gulch

1482

Twin Lakes

Boy Gul.

1472

North Fork

Mountain

Independence Mtn.

Gunnison Nat'l Forest

Portal CG

Grizzly L.

Grizzly Peak

1505

Garfield Peak

Red Mtn.

McNassar

1476

Grahan Gulch

Peekaboo

1506

Negro Gulch

Star Mtn.

Ouray Peak

394

4WD

Mc Nassar Gulch

391

South Fork

4WD

393

382

Sayres Gulch

Peekaboo Gulch

Middle Mtn.

1466

1465

Collegiate   Peaks Wilderness

391

Lake Creek

1474

La Plata Gulch

La Plata Peak

1475

Hayden Gulch

Echo Creek

Monitor Gulch

1479

Black Cloud Creek

Parry Peak

Snyder Creek

Galena Gulch

Crystal Lake Creek

Twin Peaks CG

Parry Park CG

1776

Rinker Peak

Twin Peaks

Willis Gulch

Little Willis Gulch

1473

Crystal Lake

Willis Lake

Mount Hope

1776

Quail Mtn.

Twin Lakes Res.

Sayres

Black Bear Creek

1478

San Isabel Map 3

Road Name	Road Number	Length Miles	Difficulty	Beginning Elevation	Ending Elev.	Usage	Ranger District
Peekaboo Gulch	393	2.3	Difficult	10,960'	11,600'	Moderate	Leadville

USGS Maps: Independence Pass.

Peekaboo Gulch (FDR 393) is a 2.3 mile extension from the South Fork Lake Creek Road (FDR 391). It begins at South Fork Lake Creek Road, 4.6-mile southwest of Hwy 82 and ends just below Red Mountain and FDT 1476. The road is rough and winds up into an alpine valley. Snow can block the road in the spring and winter months.

Directions from Twin Lakes Village: Travel 8 miles west on Hwy 82 to South Fork Lake Creek Road. This is FDR 391 and will be on the left or south side of the highway. Follow this 4WD road 4.6 miles to FDR 393 on the right side of South Fork Lake Creek Road. This is Peekaboo Road (FDR 393).

Road Name	Road Number	Length Miles	Difficulty	Beginning Elevation	Ending Elev.	Usage	Ranger District
McNasser Gulch	394	1.5	Difficult	10,730'	11,440'	Moderate	Leadville

USGS Maps: Independence Pass.

McNassar Gulch Road (FDR 394) begins on South Fork Lake Creek Road (FDR 391) 3.3 miles southeast of Highway 82, It ends after 1.5 miles at a gate to a private road. Beyond this gate hiking is permitted (FDT 1505) but not the use of mechanized or motorized vehicles. This is a rough road with a few steep switchbacks. Users will encounter wonderful opportunities for viewing wildflowers in the upper reaches of the valley.

Directions from Twin Lakes: Travel 8 miles west of Twin Lakes Village on Highway 82 to South Fork Lake Creek Road. This is Forest Road 391 and will be on the left or south side of the highway, Follow this four-wheel drive road 3.3 miles to Forest Road 394 on the right side of South Fork Lake Creek Road. This is McNassar Gulch Road (FDR 394).

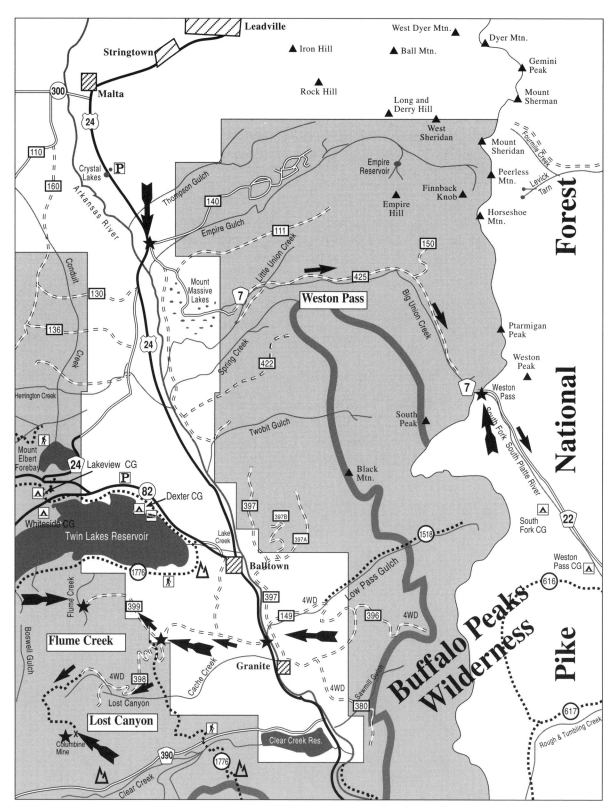

San Isabel Map 4

Road Name	Road Number	Length Miles	Difficulty	Beginning Elevation	Ending Elev.	Usage	Ranger District
Lost Canyon	398	8.5	Moderate	9,900'	12,570'	Moderate	Leadville

First 2 miles accessible by 2WD vehicle.
Ending Elevation: 12,570' @ Columbine Mine.
USGS Maps: Granite.

The road begins on Highway 24 south of the Granite store and ends at a wide alpine meadow to the northeast of Quail Mountain. The first 2 miles of road accessible by passenger vehicle, the road gets rough and rocky beyond that point. A 4WD vehicle with high clearance recommended past this point. The road winds through lodgepole stands and passes an abandoned placer mining operation on Lost Canyon Creek. Above timberline a broad alpine meadow permits visitors views of Clear Creek Valley to the south, Boswell Gulch to the west and Lake Creek Valley to the north. Excellent opportunities for observation of alpine tundra, wildflowers and wildlife abound.

Directions from Twin Lakes: Drive east on Highway 82 to the junction of Highway 24. Travel south on Highway 24 for approximately 2.75 miles to Lost Canyon Road on the right.

Road Name	Road Number	Length Miles	Difficulty	Beginning Elevation	Ending Elev.	Usage	Ranger District
Flume Creek	399	4.2	Easy	9,600'	10,200'	Moderate	Leadville

4.2 Miles - From Lost Canyon Road to road end.
USGS Maps: Granite.

Flume Creek Road is a good road that winds through the forest and climbs quickly above Twin Lakes before descending into Flume Creek. Many types of recreationists on both motorized and non-motorized transportation use it. The road climbs abruptly above the Twin Lakes with some excellent views to the north. A gate at mile four closes the road to motor vehicles.

Directions from Twin Lakes: Drive east on Highway 82 to the junction of Highway 24. Travel south on Highway 24 for approximately 2.75 miles to Last Canyon Road on the right. Flume Gulch Road begins on Lost Canyon Road (FDR 398) approximately 1.3 miles from Highway 24 and ends at Flume Gulch.

Road Name	Road Number	Length Miles	Difficulty	Beginning Elevation	Ending Elev.	Usage	Ranger District
Weston Pass	425	19.25	Easy	9,400'	9,700'	Heavy	Leadville

19.25 Miles - from Leadville.
USGS Maps: Granite, South Peak.

Approximately 11 miles to top of the pass. Road continues onto Pike National Forest down to Highway 285 leading to Fairplay. Road is not maintained for low clearance vehicles on west side of Pass. Very rough in places with a few steep pitches. Scenic route along creek with beaver activity. Climbs into high alpine valley above tree line. There is some private land around the pass summit. Passable by 2 WD on east side.

Start at Junction Hwy 24 & Weston Pass Road; continue southeast on non-gated road. Pass under the power lines and go to the end of the pavement. Enter Mt. Massive Lakes Estates. Continue SE on main road. Exit Mt. Massive Lakes Estates, cross cattle guard. Pass two road junctions and cross creek. Continue east on main road, pass Forest Service sign enter canyon. Begin 4 WD road. At 7.75 miles past road junction, continue SE on main road, at 10.5 miles you come to the top of the pass. Continue on main road until you come to Weston Pass Campground where 4WD road ends. Pass Rich Creek trailhead at 16.5 miles, pass road junction and continue NE on main road. At junction of Park Cty Rd 5 & 22, you can take Cty Rd 5, 7 miles to Hwy 285 which heads NE toward Fairplay or you can take Cty Rd 22 for 7.2 miles to Hwy 285 and head SE toward Antero Junction.

Forest Service roads open to motorized vehicles are posted with white arrows. Wilderness areas such as Collegiate Peaks and Mount Massive are by regulation permanently closed to motorized and mechanized vehicles, including mountain bikes.

Directions from Leadville: From the traffic light at 6th Street in Leadville follow Highway 24 south for 7.5 miles. Turn left (east) onto Lake County Road 7 at the sign for Weston Pass. (One Way).

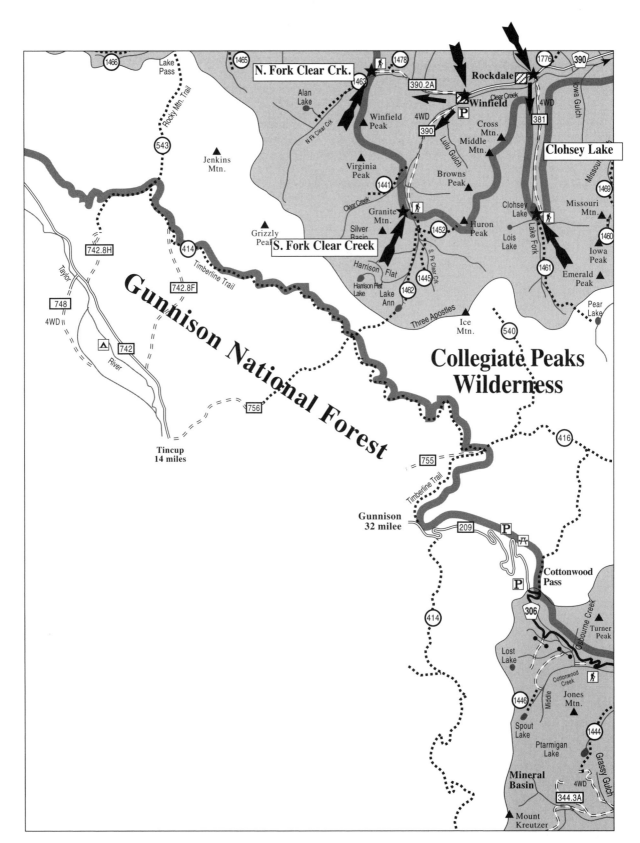

San Isabel Map 5

Road Name	Road Number	Length Miles	Difficulty	Beginning Elevation	Ending Elev.	Usage	Ranger District
Clohsey Lake	381	3.2	Difficult	9,948'	11,040'	Moderate	Leadville

Extremely rough, for high clearance vehicles only.
USGS Map: Winfield.

Clohsey Lake Road begins at Clear Creek Road in Rockdale, about 2 miles west of Vicksburg. Rockdale consists of a few cabins on the south side of the road. The road ends 0.5 mile before Clohsey Lake (Private) where the Collegiate Peaks Wilderness begins.

The road is extremely rough road recommended for high clearance vehicles only and generally not passable until at least mid-July. At the beginning of the road there is a steep, difficult stream crossing of Clear Creek where early summer high water flows occur. The entire route is heavily forested. Pear Lake Trail is accessible from Clohsey Lake.

Directions from Highway 24: Turn on to Clear Creek Road (FDR 390) which is 2 miles south of Granite, and drive 2 miles west of the historic town of Vicksburg. You will reach Rockdale another historic town on the south side of the road. Turn left on to Forest Road 381, this is Clohsey Lake Road.

Road Name	Road Number	Length Miles	Difficulty	Beginning Elevation	Ending Elev.	Usage	Ranger District
South Fork Clear Creek	390	2	Difficult	10,226'	10,700'	Moderate	Leadville

USGS Maps: Winfield.

The South Fork of Clear Creek begins at Winfield and ends at the road closure just south of the Banker Mine. The road passes the turnoff to the Banker Mine, a large privately owned patented mining claim and continues on into an open alpine meadow with some excellent undeveloped camping sites. The road is extremely rough and recommended for high clearance vehicles only. The following hiking trails may be accessed from this road: Continental Divide Trail, Lake Ann (FDT 1462), Three Apostles (FDT 1445), and Huron Peak (FDT 1452).

Directions from Leadville: Clear Creek Road is about 19 miles south of Leadville or 14 miles north of Buena Vista. Drive on Clear Creek Road (FDR 390) to Winfield, approximately 9 miles.

Road Name	Road Number	Length Miles	Difficulty	Beginning Elevation	Ending Elev.	Usage	Ranger District
North Fork Clear Creek	390.2A	2.2	Easy	10,300'	10,750'	Moderate	Leadville

USGS Maps: Winfield.

The North Fork of Clear Creek Road begins on the north side of Winfield. It ends at the Collegiate Peaks Wilderness Boundary, and is 2.2 miles in length one-way.

The ride is a gradual, bumpy climb into an open alpine valley with meadows, willows, wildlife and wildflower viewing. Hikers may access North Fork Clear Creek Trail (FDT 1463) from the road.

Directions from Leadville: Travel 19 miles south or 14 miles north of Buena Vista and turn west on Clear Creek Road (FDR 120). Road 120 is graveled and sometimes rough but satisfactory for most vehicles. Drive approximately 10 miles to the ghost town of Winfield. North Fork Clear Creek Road is the right turn immediately after Winfield.

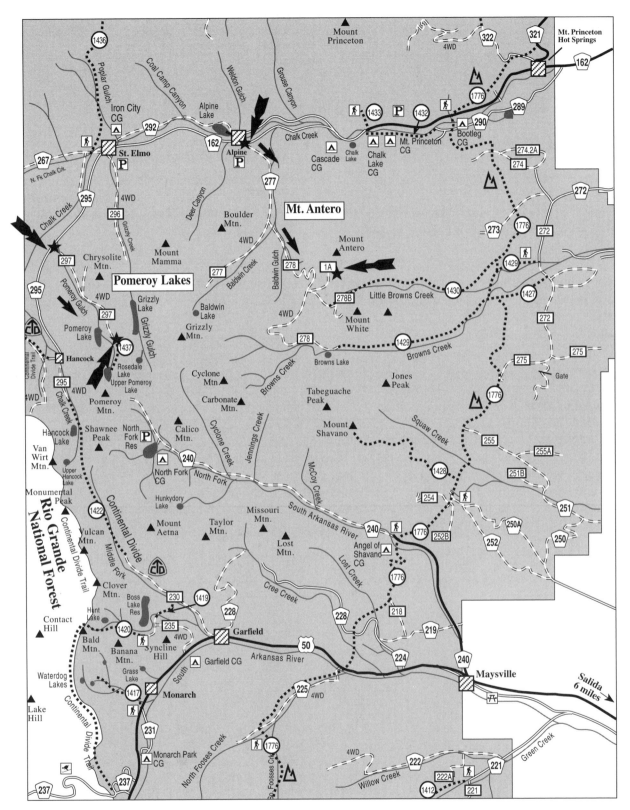

San Isabel Map 6

Road Name	Road Number	Length Miles	Difficulty	Beginning Elevation	Ending Elev.	Usage	Ranger District
Mt. Antero	278	16.2	Difficult	9,400'	14,269'	Moderate	Salida

14,269 Feet - Summit Mt Antero.
USGS Maps: Mt. Antero, St Elmo.

There are several routes to the summit of Mt. Antero. The one described here is the most popular and the least challenging. A 4WD vehicle is needed for this ascent which begins at the Baldwin Trailhead on Chalk Creek Road east of St. Elmo. There is a parking lot at the intersection of Baldwin Creek Road (FDR 277) and Chalk Creek Road (FDR 162) for those who wish to hike or bike from this point Baldwin Creek Road leads southeast from the south side of Chalk Creek Road.

Baldwin Creek Road begins at 9,400 feet and climbs steeply for the first 1.25 miles, After turning sharply to the south the road intersects with two other jeep roads. (Remain on Baldwin Creek Road to reach Mt Antero's western slopes.) The road continues to climb steadily as it follows Baldwin Creek and crosses the creek a few times. Close to mile 2.75 the road forks. Follow the eastern fork, which will soon begin to climb the western slopes of Mr. Antero. At this fork will be the third crossing of Baldwin Creek.

This is Upper Browns Road (FDR 278). At approximately mile 4.25 from the trailhead Road 278 begins to switchback. Immediately after the switchbacks the road turns sharply to the south leading toward the southern ridge of Mt Antero. Approximately 1 mile after the last switchback the road forks again. Follow the left fork, which leads east. After this fork the road remains at 13,000' for a short distance, descends a few hundred feet and then it begins to climb the final flanks to 13,760. From the road's end the summit is .25 miles north. Nearly 50% of this road is single lane without a pull off or places to turn around. It is not recommended for novice drivers.

Directions from Salida: From Salida drive 15 miles north on Highway 285 to County Road 162, Drive west on County Road 162 for 12 miles to the junction of Baldwin Creek Road (FDR 277).

Road Name	Road Number	Length Miles	Difficulty	Beginning Elevation	Ending Elev.	Usage	Ranger District
Pomeroy Lakes	297	2	Easy	12,080'	12,250'	Heavy	Salida

USGS Maps: St. Elmo.

Pomeroy Lakes Trail is a short trail to a pair of alpine lakes. The trailhead (FDT 1437)is located south of St. Elmo, and a 4WD vehicle is necessary to reach it. The trailhead lies at an elevation of 12,080 feet. Pomeroy Lake lies .25 miles south of the trailhead at 12,035 feet. Upper Pomeroy Lake lies 1 mile south of the trailhead at an elevation of 12,250 feet.

The lakes have very good fishing for cutthroat and rainbow crossed with cutthroat. It is stocked every 1 to 2 years and the average size fish is 10-12 inches. The ice does not completely melt on Upper Pomeroy Lake until late June or early July.

Directions from Salida: Travel on Hwy 285 north to Nathrop. Turn west at Nathrop and drive about 15 miles on County Rd 162.Immediately before St. Elmo turn left on to County Road 295. Travel 3 miles to County Road 297. Turn left on FDR 297 which will bring you to the trailhead. A 4WD vehicle is needed to drive this road.

Road Name	Road Number	Length Miles	Difficulty	Beginning Elevation	Ending Elev.	Usage	Ranger District
Mt. Princeton	322	5.5	Moderate	8.900'	14,197'	Moderate	Salida

14,197 Feet - Summit Mt. Princeton.
USGS Map: Mt. Antero.

Mt Princeton is one of the most visible mountains in the Sawatch Mountain Range. The broad eastern face of the mountain dominates the landscape as visitors to the Arkansas River Valley enter Johnson Village on Highway 24/285.

There is a large parking lot at the base of Mt. Princeton Road. It is recommended that anyone driving a passenger car park here. Limited parking exists along the road and it is difficult to turn around or pass other vehicles. Those 4WD vehicles should have few problems driving to 11,800 feet on the Lucky Mine Road. An easy to follow road without much difficulty until the last half mile where the road becomes a narrow shelf. If you plan to hike the rest of the way park here. The Mt. Princeton Road is steep and narrow with few turnouts and turn around points. Avoid it until all snow has melted.

Beyond the road the trail starts mildly, you will gain elevation slightly and cross the Southern ridge of "Tigger Peak", Point 13,300 feet. A rocky trail leads .25 miles into the basin below Mt. Princeton's Peak. The last .25 mile is a scramble to the summit through boulders with no defined trail. Not a very exciting hike except for the scenery.

Directions from Buena Vista:
Drive south from Buena Vista on Highway 285, 8 miles. Turn west (right) on County Road 162, and drive about 4.5 miles to Mt. Princeton Hot Springs. Turn north on County Road 321 opposite the Hot Springs. Follow County Road 321 1.5 miles to County Road 322. Turn left onto County Road 322 and drive one mile southwest to Young Life Camp (follow signs). There is a large parking lot immediately before the beginning of the Mt. Princeton Road. Within 3 miles you'll reach the radio towers and parking for a few vehicles.

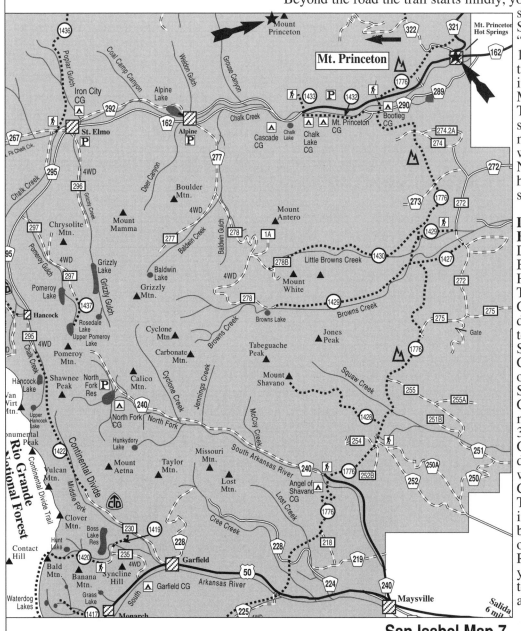

San Isabel Map 7

Road Name	Road Number	Length Miles	Difficulty	Beginning Elevation	Ending Elev.	Usage	Ranger District
Music Pass	119	2.1	Difficult	9,260'	10,500'	Heavy	San Carlos

Beginning Elevation: Southern trailhead for the Rainbow Trail.
Ending Elevation: Music Pass Trailhead.
USGS Maps: Crestone Peak, Beck Mountain.

A short difficult 4WD road to Music Pass Trailhead. At the Music Pass Trailhead you will find a parking area and dispersed camping sites. In the fall this area is popular with hunters. This area also offers opportunities for horseback riders.

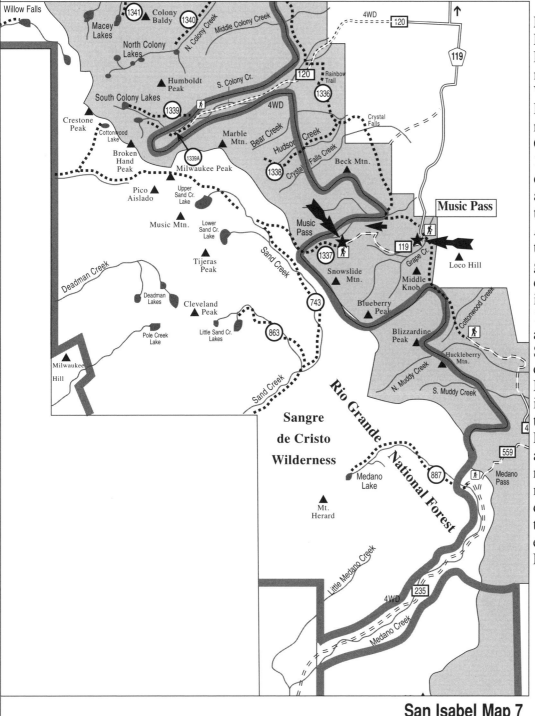

Directions from Highway 69:
Less than 6 miles south of Westcliffe on Highway 69 turn right onto County Road 119 and continue due south for about 5 miles on the paved road. At the junction turn left on the gravel road and continue following County Road 119 south for about 5 miles. Shortly after entering the National Forest is the southern trailhead for the Rainbow Trail and the beginning of the 2-mile four-wheel drive portion of the road which ends at Music Pass Trailhead.

San Isabel Map 7

Road Name	Road Number	Length Miles	Difficulty	Beginning Elevation	Ending Elev.	Usage	Ranger District
South Colony	120	5	Most Difficult	9,000'	11,400'	High	San Carlos

USGS Maps: Medano Pass, Beck Mountain.

About 1 mile from County Rd 119, on South Colony Road is the parking area where all vehicles must stop. If you have a high-clearance, 4WD vehicle, make sure you are prepared for 5 miles of what could be the worst road you have ever driven. Even so, this road is used rather heavily. Please help preserve Nature's beauty for the others yet to come.

There are steep areas, big rocks, small rocks, slabs of rock and water bars as you follow South Colony Creek. Give yourself at least two hours driving time to get to South Colony Trailhead, where the road dead-ends. For most of the last 3 miles you will be driving through a designated corridor about 150 yards wide. This corridor is a passage through the Sangre de Cristo Wilderness.

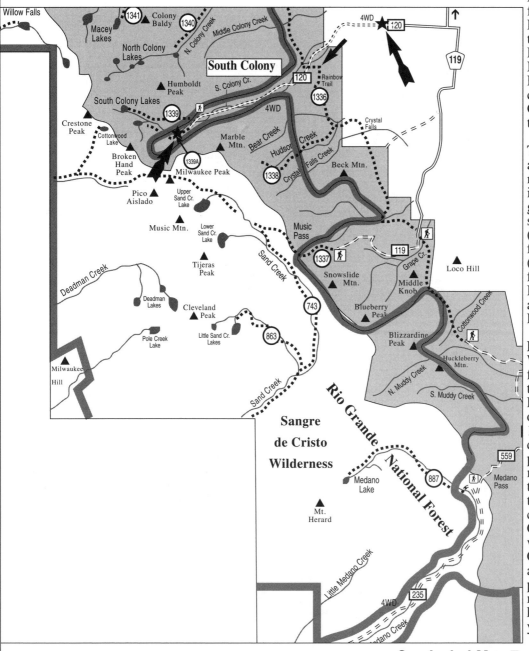

Many hikers can be found on the road. People attempting to summit Crestone Peak, Crestone Needle or Humboldt Peak camp at South Colony Lakes or the parking lot.

This is a beautiful area, surrounded by mountains. Starting in the north and going west, you can see Humboldt Peak (Elevation 14,064 feet), the Crestone's (all over 14,000 feet) and then Broken Hand Peak and Milwaukee Peak.

Directions from Westcliffe: South from Westcliffe less than 6 miles on Hwy 69 turn right onto County Road 119 and continue due south on the paved road for 5-6 miles. At the junction, turn right on the gravel road and continue following County Road 120, which is South Colony Road. It is about 1 mile to the parking area. Five miles of the worst kind of 4WD awaits you.

San Isabel Map 7

Road Name	Road Number	Length Miles	Difficulty	Beginning Elevation	Ending Elev.	Usage	Ranger District
Trinchera Peak	436	5.5	Moderate	10,500'	13,517'	Moderate	San Carlos

Beginning Elevation: Blue Lake.
Ending Elevation: Summit of Trinchera Peak.
USGS Maps: Trinchera Peak.

This road is located above Cuchara on the left side of Blue Lake, which is part of the Cuchara Recreation Area. There is some parking for 2WD vehicles at the trailhead. Some high clearance vehicles can make it to tree line. There are a few switchbacks and waterbars, but otherwise pretty easy traveling. At tree line, about 11,800 feet is a parking area and dispersed camping. If traveling past tree line, a high clearance 4WD vehicle is a must.

The 4WD portion of the road climbs steeply after the first switchback, going through scree and tundra. It then drops into a cirque (where a waterfall can be seen in early spring).

The road then climbs with narrower switchbacks over large scree and slice rock. The portion of the road from tree line to the dead-end 12,600 feet, takes you to just below the ridge at an old mine. This part is about l mile in length with a 1,000 foot vertical rise.

The trail to Trinchera Peak begins just after the mine and the summit is about .75 of a mile (40 minutes) from the mine. Gain the steep and rocky ridge and follow it to the summit. Trinchera Peak is part of the Sangre de Christo Range and sightings of a large herd of bighorn sheep are common.

Directions from La Veta: Take Hwy 12 south, through Cuchara and past the turnoff for Cuchara Mountain Resort. Cuchara Recreation Area is a right turn onto FDR 422. About 2 miles up the road are the Day Use and Parking Area, after about 5 miles you reach Blue and Bear Lakes. It is a typically rutted gravel road; watch yourself going up when the switchbacks turn, some are very deeply rutted. Trinchera Peak 4WD Road (FDR 436) begins across from the entrance to Blue Lake Campground, on the left side. There is some parking for 2WD vehicles just before the 4WD road begins.

San Isabel Map 8

WHITE RIVER NATIONAL FOREST

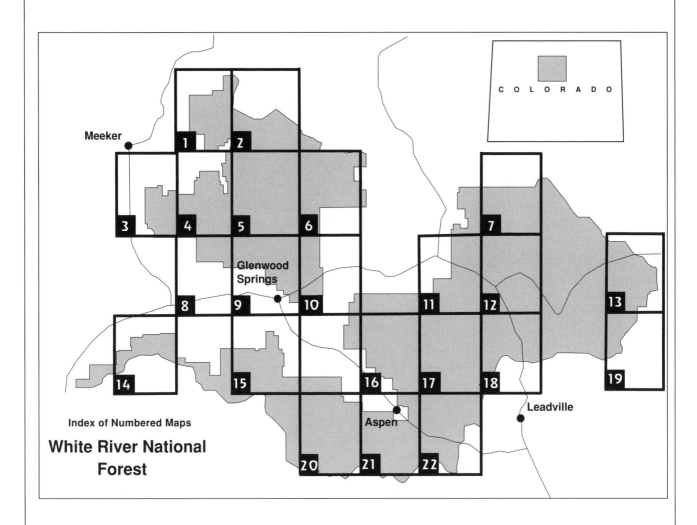

Meeker

1 2

3 4 5 6

Glenwood
Springs

7

8 9 10 11 12 13

COLORADO

14 15 16 17 18 19

Index of Numbered Maps

**White River National
Forest**

Aspen

Leadville

20 21 22

WHITE RIVER NATIONAL FOREST

On October 16,1891, President Benjamin Harrison signed a Proclamation setting aside public lands for the public good. The lands President Harrison set aside were called the White River Plateau Timber Reserve and were among the first lands established in support of a historic conservation movement. They were, in fact, the very first Timber Reserve lands established in the State of Colorado and the second in the United States (The Shoshone Timber Reserve being the first). That early conservation movement, and subsequent decisions, established what we know today as the National Forest System, a system of over 190 million acres managed under a multiple use principle designed to provide the greatest good for the greatest number in the long run.

CULTURAL HISTORY

The White River National Forest is rich in cultural history. The first human use probably occurred between 5,000 and 10,000 years B.C. The Ute Indians were the most recent Native Americans inhabiting the Forest until the late 19th Century, when they were removed to live on a reservation. Evidence of their presence can still be found in the form of an extensive trail system. The main Ute Trail from Meeker to Dotsero is being re-marked so that hikers will know they are treading where the Utes once roamed. Early day ranching, mining and agricultural uses developed on the lands after the Native Americans. Signs of these early uses are old mines, pack trails, wagon roads, narrow and standard gauge railroad routes, and prospector, trapper and homestead cabins. If you discover any remnants and relics of our past, leave them in place for the next visitor to appreciate. Cultural artifacts may not be collected from Federal lands; please report them to the local district office.

CRADLE OF WILDERNESS

The Wilderness concept was born and the principle was first applied in 1919 at Trappers Lake, White River National Forest, Colorado by Arthur H. Carhart.

Carhart was assigned the task of surveying the Trappers Lake area to plot several hundred home sites on the lake shore and to plan a "through" road around the lake. Carhart completed the surveys but made it known to his supervisor that he opposed further "improvement where natural landscape would suffer."

The first landscape architect employed by the Forest Service, Carhart foresaw the damage to our wilderness heritage if waste and undesirable exploitation were not curtailed. He provided the first blueprint for practical development of recreational resources in the National Forests. He was a man who worked behind the scenes influencing others in positions of authority to further the cause of wilderness preservation.

A chain of events dating from 1919 to 1964 developed into what became known as the wilderness preservation movement. This movement culminated in 1964 with the passage of the Wilderness Act.

Today the White River National Forest manages all or part of seven Wildernesses. They are managed to protect their natural ecosystem. They also offer opportunities for human isolation, solitude, self-reliance, and challenge while hiking cross-country or on trails. Please practice low impact camping techniques and follow local regulations for use of these areas.

1. Moeller Creek/Sleepy Cat

White River

Road Name	Road Number	Length Miles	Difficulty	Beginning Elevation	Ending Elev.	Usage	Ranger District
Moeller Creek	290	11	More Difficult	8,050'	9,550'	Light	Blanco

Sleepy Cat Trail FDR 250.
USGS Maps: Fawn Creek, Lost Park.

Sections of Moeller Creek Road are narrow and steep with several tight corners and few turnouts. The Moeller Creek Road travels through scattered stands of conifer, open parks and aspen. Two short side roads diverge from the road. The Log Springs Road begins roughly 2 miles up the Moeller Creek Road and heads southeast to its deadend at Logs Springs, approximately 1 mile away. After another mile on the Moeller Creek Road (FDR 250), the Pattison Park Road drops down a small drainage to its destination, about 1 mile away at Pattison Park. Proceeding up FDR 290 about .5 mile the road emerges into Little Lost Park. After crossing this 160 acre grassy meadow and traveling another .25 mile, the Lost Park Road (FDR 293) junctions the Moeller Creek Road. For the next 7 miles FDR is called the Sleepy Cat Trail land is a four-wheel drive road being extremely difficult because of rock and boggy terrain. The road then junctions with East Beaver Road and in either direction the roads are drained and periodically graded.

The Lost Park Road (FDR 293) continues 1 mile to its terminus in Lost Park. The Lost Park Trail (FDT 1805) provides access by foot through Lost Park onto the Routt National Forest or down Lost Creek. From June 15 through August 31 a motorized ATV trail (under 50") crosses Lost park and Lost Creek ending at FDR 231 at Trough Gulch.

Directions from Meeker: Drive east of Meeker on State Highway 13, 1 mile to the junction of County Road 8, turn right on County Road 8 for 27 miles to the Fawn Creek Road (FDR 280). Follow the Fawn Creek Road for 2.4 miles to the Moeller Creek Road.

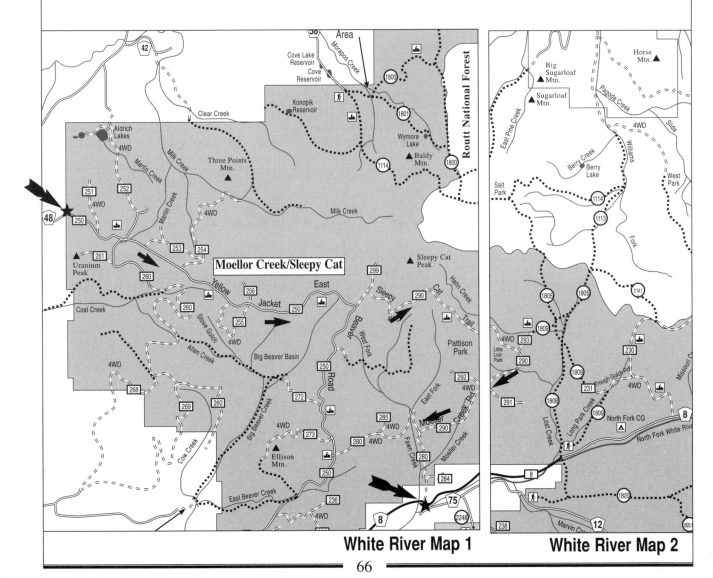

White River Map 1   **White River Map 2**

66

White River

Road Name	Road Number	Length Miles	Difficulty	Beginning Elevation	Ending Elev.	Usage	Ranger District
Dead Horse/Long Park Loop	230	11.7	Most Difficult	7,600'	8,078'	Light	Blanco

USGS Maps: Lost Park, Ripple Creek.

Starting at the west entrance to the Dead Horse Loop, you follow switchbacks up a steep south facing slope. Gaining elevation you have a view of the valley of the North Fork of the White River. After approximately 2 miles you emerge into Long Park. The road then divides, the left fork Trough Gulch Road (FDR 231) takes you west down Long Park Creek until it ends at Trough Gulch. Following the other fork you proceed up Long Park Creek to the divide between the White River and Williams Fork drainage. As you follow the divide to the north you see the Elk Head Mountains while the South Fork of the Williams Fork lies directly below. To the east and south, you see the White River Valley and the Flat Tops. After following this divide for approximately 3 miles you drop back into the White River Drainage. As you proceed down the road you come to another junction. The west fork (FDR 234) ends at Missouri Creek, while the east fork takes you to the Dead Horse Creek end of the loop. You lose elevation quickly, over a steep, rough, and narrow road until you meet County Road 8. Much of this road is rough, narrow and steep. There are steep switchbacks, large water bars and few turnouts.

Directions from Meeker: Drive east of Meeker for 2 miles to the junction of County Road 8, turn right and proceed 35 miles to the west terminus or 38 miles to the east terminus.

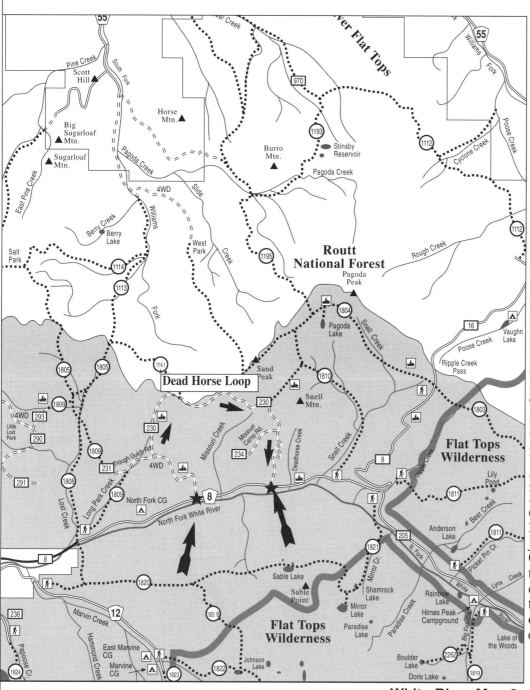

White River Map 2

Road Name	Road Number	Length Miles	Difficulty	Beginning Elevation	Ending Elev.	Usage	Ranger District
Hay Flats	211	13.5	Moderate	6,690'	9,000'	Light	Blanco

USGS Maps: Veatch Gulch, Red Elephant Point.

The Hay Flats Road climbs the Gooseberry Creek drainage through oak brush and aspen for 2 miles until it emerges onto Hay Flats. Hay Flats is a rolling, brush and grass covered plateau with scattered patches of aspen. Vistas of the White River drainage are occasionally visible with Sleepy Cat Peak being the dominant land feature. To the northeast several stock watering ponds are built near the road at Indian Springs, Janes Springs and Machine Springs. Crossing Hay Flats, the elevation rises gradually to 9,000 feet. After 1.5 miles the road divides with the left fork dropping into a gulch 1 mile to the east. This fork ends at private land after 2.5 miles. The main fork continues south, 6.5 miles from the forest boundary is the Flag Creek Road (FDR 220).

(The Howey Reservoir Road junctions about 1.5 miles beyond the FDR 220 junction) The road continues 12 miles through aspen and coniferous stands end at the Buford New castle Road (FDR 245) in Triangle Park. Refer to Forest Service map for several loop routes.

Directions from Meeker: Drive south on 10th street out of Meeker and after crossing the White River, turn right onto the Flag Creek Road for 7.5 miles to the East Flag Creek Road (County Road 38). The Hay Flat Road FDR 211 begins at the forest boundary 3.5 miles up County Road 38.

White River Map 3

Road Name	Road Number	Length Miles	Difficulty	Beginning Elevation	Ending Elev.	Usage	Ranger District
Four Mile	214	6	Moderate	7,200'	9,300'	Light	Blanco

USGS Maps: Triangle Park, Red Elephant Point.

The Four Mile Road rises out of Miller Creek, following Four-Mile Creek through oak brush and stands of spruce and fir. After 1 mile of this type of terrain the road levels off on a rolling plateau.

The remaining 4 miles to junction of the Bar HL Road (FDR 211) the vegetation interchanges from open parks to aspen stands with scattered patches of conifers. Sections of the Four Mile are steep and narrow. The road borders private property, respect their rights. Leave gates as you found them.

Directions from: Meeker: Drive east of Meeker on State Highway 13, 1 mile to the junction of County Road 8; turn right on County Road 8 for 10 miles to the Miller Creek Road (County Road 57 and FDR 215). Stay on the Miller Creek Road for 7 miles to the junction of the Four Mile Road (FDR 214).

White River Map 4

Road Name	Road Number	Length Miles	Difficulty	Beginning Elevation	Ending Elev.	Usage	Ranger District
Clinetop/Hiner Springs	601/603/651	33	More Difficult	6,177'	9,900'	Moderate	Rifle

Beginning Elevation: Forest Boundary on FDR 603.
Ending Elevation: Intersection of Buford/New Castle Road and FDR 601.
USGS Maps: Deep Creek Point, Adams Lake, Blair Mountain, Meadow Creek Lake.

The area has some scenic and beautiful meadows covered with wildflowers. The route crosses Blair Mountain at about the halfway point. From Blair Mountain you can see across the Flat Tops Wilderness Area and down into Jet, Blair and Crater Lakes. Located along FDR 601, Cliff Lakes Overlook offers an excellent view of the South Fork of the White River.

The Clinetop road ascends for 10 miles to the top of the mesa. This section of the road is very wash boarded with numerous switchbacks in the road but may be traveled by two-wheeled drive vehicles. As you turn off FDR 603 onto FDR 651 the road becomes very rocky and rutted and four-wheel drive will be necessary. You will then pickup FDR 601 just above Elk Lakes. At this point FDR 601 continues up the side of Blair Mountain. This section of road is very rocky and steep with rock ledges that would challenge any 4-wheeling enthusiast. After reaching the top of Blair Mountain the road has some rocky and rough sections, but continues to get better the closer you get to the Buford/New Castle Road (FDR 245).

Directions from Rifle: Go east of Rifle to New Castle, turn left on 7th Street which turns into Buford/New Castle Road. Continue for 3.5 miles to Main Elk Creek (FDR 243), turn right and continue to the White River National Forest via the Clinetop Road (FDR 603).

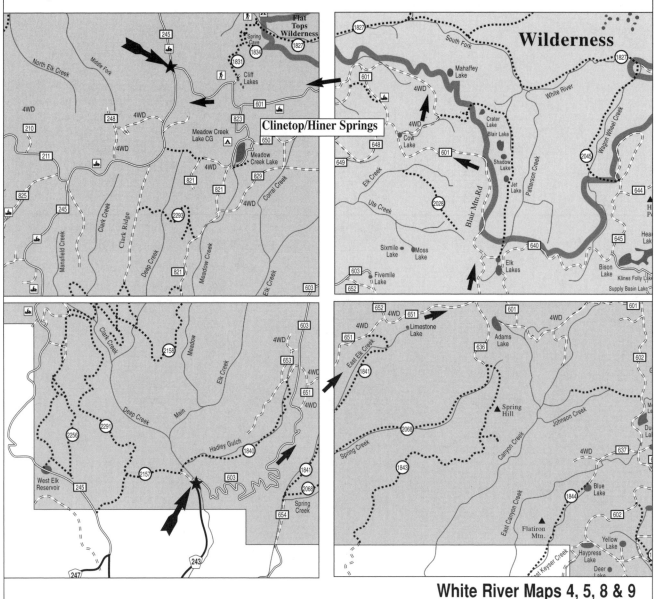

White River Maps 4, 5, 8 & 9

Road Name	Road Number	Length Miles	Difficulty	Beginning Elevation	Ending Elev.	Usage	Ranger District
Ten Mile Park	618/619	8.4	Moderate	10,642'	10,700'	Low	Eagle

USGS Maps: Sweetwater, Deep Lake, Broken Rib.

This tour starts near Deep Lake on FDR 618 with a bird's eye view of Deep Lake. After easy grades for 3 miles the road forks to the right where a steeper and rockier section will make for difficult travel if conditions are wet. If conditions are dry you should have no problems you have just past the roughest part of the trip. Your reward comes at the end of FDR 619 where the views are the best. The entire route stays above 10,500 feet, winds can be strong and storms can arrive on very short notice.

After parking your vehicle at the end of FDR 619 you can enhance the view by hiking along the ridge which runs east. A faint trial can be hiked for about a mile through aspen trees, cresting at the edge of a meadow. When the fall colors arrive, this is an excellent vantage point. While many visitors travel the south side of Deep Creek for its spectacular scenery, the roadways north of the canyon combine the pleasures of breathtaking views and greater solitude.

With its mix of forest and meadow, both deer and elk can be spotted early in the morning or late in the day, predatory birds are common. As the winds calm down in the evening, the sound of coyotes might even be heard. Late July and early August are the best times to see alpine wildflowers in full bloom. Stay only on designated roads. Stay on the road, vegetation in these high elevation meadows is easily damaged and takes many years to recover.

Directions from Eagle: Follow I-70 westbound 12 miles to the Dotsero exit (133). Continue north 1.5 miles and turn left onto the Coffee Pot Road (FDR 600). Travel on FDR 600 about 30 miles past the turnoff for Deep Lake, a sign will indicate the start of FDR 618. This road should be followed until it turns right and downhill to Sam's Springs (about 7 miles past the start of FDR 618). Instead of turning right, drive straight ahead to begin FDR 619. This road will end 1.4 miles down the road where there is space to park and turn around.

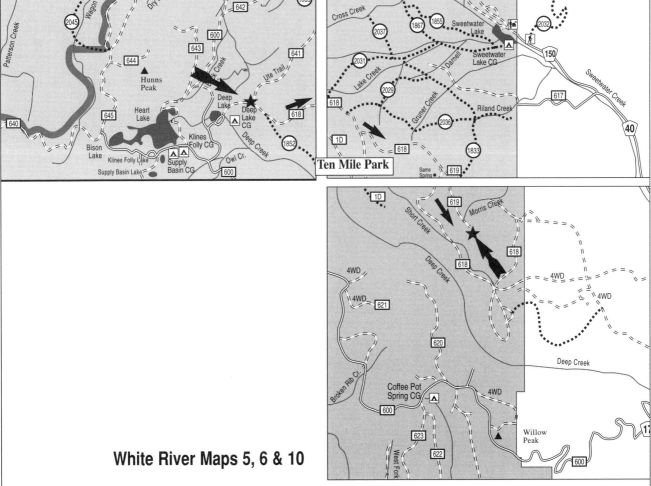

White River Maps 5, 6 & 10

Road Name	Road Number	Length Miles	Difficulty	Beginning Elevation	Ending Elev.	Usage	Ranger District
South Derby	613	11.2	Most Difficult	8,200'	10,730'	Heavy	Eagle

USGS Maps: Burns North, Dome Peak, Trappers Lake.

The South Derby Road (FDR 613) starting from the Derby Loop and ending at Crescent Lake is considered the roughest, most difficult 4WD road in the Eagle Ranger District. The road begins in a meadow, passes through aspen and then some ponderosa pine and douglas fir. For several miles after, it goes through a large burn area with new aspen growth. As the road nears Emerald Lake, it enters pockets of spruce/fir and aspen, and passes the 90-acre Derby Fire area of 1990. Up to Crescent Lake, the road continues through meadows and spruce/fir forest. There are steep sections, stream crossings with no bridges and large jutting rocks in the road and a 1.5 miles of bog near Crescent Lake. Some of the road is solid rock. The rugged condition of this road makes it extremely difficult for even 4WD jeeps. ATV's and motorcycles can handle the terrain easier. From Mackinaw Lake hikers can access the Flat Tops Wilderness.

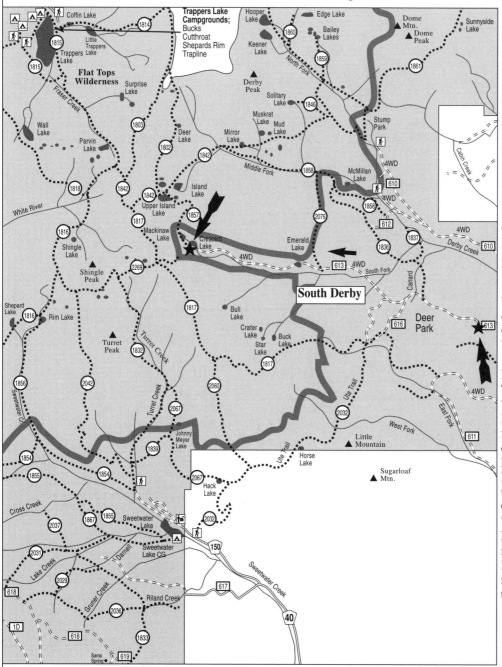

Burn Areas: About 1.5 miles up the road, the Red Dirt Fire of 1975 burned approximately 4,500 acres. Now the area has lush green aspen regeneration and some areas were replanted with lodgepole pine. It is advised not to walk in the area for the burned snags can fall at any time.

Fishing: Emerald and Crescent Lakes receive high fishing pressure. Ten-acre Emerald Lake has brook trout. Crescent Lake, 38 acres, has mackinaw, brook and Colorado native cutthroat trout. The Colorado Division of Wildlife stocks both lakes.

Directions from Eagle: Travel 12 miles west on I-70, getting off at the Dotsero exit. Follow signs for Burns, turning north onto the Colorado River Road. Go about 20 miles to Burns, taking a left before the post office onto the Cabin Creek Road. Go up 7 miles to the South Derby Road (FDR 613). An information board and a parking lot large enough to accommodate horse trailers is at the beginning of the road.

White River Map 6

Road Name	Road Number	Length Miles	Difficulty	Beginning Elevation	Ending Elev.	Usage	Ranger District
Stump Park	610	6.7	Most Difficult	8,000'	10,000'	Heavy	Eagle

USGS Maps: Burns North, Dome Peak.

Stump Park Road (FDR 610) provides access to the North Fork Valley. The road is one of the most rugged and beautiful 4WD roads on the Eagle Ranger District. Starting off the Derby Loop, it travels through dry pinyon pine and juniper country, into ponderosa pine and on through aspen, spruce and fir forest. This road has large protruding rocks in it, can be very narrow and steep at times and it has 3 to 4 stream crossings which can be difficult during spring runoff. There are some areas where the road is solid rock that has several ridges and ledges to drive over. The Stump Park road passes through cattle grazing country, so be wary of cattle in the road. The road ends just before 2 small cabins at Stump Park, the only meadow near the road.

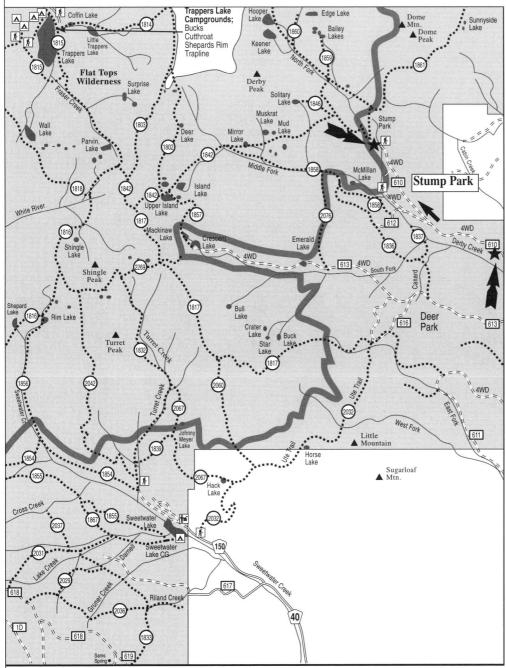

For several miles, it travels along a ridge that offers views of new forest regeneration from the 10,063 acre Emerald Lake Fire of 1980. Around the first mile of the road, it passes through a unique stand of very large ponderosa pine trees with juniper, pinyon pine and aspen. Such vegetative variety attracts abundant and diverse wildlife.

The North Fork Valley receives extremely high fishing pressures on the area's lakes and hunting is popular. Campers will find several undeveloped sites along the road, no potable water. The road provides hikers access to trails into the Flat Tops Wilderness.

Directions from Eagle: Travel 12 miles west on I-70, getting off at the Dotsero exit. Follow the signs for Burns/Sweetwater, turning onto the Colorado River Road. Go about 20 miles to Burns, then take a left before the post office onto the Cabin Creek Road and go 6 miles up to the Stump Park Road (FDR 610). At the beginning of the road, there is an information board and a parking lot large enough to accommodate small horse trailer.

White River Map 6

Road Name	Road Number	Length Miles	Difficulty	Beginning Elevation	Ending Elev.	Usage	Ranger District
Spring Creek	23/1831	14	Moderate	7,680'	8,995'	Moderate	Dillon

Beginning Elevation: Spring Creek Rd (Cty Rd 23), N of Green Mountain Res. off Co. Hwy 9.
Ending Elevation: Mahan Lake.
USGS Maps: King Creek, Sheephorn Mountain.

The first 12 miles are 2WD (numerous bogs in early summer). Travel 5.5 miles west through private land until entering public lands at the Dice Hill intersection. Continue straight for 1 mile traveling through BLM land, into White River National Forest, until reaching an intersection. Turn right up hill following the sign to Sheephorn-Divide Mahan Lake (FDR 1831). Continue up hill for 3 miles until reaching another intersection. Turn left and travel south along Elliot Ridge for 0.5 mile (turning right instead takes you down to the Colorado River via Sheephorn Creek). Veer to the right at the next intersection (turning left instead takes you back down to road FDR 1831 - use when returning). Continue along Elliot Ridge for 1 mile to the Mahan Lake - Elliot Ridge intersection sign. Turn left onto the 4 WD road to Mahan Lake (turning right instead dead ends in .1 mile at Blue Lake, but has beautiful views of Piney Ridge and Sheephorn Creek drainage). Continue for 3.5 miles to Mahan Lake where road deadends .5 mile before the lake.

Directions from Silverthorne: Twenty Seven miles north on Highway 9 (I-70 exit #205) past Green Mountain Reservoir. Turn left onto Spring Creek Road (County Road 23). County Road 23 travels through private property, respect private property.

White River Map 7

Road Name	Road Number	Length Miles	Difficulty	Beginning Elevation	Ending Elev.	Usage	Ranger District
Hubbard Cave		4.5	More Difficult	6,950'	8,400'	Moderate	Sopris

Beginning Elevation: Left fork of County Road 115.
Ending Elevation: Hubbard Cave Trailhead.
USGS Maps: Glenwood Springs, Shoshone.

Hubbard Cave Road takes you to within .25 mile of Hubbard Cave. Hike the trail to the cave, which has approximately 3,000 feet of passage with a vertical relief of only 50 feet. Geologists think the cave was formed by an explosion caused by a stream derived from ground water in the lower beds of Leadville Limestone and Dyer Dolomite. The cave is a rectangular network of three parallel passages, each with its own entrance. There are large quantities of cave coral, but it is mostly restricted to the upper level. The Grape Room, deep in the cave has unusual small, rounded botryoid formations. The Gypsum room has a large concentration of gypsum flowers, gypsum blisters, selenite needles and angels hair. Remember law protects all cave features. Help preserve this natural wonder for future generations to enjoy.

Directions from Glenwood Springs: Follow Highway 82 east from Glenwood Springs for 3 miles. Take a left onto Red Canyon Road (County Road 115). Go 2.5 miles and take a left into an open area and past a gravel pit. Travel 2 miles and take a right on to a rough four-wheel drive road that winds up the hill.

CAUTION: this road is impassable when wet. The road is also extremely narrow, with scrub oak hanging into the road which will scratch wider vehicles. After going 4.5 miles there is a parking area with a trail register near the entrance of the cave. There are no facilities at this site.

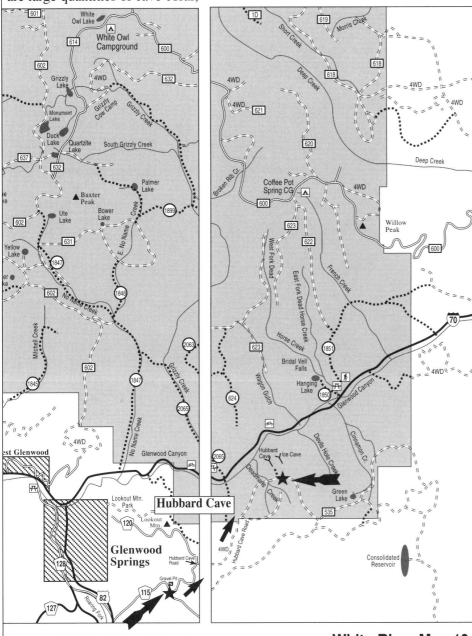

White River Map 9

White River Map 10

Road Name	Road Number	Length Miles	Difficulty	Beginning Elevation	Ending Elev.	Usage	Ranger District
West Deep Creek Rim	620	4	More Difficult	10,130'	10,490'	Low	Eagle

USGS: Broken Rib Spring.

This two-track road leaves the Coffee Pot Road (FDR 600) to climb up a southern slope meadow and follow along the west rim of the Deep Creek Canyon. The road erodes easily and often has deep ruts in the clay soil. Because of the soft nature of clay, this road becomes difficult to drive when wet. Mostly traveling is in open grassy meadows, though the road does pass through a couple of small patches of aspen and spruce/fir forest. On the steeper inclines, there are likely to be large protruding rocks. There are two intermittent stream crossings, which are relatively easy to cross. This old logging road ends at a stand of timber. This 4WD road receives most of its use during hunting season. It provides access to the Deep Creek Canyon rim where deer and elk often go to seek refuge.

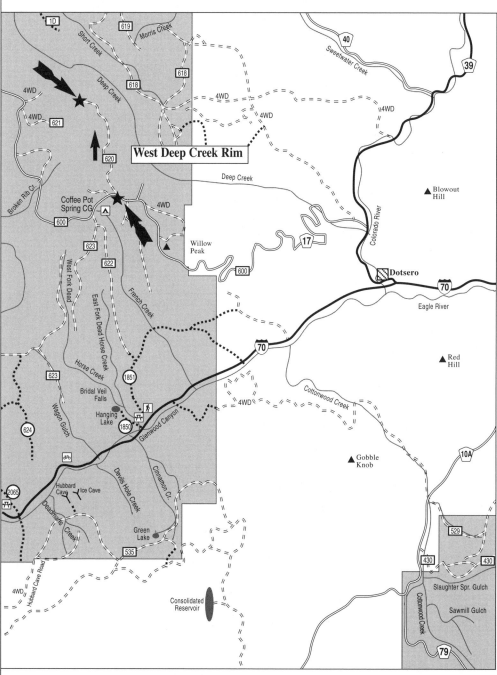

Several areas along the road offer nice views of the 2,200 foot deep canyon. The cliffs show many layers of sedimentary sandstones and limestones. Late July and August wildflowers are spectacular.

Directions from Eagle: Travel 12 miles west of Eagle on I-70 to the Dotsero exit. Follow signs for Sweetwater and Burns turning onto the Colorado River Road (FDR 600). Stay on this road for 1.8 miles, then turn left on the Coffee Pot Road, and go 16.5 miles up. Make a right turn onto FDR 620.

White River Map 10

Road Name	Road Number	Length Miles	Difficulty	Beginning Elevation	Ending Elev.	Usage	Ranger District
Red & White Mountain	734	11.4	Easy	9,600'	10,350'	Heavy	Holy Cross

Length: 11.4 Miles to Muddy Pass/June Creek Junction.
USGS Maps: Vail West, Edwards.

This all day excursion is perfect for families, or those wanting a little practice with their 4WD road skills. The road leaves from Vail, and shortly joins Red Sandstone Road County Road 701/FDR 700, a two-wheel drive dirt road with great scenery. You will encounter a lot of traffic on this road, including bikers and hikers. Please exercise caution.

There are places with views of Vail Ski Mountain, but they are easy to miss if you do not pull over at the right spot. Continuing on the road, you will come to an intersection at mile 11.4. The right spur will take you over Muddy Pass, the left down through June Creek.

The road to Muddy Pass becomes more difficult from here, and you should plan a full day to complete this loop. June Creek also becomes a bit more difficult at this point, but stays close to town, and will only take about an hour from this point.

You cannot access the Town of Edward from June Creek. The road is closed at the bottom.

Directions from Vail: From main roundabout, travel west on North Frontage road for 1 mile. You will see a sign on the right side of the road marked "Piney Lake/Red Sandstone Road". Turn right at the sign (County Road 701/FDR 700). Continue on the main road (FDR 700), 5 miles from the start of the dirt road, you will see a large meadow and take a left (FDR 700). Continue down the road until you reach a "Y". The right fork is the Red and White Road (FDR 734). June Creek or Muddy Pass can be accessed from this area.

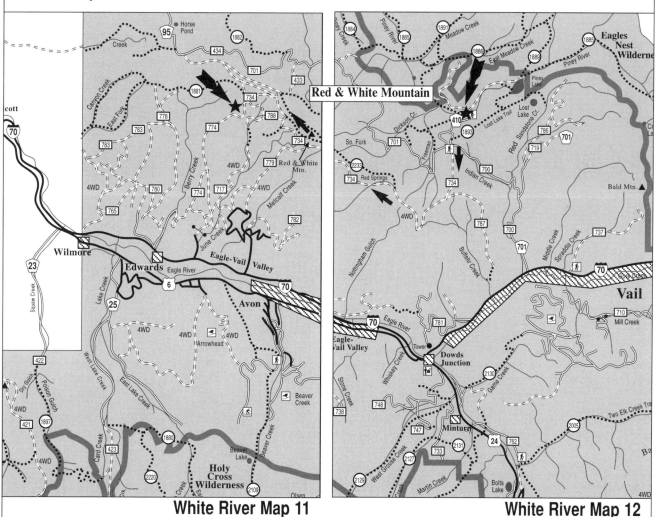

White River Map 11   **White River Map 12**

Road Name	Road Number	Length Miles	Difficulty	Beginning Elevation	Ending Elev.	Usage	Ranger District
Davos	781	4.2	Moderate	8,200'	8,900'	Heavy	Holy Cross

USGS Maps: Minturn and West Vail.

Some steep climbs and a few tight bends make this road fun, but not overly challenging. The road is mostly on a sunny hillside that winds through aspen forests where elk are frequently spotted. This road is most popular with mountain bikers, and local races are held on this road.

As the top of the last steep climb, you will be at the base of a large radio tower. There are great views to the west, south and east, with the focus towards the west past the town of Avon and Beaver Creek Ski Area.

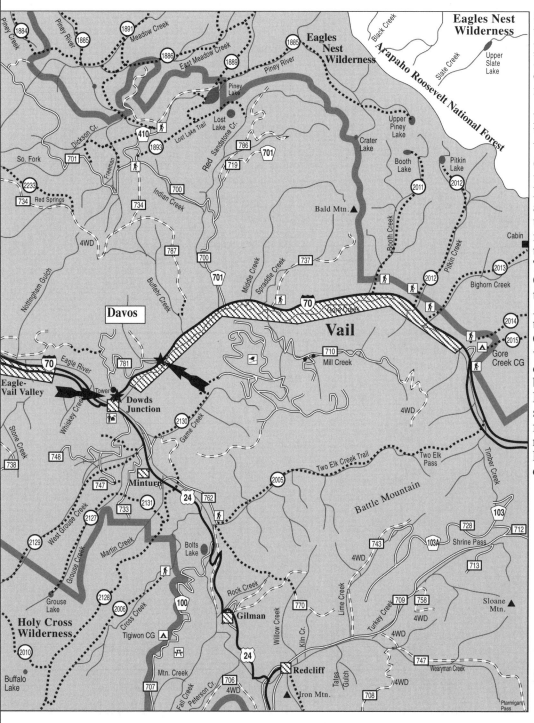

Stay in "four-low" to avoid spinning your wheels on the loose, rocky climbs. Watch for mountain bikers.

Directions from Vail: Take the West Vail exit (173) and travel west on North Frontage Road about .25 mile until the road makes a hairpin turn to the right. Turn right onto Chamonix Road, then right onto Arosa Drive. Stay to the right onto Cortina Lane, it will turn into the dirt road that becomes Davos Road. There is a spur at 4 miles from the paved road, stay to the left at this point to complete the road.

White River Map 12

Road Name	Road Number	Length Miles	Difficulty	Beginning Elevation	Ending Elev.	Usage	Ranger District
Lime Creek	743	3.9	More Difficult	8,850'	10,750'	Low	Holy Cross

Ending Elevation: 10,750 Feet at old mill ruins.
USGS Maps: Redcliff, Minturn.

This is a rough and challenging road leading to scenic meadows and an old saw mill. This road has a few rough spots, primarily at the beginning. There are rock holes and shelves that angle across the road and test your suspension system. A short climb leads to a creek crossing then climbs from a wooded area to a grassy bowl. It ends at an area that is a favorite for campers. At this point, look for the remnants of old saw mill.

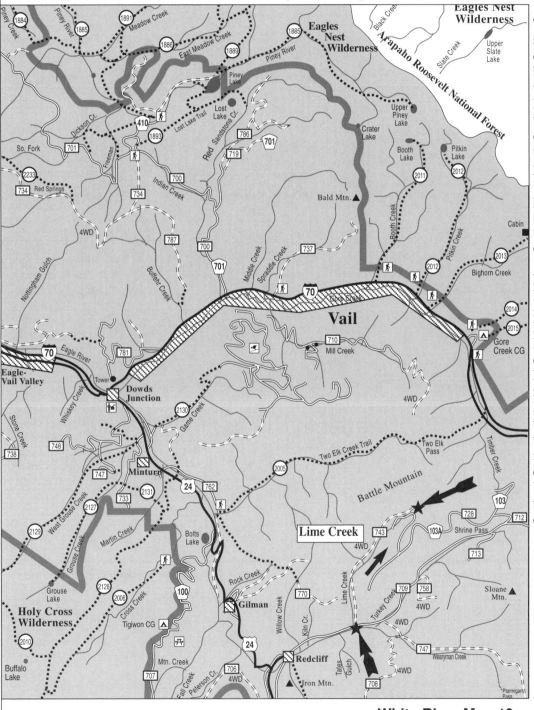

There are a few sections with steep drop-offs that may be tough for those with a fear of heights. Some sections exist where opposite wheels will lose traction if you are not careful with your wheel placement. Stock suspension system is not recommended for this road.

Directions from Minturn: Eight miles south of Minturn on Highway 24 east on Shrine Pass Road take the first road to the left. Depending upon time and desire, this spur can he reached from either the top of Vail Pass, or through the town of Redcliff.

White River Map 12

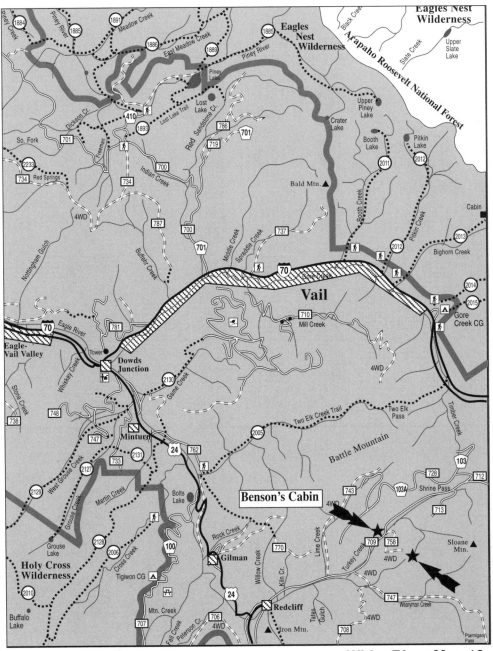

White River Map 12

Road Name	Road Number	Length Miles	Difficulty	Beginning Elevation	Ending Elev.	Usage	Ranger District
Bensons Cabin	758	2	More Difficult	9,600'	10,600'	Moderate	Holy Cross

USGS Maps: Red Cliff.

This four-wheel drive road starts out on a two-wheel drive dirt road and is primarily used by those who wish to take a short spur off of the main road. One of the least traveled roads in this area, it is often very overgrown with shrubs and plants and can scratch vehicle paint (Colorado pin stripe). The road spends most of its route in the shade, and is a good option on very hot days for a picnic spur.

It will take only about five minutes to reach the trailhead from the town of Redcliff. This road is recommended for smaller vehicles, the road is very narrow with trees on both sides.

This road can be very difficult due to erosion and overgrowth. If in doubt, walk the spur first! It is 2 miles in length one way to a private hunting camp. Almost immediately at the start of Benson's Cabins spur there is a challenging hardscrabble rock switchback. Do not attempt if wet!

A scenic day trip is a loop to Shrine Pass after enjoying the Benson's Cabins spur. Just continue on the two-wheel drive road that got you to the trailhead and after about 11 miles you will reach the summit of Vail Pass. Drive through the rest area and you will be back at I-70, 10 miles east of Vail. This loop can be done backwards if desired.

Directions from Vail: From Vail, proceed west on I-70 to the Minturn exit (171). Turn right (south) from the off-ramp onto Highway 24. Follow Highway 24 south through the town of Minturn to the Redcliff exit (unmarked) approximately 9 miles from the interstate turnoff.

Watch for this turnoff before the large and beautiful suspension bridge. The turn is to your left (east) just before the bridge begins. Follow this narrow paved road to the town of Redcliff, but keep your speed low due to speed control dips. This road turns into Eagle Street when you reach the town about .5 mile from the bridge. Look for the first left turn for Shrine Pass, the two-wheel drive dirt road that accesses this spur FDR 758.

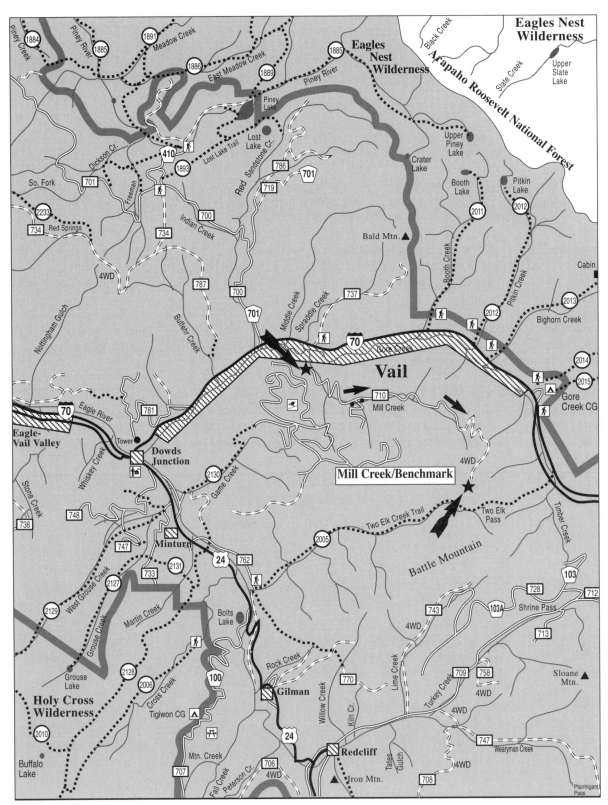

White River Map 12

Road Name	Road Number	Length Miles	Difficulty	Beginning Elevation	Ending Elev.	Usage	Ranger District
Mill Creek/Benchmark	710	9.1	Varies	8,600'	11,715'	Heavy	Holy Cross

Difficulty: Easiest to more difficult.
USGS Maps: Vail East, Redcliff.

A unique, scenic and really fun four-wheel drive trail used frequently by bikers, hikers and four-wheelers. This trail starts from the heart of Vail Village, and runs right up the face of the Ski Mountain, switching back on the international race hill aptly named "International".

This section is the best place in the area for large-scale pictures of Vail Village and the beautiful Gore Range to the east. The first portion of the trail is a graded dirt road, and many ski resort trucks and mountain bikes race through this area; watch out!

The road takes you past several small waterfalls and creeks, and is lush and green in the summertime. At 5.5 miles from the start, you will see a major spur road to the left (east), take this trail, it is the start of Benchmark. You can not continue on the ski mountain road from this point due to a locked gate, no access to public vehicles.

At this point the road becomes a true four-wheel drive road and is gets continually tougher, culminating with a very steep and bumpy climb to the summit.

There is an abundance of wildlife on this trail; keep your eyes open and you may see any variety of wildlife. From the turn-off onto Benchmark, there are numerous spurs; always take the left fork! Other spurs quickly become mud bogs or end at hunting camps.

Take your time, and stay out of the ruts to avoid becoming high centered. The road finishes with a very steep hill climb to the top of the world with 360-degree views. Unobstructed views in every direction; Mount of the Holy Cross, Battle Mountain, the Gore Range and the back bowls of Vail Mountain can be seen.

This mountaintop often hosts large herds of sheep, their herders and dogs; a neat experience. Follow the road around, it will loop back to the start of the last steep climb. Backtrack your way to Vail Village.

Be sure to watch out for heavy traffic on this road. Bikers especially tend to travel fast, and aren't always aware of traffic. There are many "speed bumps" on the start of the four-wheel drive section. These large mounds with deep dips after them are for water flow. Be sure to travel them slowly, as the dip size varies, and can do damage to shocks and under carriages of vehicles.

The last 2 miles of this road can he snowy or wet. Do not attempt under these conditions as large ruts and holes will be hidden and potentially can cause major problems. Be sure to use "4-low" and gear down appropriately before attempting the last steep climb to avoid slipping and spinning.

Directions from Vail: From the main Vail I-70 exit turn toward Vail Village and the ski area. At the main (south) roundabout, turn onto Vail Road, headed straight towards the Ski Mountain. A half block later, you'll be at a four-way stop. Go straight through the stop past the bank and church, and follow the road as it curves slightly to the left. You will see a dirt road to your right, up a small hill. Follow this dirt road to the ski lift, and take the first right turn up the mountain. At the top of this hill, take your first left, and follow the road from that point. At all spur intersections follow the main road to the left.

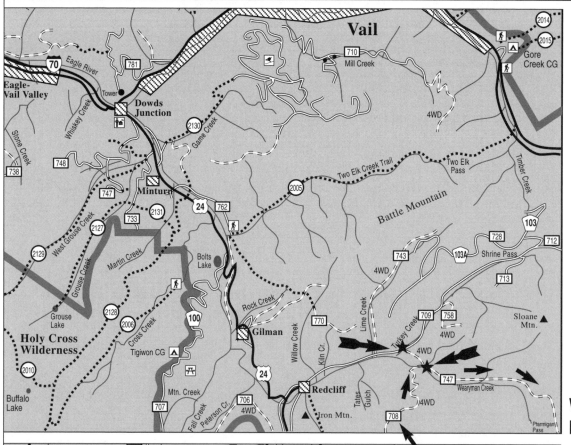

**White River
Map 12**

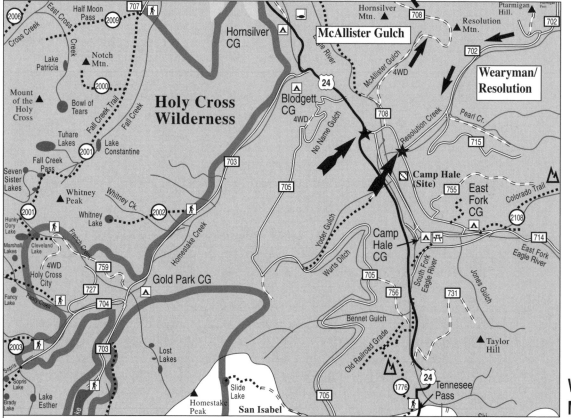

**White River
Map 18**

Road Name	Road Number	Length Miles	Difficulty	Beginning Elevation	Ending Elev.	Usage	Ranger District
Wearyman/Resolution	747	12.7	Most Difficult	9,600'	11,000'	Moderate	Holy Cross

Length: 5.7 Miles from Shrine Pass Road to Ptarmigan Pass. 12.7 Miles from Shrine Pass Road to Camp Hale.
USGS: Red Cliff, Pando.

This is truly a classic jeep road for this area, featuring some steep climbs, tight forest areas, and sweeping alpine meadows, topped off with everyone's favorite, a small bridge over a perfect mountain creek at the start (great for pictures). The beginning of this trail is the most difficult part with a formidable rocky road and the bridge crossing. The second bridge was not built by the Forest Service, be sure to check the bridge before continuing.

From mile point 3 you will enjoy a steep climb to the summit of Ptarmigan Pass, a great spot for all backcountry enthusiasts. This pass is aptly named for the large number of Ptarmigans in this area. From the summit of this Ptarmigan Pass the Wearyman 4WD Road turns into Resolution Road (FDR 702). Continue straight (south) on the graded, two wheel drive dirt road for 7 miles to Camp Hale. From the exit of Camp Hale, you will rejoin Hwy 24.

About 3 miles from the start of this road, you will see a pullover spot on your left. Be sure to take a short walk on the footpath from this spot. It leads to a large meadow usually filled with wildflowers in the summer. Ptarmigan Pass is named for the large grouse-like bird that inhabits the area. Ptarmigan change the color of its feathers from brown and white in the summer to pure white in the winter. If you are lucky enough to spot a one, they are white with black dots.

You may notice remnants of buildings in this area. They are old sawmills that operated near the turn of the century, and supplied many of the ranches and farms in this area with building supplies.

Please help us control erosion, and stay on this road at all times. This is especially true at the beginning creek crossing! The beginning of this road is very narrow, watch for vehicles traveling in the other direction.

Directions from Vail: Travel west on I-70 to the Minturn exit (171). Turn right (south) from the off-ramp onto Hwy 24. Follow Hwy 24 south 9 miles through the town of Minturn to the Redcliff turnoff (unmarked). Watch for this turn off before the large suspension bridge. Turn to your left (east) just before the bridge begins. Follow this narrow paved road to the town of Redcliff. In Redcliff this road turns into Eagle Street about 0.5 mile from the bridge. Look for the first left turn for Shrine Pass, the two wheel drive dirt road that accesses Wearyman Road. The trailhead is the first turn on the right off Shrine Pass Road. You'll see two creeks joining at the trailhead, as well as a Forest Service sign. Stay on the main road, avoiding spur roads that usually lead to hunting camps.

Road Name	Road Number	Length Miles	Difficulty	Beginning Elevation	Ending Elev.	Usage	Ranger District
McAllister/Hornsilver	708	10	Moderate	9,200'	8,650'	Moderate	Holy Cross

USGS Maps: Pando and Redcliff.

Follow the road .5 miles from Highway 24 take a left at the Y and then a left at the immediate next Y (FDR 708). Follow FDR 708 north along the mountainside until you enter the pine forest. At the beginning of this trail you will notice that the trail crosses private land. Please respect this crossing and stay on the trail. The summit is about 8.5 miles from the private land area, and Hornsilver Road ends in a junction with Wearyman Jeep Road (FDR 747). Turn left (north) onto Wearyman, which will quickly end at a junction with Shrine Pass Road (FDR 709). Take a left onto Shrine Pass Road and follow the graded dirt road into the town of Redcliff. Go through Redcliff, and you'll be at Highway 24, just north of Camp Hale.

The rough sections are a steep rocky climb at mile point 4.3 and some narrow sections on the ridge top. This trail difficulty primarily comes from the steep switchbacks on both the ascent and descent. The trail switchbacks through thick narrow pine forests.

The summit rewards you with spectacular views of the Sawatch Range, Gore Range, Mount of the Holy Cross, Camp Hale and Mount Elbert. One of the 10th Mountain Huts is visible from a short walk east at the summit on the descent where the trail becomes Hornsilver Mountain. You will see remnants of an old Warrens Sawmill at mile 8.6.

DO NOT ATTEMPT THIS TRAIL WHEN WET! Due to erosion, and loss of traction from the oily, muddy dirt. This trail is very steep. Keep your vehicle in 4-low at all times, and avoid spinning your wheels. The trail has many switchbacks. Please stay on the trail.

Directions from Vail: Follow I-70 west to the Minturn exit (171). Follow Highway 24 south through the town of Minturn 14 miles from the interstate until you reach a valley opening. Look for the first major turnoff on the left (east) side onto the road entering Camp Hale.

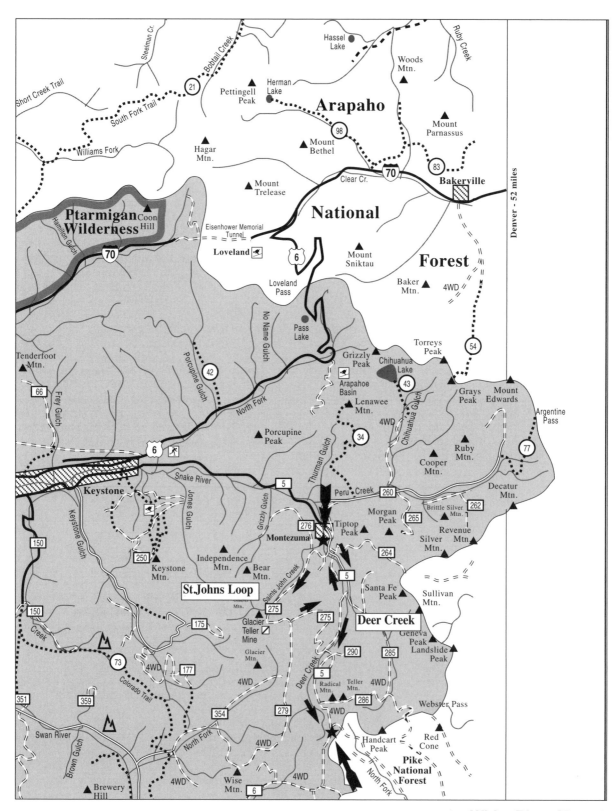

White River Map 13

Road Name	Road Number	Length Miles	Difficulty	Beginning Elevation	Ending Elev.	Usage	Ranger District
Deer Creek	5	7.5	Moderate	10,268'	12,400'	Moderate	Dillon

USGS Maps: Montezuma.

The Deer Creek drainage serves as the backbone to an extensive system of 4WD roads branching in all directions from the main trail. We suggest you obtain USGS topographic maps for orientation.

The Deer Creek road provides access to the Pike National Forest via the Continental Divide and Hall Valley to the south. A spur road also branches off southwest to Sts. John. For the experienced 4-wheeler, more hazardous roads branch off east to the Webster Pass area, and southwest to the Swan River drainage.

Throughout this system of trails, the scenery is spectacular with views of the Tenmile Range, the Gore Range, Grays and Torrey Peaks and the vast expanse of South Park. In mid-summer, tundra wildflowers abound above 12,000 feet, so bring a camera.

Directions from Keystone: Travel on US 6 to Montezuma Road east of Keystone. Turn right then veer left, following the road past Montezuma. The Deer Creek Road begins 2.5 miles past Montezuma.

Road Name	Road Number	Length Miles	Difficulty	Beginning Elevation	Ending Elev.	Usage	Ranger District
Saint Johns Loop	275	14	Moderate	10,268'	12,400'	Moderate	Dillon

Beginning Elevation: Montezuma.
Ending Elevation: General Teller Mines.
USGS Maps: Montezuma, Keystone.

The Sts. John drainage offers a wide variety of recreation opportunities, for the 4WD enthusiast, as well as trail bikers and hikers. 2WD vehicles can easily make it to within .25 mile of historic Sts. John, making this area as ideal place for short day hikes.

From Sts. John the road continues on to the Wild Irishman and General Teller Mines. From General Teller the road becomes more difficult, but continues on to connect with the Deer Creek drainage, and eventually north back to Montezuma.   As an alternative, to returning to Montezuma, you may continue south into Hall Valley and the Pike National Forest. For the experienced 4-wheeler, there is also a somewhat dangerous road going east to connect with the middle fork of the Swan River. This road becomes evident as you head south toward Hall Valley.

Directions from Keystone: Travel on US 6 to the Montezuma Road 5 east of Keystone. Turn right, then veer left, continuing to the Saints John road intersection in the center of Montezuma. Turn right at the intersection. The area up to and including Sts. John is private. Please respect private property.

Trip Planning
Individual Forest maps are available at sporting goods stores, maps stores, and from U.S. Forest Service offices. The maps provide an overview of the National Forest road system. Purchase a Forest Map.

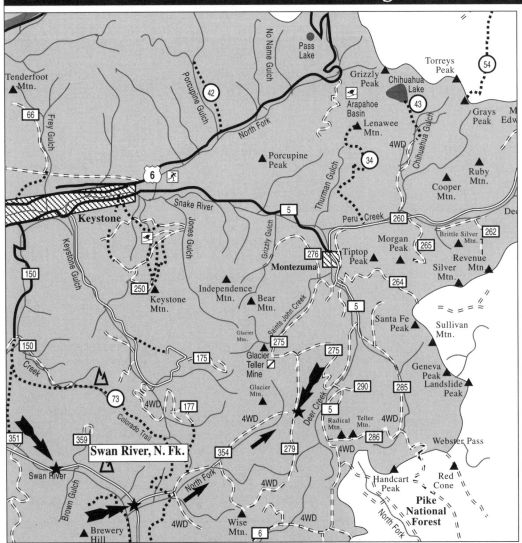

White River Map 13

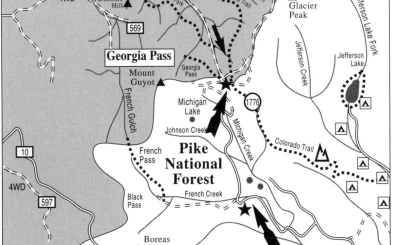

White River Map 19

Road Name	Road Number	Length Miles	Difficulty	Beginning Elevation	Ending Elev.	Usage	Ranger District
Swan River, North Fork	356	5	Moderate	9,773'	11,600'	Moderate	Dillon

Beginning Elevation: Tiger Road.
Ending Elevation: Base of Glacier Mountain.
USGS Maps: Keystone.

The North Fork drainage provides access to the ruins of the old mining camp of Rexford. Although the trail dead ends at the base of Glacier Mountain, and you must retrace your route, it does lead to seldom use back-country camping areas. The route is ideal for day hikes.

Directions from Breckenridge: Turn east onto Tiger Road off of Colorado 9, 4 miles north of Breckenridge. Continue 7 miles to the North Fork Swan River road.

Road Name	Road Number	Length Miles	Difficulty	Beginning Elevation	Ending Elev.	Usage	Ranger District
Georgia Pass	355	10	Most Difficult	9,770'	11,585'	Moderate	Dillon

Length: 10 Miles. (23 Miles)
Beginning Elevation: Tiger Road.
Ending Elevation: Georgia Pass.
USGS Maps: Frisco, Boreas Pass, Keystone, Montezuma.

The Georgia Pass Road provides an excellent day trip for motorcycles and 4 WD's. The road progresses through lodgepole pine forest, to spruce/fir with beautiful flower filled meadows, to lush tundra with breathtaking scenery. The trip passes through the mining camps of Parkville on the South Fork, and Swandyke on the Middle Fork. A short side trip up Glacier Peak allows a spectacular view of South Park, Greys and Torreys Peaks, and the Tenmile Range.

Georgia Pass is located on the Continental Divide at the north end of the Park Mountain Range. Georgia Pass was one of the first transportation routes to the Breckenridge area during the region's gold discovery era. However, both Hoosier and Boreas Pass proved to be easier access routes and Georgia Pass were soon abandoned.

The pass provides travelers with spectacular views of South Park. Mt. Guyot lies to the west of the pass on the Continental Divide. Today the Colorado Trail leads across Georgia Pass. This pass is open from June until October weather permitting. Sections of western portion of road are rocky and narrow.

Lower portions of both the Middle and South Forks are accessible to 2 WD, and provide ideal tent and trailer camping.

Directions from Breckenridge: Turn east onto the Tiger Road off of Colorado 9, 4 miles north of Breckenridge. Continue past the North Fork Swan River Road to either the Middle Fork or South Fork Roads. Both lead to George Pass.

Directions from Fairplay: From Fairplay drive north on Highway 285 for 16 miles to the small town of Jefferson. Turn left on to County Road 35. Continue driving until you reach County Road 54, which will turn into Pike Forest Road 54. The dirt road to the top of Georgia Pass is relatively accessible with a passenger vehicle however, to continue onto the western portion of the mountain, four-wheel drive, high-clearance vehicles are recommended.

Road Name	Road Number	Length Miles	Difficulty	Beginning Elevation	Ending Elev.	Usage	Ranger District
Battlement	847	2.2	Most Difficult	7,920'	10,200'	Moderate	Rifle

USGS Maps: Rulison, Hawkhurst Creek.

The Battlement area is truly unique in that it is still rather primitive in nature. The Battlement Road is very rocky with large lava boulders to navigate around and over. This road should be traveled only during dry weather and is extremely rough and challenging to any 4-wheeling enthusiast. You should plan to have plenty of time to travel this road. Campsites and water are available. You may encounter closed gates, here you are crossing private property, please close the gates behind you.

Battlement Road is one of the most challenging 4-wheel drive roads that you will travel on the Rifle Ranger District. The first 2 miles is a twisting, rocky uphill climb through spruce/fir forest road with several small stream crossings. There are a number of difficult obstacles that you will encounter on this route. Once at the Battlement Reservoirs, it makes the rough trip worth it. There are a number of good campsites at the Reservoirs. Please remember to pack your trash out with you when you leave.

Directions from Rifle: Go west of Rifle on I-70 for 16 miles (exit 75) to Parachute turn left on County Road 301, continue across the Colorado River for 4 miles to the Project Rulison Site. From this point on the road requires a 4-wheel drive vehicle to the Battlement Reservoirs. The road is very rough, and it is recommended that you be an experienced 4-wheel driver before taking this road.

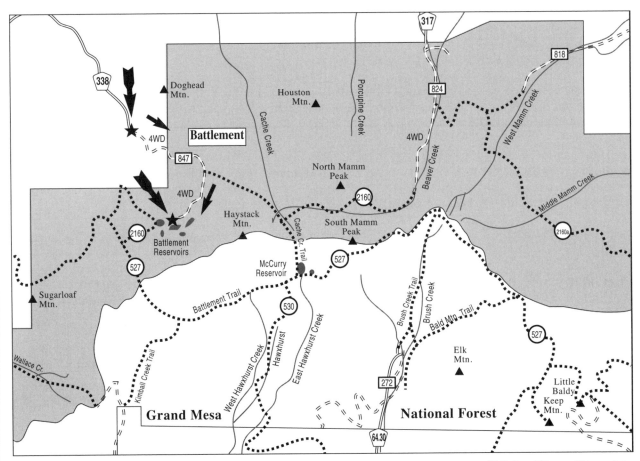

White River Map 14

24. Thompson Creek

White River

Road Name	Road Number	Length Miles	Difficulty	Beginning Elevation	Ending Elev.	Usage	Ranger District
Thompson Creek	305/306	12.1	Moderate	7,808'	8,440'	Moderate	Sopris

USGS Maps: Cattle Creek, Stony Ridge, Quaker Mesa.

Thompson Creek Road provides access for many hiking and biking trails including the following: South Thompson (FDT 1952), Lake Ridge Lakes (FDT 2093), Middle Thompson (FDT 1950), South Branch of Mid Thompson (FDT 1951) and Dexter Park. Bicyclist, horseback riders and hunters primarily use this area. It passes through aspen groves and crosses many small streams.

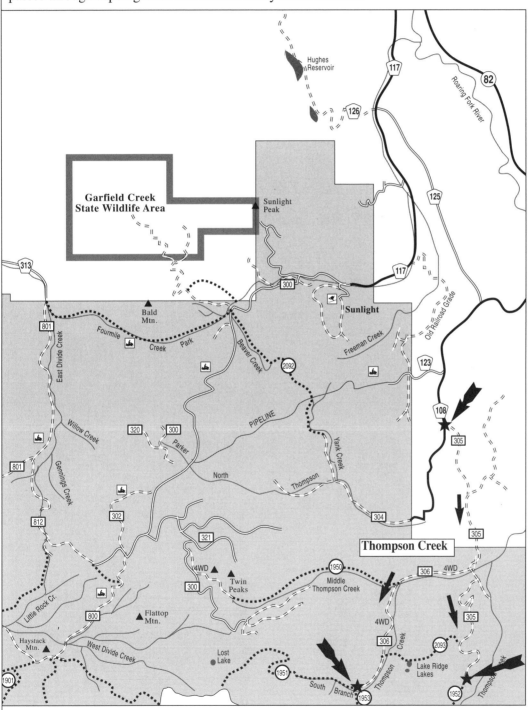

Thompson Creek Road is impassable when wet, so do not drive it if rain is in the forecast. The road is accessible to two-wheel drive vehicles until reaching the stream crossing at Middle Thompson. Users will need a high-clearance four-wheel drive to cross the stream and for the road afterward. Continue driving 3.9 miles on road FDR 305 until you reach a fork in the road. Take the right fork to access road FDR 306 and Mid Thompson, the South Branch of Mid Thompson, Dexter Park and Lake Ridge Lake Trails. Take the left fork to stay on road FDR 305 to access South Thompson.

Directions from Carbondale:
Follow County Road 108 west past the stoplight for 7.5 miles and turn left on to Mid Thompson Creek Road FDR 305.

White River Map 15

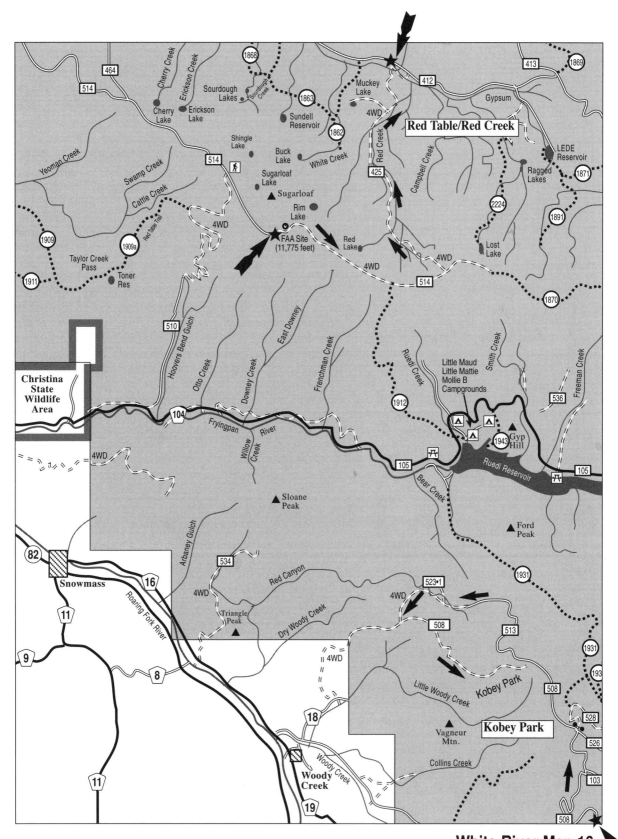

White River Map 16

Road Name	Road Number	Length Miles	Difficulty	Beginning Elevation	Ending Elev.	Usage	Ranger District
Red Table/Red Creek Loop	514/425	50	More Difficult	6,600'	6,600'	Low	Eagle

Length: 50 Miles. (Approx. 13.5 miles of 4WD road.)
USGS Maps: Suicide Mtn., Cottonwood Pass, Leon, Toner Res., Red Creek.

All along the Red Table Mountain ridge top, there are spectacular panoramic views. The Gypsum Creek drainage, a series of cirque lakes and the Sawatch Mountain Range are visible to the northeast. To the southwest, the Roaring Fork Valley, Ruedi Reservoir and the Maroon Bells of Aspen are in view.

There are good chances of spotting big game such as elk or mule deer in the meadows or aspen woods of Red Table Mountain. Yellow-bellied marmots, golden-mantled ground squirrels and chipmunks are common in the rocky areas.

Begin the loop by taking a right onto County Road 10A at the Cottonwood Pass sign off of Gypsum Creek Road. CAUTION: This gypsum base dirt road through sagebrush and oak becomes impassable when wet. Travel 11 miles and take a left onto the Red Table 4-wheel drive Road (FDR 514) just before Cottonwood Pass. This road which follows the ridge top of Red Table Mountain is moderately rough with some narrow spots. The 4WD section of FDR 514 begins at the FAA Site (elevation 11,775 feet) approximately 5 miles west of FDR 425. The road travels through aspen and spruce/fir forest and into alpine meadows. The last mile or so of FDR 514 is difficult shelf driving. The road is built on loose rock that slants to the outside. Often times rocks need to be cleared from this section before continuing on. Take a left just after the switchbacks and before the Red Table Road ends onto Red Creek Road (FDR 425). This road begins in dense spruce/fir forest and descends into aspen following the Red Creek drainage. The Red Creek Road is very steep and narrow in areas with many large protruding rocks. The middle 2-3 miles are slow going, only 5 mph at most. Once completing the 8.8 miles on FDR 425, it ends at the Gypsum Creek Road (FDR 412). Take a left and continue north to town.

Directions from Eagle: Go 7 miles south of Eagle on I-70 to the Gypsum exit. Turn left onto Hwy 6 for 1 mile, then turn right at the Forest Access sign. Travel 2.5 miles up the Gypsum Creek Road, turn right onto County road 10A. There is parking at the beginning of Red Table Road for vehicles and trailers.

Road Name	Road Number	Length Miles	Difficulty	Beginning Elevation	Ending Elev.	Usage	Ranger District
Kobey Park	508	6	Moderate	8,600'	10,989'	Moderate	Aspen

USGS Maps: Aspen, Ruedi.

Kobey Park is an old logging area with many spur roads winding through it. There are beautiful views of the Elk Mountains to the south. This is a fairly well maintained 4WD road, used by mountain bikes, 4WD's, dirt bikes, and snowmobilers in the winter. From Lenado continue up the 4WD road. This road is sometimes called Christmas Tree Road since it winds back and forth around the mountain. It provides a superb view of the Elk Mountains, Williams Mountains, and the Sawatch Range. A great view of Mt. Yeckel can be found at the end of FDR 526. There are numerous spur roads, stay on the main road. At the intersection, between Road FDR 103 and FDR 508, keep straight on FDR 508 to Kobey Park (Road FDR 103 goes to the right and heads to Margy's Hut). Camping spots are numerous, water is scarce.

Directions from Aspen: From Aspen travel west 7 miles on Highway 82 to the Woody Creek turn-off on your right. At the bottom of the hill and across the bridge left to the Woody Creek Tavern. About a .25 mile past the tavern make a sharp right onto FDR 103 and drive 10 miles to Lenado. From there continue on the road to Kobey Park.

Road Name	Road Number	Length Miles	Difficulty	Beginning Elevation	Ending Elev.	Usage	Ranger District
Mid-Cunningham Creek	532	6	Moderate	9,600'	10,720'	Moderate	Sopris

USGS Maps: Meredith, Nast.

Sellar and Diemer Lakes are near the west-end of Forest Road FDR 532, There is fishing and some dispersed camping opportunities at these lakes. A good place to view alpine scenery is at the eastern end of Mid Cunningham Creek Road

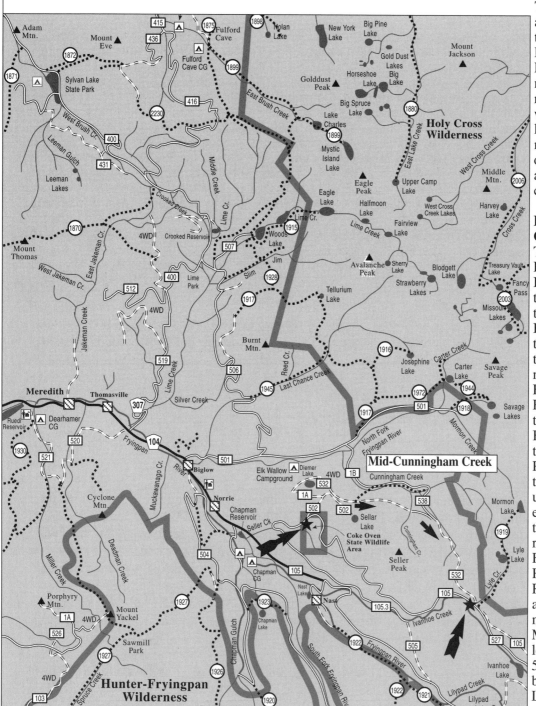

This route provides a challenging side trip from the Hagerman Pass Road. It has some narrow, steep and rocky sections that will provide a challenge suitable for many four-wheel drive vehicles with adequate ground clearance.

Directions from Carbondale:
Travel east on Highway 82 to Basalt. Turn left at the stoplight and travel through Basalt following the main street through town, this road is the Fryingpan River Road. The road travels out of Basalt following the Fryingpan River. From Basalt travel 27 miles until the pavement ends, turn left at the fork in the road, staying on FDR 105 the Hagerman Pass Road. Travel on the all weather road 4 miles to Sellar Meadow and take a left on to road FDR 502, This will bring you to Sellar Lake.

White River Map 17

Road Name	Road Number	Length Miles	Difficulty	Beginning Elevation	Ending Elev.	Usage	Ranger District
Holy Cross City	759	3.5	More Difficult	9,300'	11,400'	Heavy	Holy Cross

USGS Maps: Mount of the Holy Cross, Pando.

The trailhead is identifiable by the parking lot in front of a "road of rocks", the only pullover like this on Homestake Road. The road follows the rock road without any side spurs to confuse you until about 2 miles from the trailhead, where a spur to the left (south) drops downhill to a two-wheel drive access road. Continue on FDR 759 up the road and you will he rewarded by the river crossing, the most challenging obstacle on this road. Most small vehicles will find that crossing the river on the left (south) side easier, while some long bedded vehicles enjoy the right side. Note that usually until mid-June at the earliest, the river crossing is not passable due to high water. Immediately after conquering the river crossing, take the left road (there is a "Y" without a sign). From this point, you are almost a .5 mile from the destination - Holy Cross City. Enjoy the road from this point, and be sure to follow the footpath to the cabins. Backtrack on the same road to complete your trip.

Holy Cross Road is extremely challenging and should be attempted by experienced drivers with modified vehicles only. Hi-Lift jacks, a fire extinguisher, extra clearance and locking differentials are basic requirements for this road.

This road is not for the faint of heart or scared of heights, either, since many of the tougher sections requires serious side-hill driving. If in doubt, hike it first. It is only about 3.5 miles. Because of the bouncy rock road, most drivers lower their tire pressure to between 10-15 PSI, but be sure you still have clearance. Although short in mileage, this road takes most vehicles a full day from the trailhead. Allow adequate time, since this road is much more difficult if you find it took longer than you thought.

This historic stage coach route to the ghost town of Holy Cross has quite a past and includes some of the most spectacular and challenging driving in Colorado.

This road is not gated closed but is considered one of the most difficult 4-wheel drive roads in Colorado. A winch may be required in places to haul your vehicle up. Snow patches may be encountered and muddy conditions. The road is very steep and rocky, many huge rocks also, potholes and mud bogs. Bighorn Jeep Club has adopted this road with the help of a grant in 2000. The club placed anchor bolts in the road, please use winch anchors, don not anchor from trees. Drivers need to stay on road and out of bog below city.

In the city's heyday in 1800's Holy Cross was proud of its two gold mills that processed ore from 30 mines in this area. It is truly amazing to see all of the heavy equipment that was dragged to this location considering how hard it would have been for wagons and horses to get here. This area has also recently regained notoriety by being within one mile of the crash site of an A-1O air force bomber in the spring of 1997.

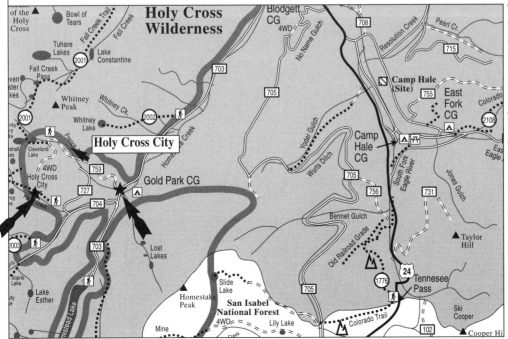

This road is used to reach the city and to return. Be aware of vehicles headed in the opposite direction!

Directions from Vail:
Follow I-70 to the Minturn exit (171). Turn right (south) from the off-ramp onto Hwy. 24. Follow Hwy 24 south approximately 11.5 miles from I-70 to the turn-off on the right (west) side onto Homestake Creek Road (FDR 703). From Highway 24 travel southwest on Homestake Road (FDR 703) approximately 8 miles to the trailhead on the right (west).

White River Map 18

Road Name	Road Number	Length Miles	Difficulty	Beginning Elevation	Ending Elev.	Usage	Ranger District
No Name/Wurtz	705	2.1	More Difficult	9,000'	10,816'	Moderate	Holy Cross

USGS Maps: Pando, Mt. Of the Holy Cross, Leadville North.

This road leads to high mountain meadows where snow tends to stay in patches year round. You will also notice many logging areas, especially on the two-wheel drive dirt road that brings you to the trailhead.

Most of the road is through thickly forested area, with occasional glimpses of mountain ranges to the west. The actual road is primarily embedded rock, with good traction and a few very steep sections. There is a spur road to your right at .75 mile from the trailhead. This spur is not really worth exploring and ends almost as soon as it starts in private, fenced land.

At two miles into the road, there is a "Y" intersection, stay to the right. Although this spur into Yoder Gulch looks passable by 4WD, it is best left to hikers and bikers, as the road quickly disintegrates into impassable bogs, impassable side-hill sections and ends with a "jump" of about 15 feet that is very dangerous to vehicles.

This road provide access to a good view from Yoder Gulch Meadows. At mile point 1.3 there is a drainage crossing with excellent views of Sheep Mountain and Chicago Ridge. At mile point 1.0 a rocky section of road reaches a ridge top and road junction. There is sign directing you to the left. The right hand road dead ends in .7 mile at the tundra where a fence denotes closure at the wilderness boundary. The road to the left continues on to Wurtz Ditch Road that leads to the Continental Divide back to Highway 24.

Travel Tips: Be advised this road typically retains snow and Wurtz Ditch may not be accessed. Check with the Holy Cross or Leadville Ranger Districts.

Directions from Vail: Follow I-70 to the Minturn exit (171). Follow Hwy 24 through the town of Minturn and continue 13 miles to FDR 705. The turn off on the right (west) side of the road is hard to see, look for a dirt parking area immediately before the road sign. Follow the two-wheel drive dirt road for 7 miles until you come to the marked trailhead on the right side (south) of the road. The road quickly becomes very rocky and steep at this point, but it is also one of the toughest parts of the entire trail. Follow the trail either to the summit, then back track, or try Wurtz Ditch. Watch out on the spur roads, they turn into mud bogs immediately. The main trail is much more rewarding.

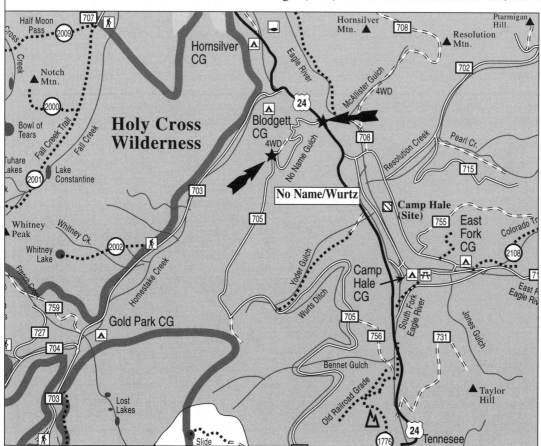

White River Map 18

Road Name	Road Number	Length Miles	Difficulty	Beginning Elevation	Ending Elev.	Usage	Ranger District
Ranch Creek	755	4	Most Difficult	9,200'	11,000'	Moderate	Holy Cross

USGS Map: Pando.

This road leaves historic Camp Hale training ground primarily used by the military during World War II. Camp Hale is partially responsible for the creation of Vail and Beaver Creek Ski resorts, as some of the soldiers who trained at Camp Hale returned to start these world class ski areas. Be sure to read the information sign posted at a turnoff on Hwy 24, near the south end of Camp Hale.

Ranch Creek Road (FDR 755) trail is quite steep in many sections but is a great choice for those looking for challenging four-wheeling. A trip for those that do not want to spend all day in their vehicle. This road gains elevation quickly and visitors frequently see wildlife including marmots, deer and elk. After .25 mile, the road weaves in and out of a mature aspen forest, alternating with open meadow featuring great views to the west and south. At 2 miles, is the ruins of a sheep herding camp. It is estimated that these cabins were built around 1870 because of the square headed nails that were used.

At just under 4 miles, you will reach the summit with amazing views of the Sawatch Range, and fourteen thousand-foot peaks to the south. If you stop in this meadow please be aware of the fragile tundra, and enjoy the abundance of wildflowers from the road, so that others may do the same in the future.

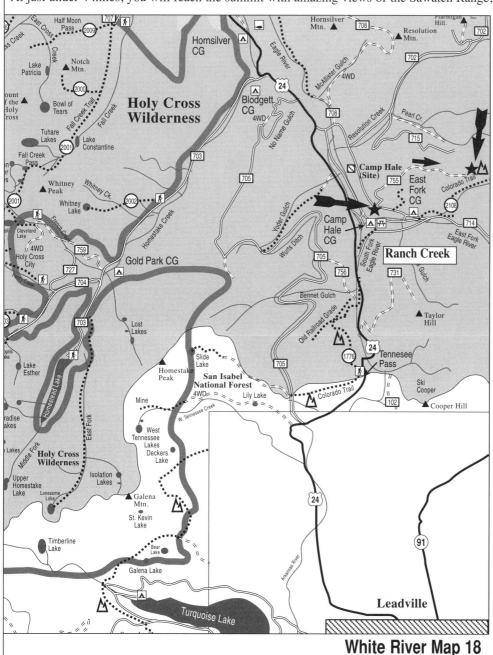

You may wish to walk a little further down this road, there is a 10th Mountain Division Hut here. Jackal Hut is one of the nicest in this link of huts used by cross-country skiers and hikers, and boasts a spacious main floor and a sauna. Call the 10th Mountain Division Hut System for more information.

At this point, carefully turn your vehicle around, and enjoy the trip back the way you came.

Directions from Vail: Take I-70 to the Minturn exit (171). Follow Hwy 24 south, through the town of Minturn, a distance of 14 miles from the interstate until you reach a valley opening. Look for the first major turnoff on the left (east) side onto a dirt road entering Camp Hale. Follow the road to the immediate right and at .5 miles from Hwy 24 take a left at the "Y" and then a right at the immediate next "Y". Follow this road south approximately .5 miles until it curves left (east) and look for the Ranch Creek Jeep Road sign on your right (north).

White River Map 18

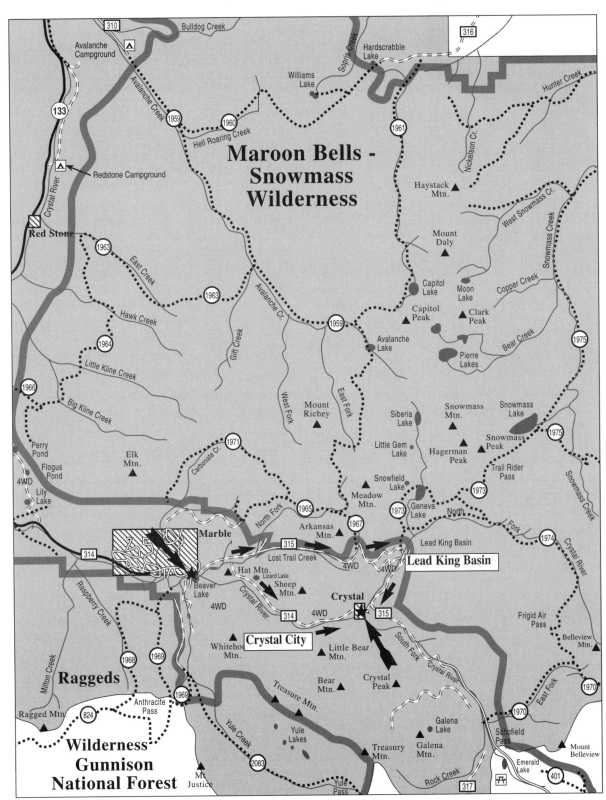

Maroon Bells - Snowmass Wilderness

Lead King Basin

Crystal City

Raggeds

Wilderness Gunnison National Forest

White River Map 20

Road Name	Road Number	Length Miles	Difficulty	Beginning Elevation	Ending Elev.	Usage	Ranger District
Lead King Basin	315	8	More Difficult	7,956'	8,800'	Moderate	Sopris

High Point: 10,800 Feet - Silver Creek Trailhead.
USGS Maps: Marble, Snowmass Mtn.

The segment from Marble along Lost Trail Creek to Lead King Basin should not be traveled when it is wet! The road is built on slick shale and slopes towards the valley bottom. Four-wheel drive is required. From Lead King to Crystal City the road is very narrow and extremely rocky. There is a very steep drop-off into the Crystal River Canyon. There are few pull-offs on this road and drivers may be required to back-up for considerable distances when another vehicle is met. A high clearance four-wheel drive vehicle is required for this segment. A loop can be made from Marble by traveling the Crystal River Road (FDR 314) from to Crystal City to Marble.

Lead King Basin road passes very close to the boundary of the Maroon Bells-Snowmass Wilderness and affords some spectacular views of mountains, meadows, and canyons. The basin is a great place to view a variety of wildflowers during the late summer. Three trailheads into the Maroon Bells-Snowmass Wilderness are located along this road. Be wary of the old bridge over the Crystal River between Crystal and Lead King Basin is not maintained by the Forest Service and located on private land. Please respect the privacy of these landowners.

Directions from Carbondale: Travel south on Colorado Highway 133 for 22 miles to the Marble turnoff, Go east on the Marble road, through Marble, and past Beaver Lake. The four-wheel drive section begins just past the Gold Pan Gallery. The road begins to head uphill and passes over shale rock. About one mile outside of Marble there is a fork in the road, take the left fork (FDR 315), the road immediately heads uphill.

Road Name	Road Number	Length Miles	Difficulty	Beginning Elevation	Ending Elev.	Usage	Ranger District
Crystal City	314	5.5	Difficult	7,956'	8,800'	High	Sopris

USGS Maps: Marble, Snowmass Mtn.

The city of Crystal is an old mining town and is now somewhat of a ghost town. The Dead Horse Mill, or Crystal Mill, a historical landmark, stands next to the Crystal River west of town as a reminder of the mining economy that brought settlers to the region. The mill stands on private property and is not open to the public.

The Crystal River Road (FDR 314) parallels the Crystal River from Beaver Lake to Crystal City. Although most of the road is not too difficult, there are several narrow, rocky and steep sections where it may he necessary for the downhill driver to back up when encountering another vehicle. This is not a road for passenger automobiles or inexperienced drivers.

For the most experienced four-wheeler, it is possible to continue beyond Crystal City to Schofield Pass (FDR 315), or to make a loop back to Marble via the Lead Basin Road.

Directions from Carbondale: From Carbondale travel south on Colorado Highway 133 about 22 miles to the Marble turn off. Go east on the Marble road, through Marble, and past Beaver Lake. The four wheel-drive portion begins just past the Gold Pan Gallery. The road begins to head uphill and passes over shale rock. About one mile outside of Marble there is a fork in the road, take the right fork (FDR 314). The road immediately heads downhill.

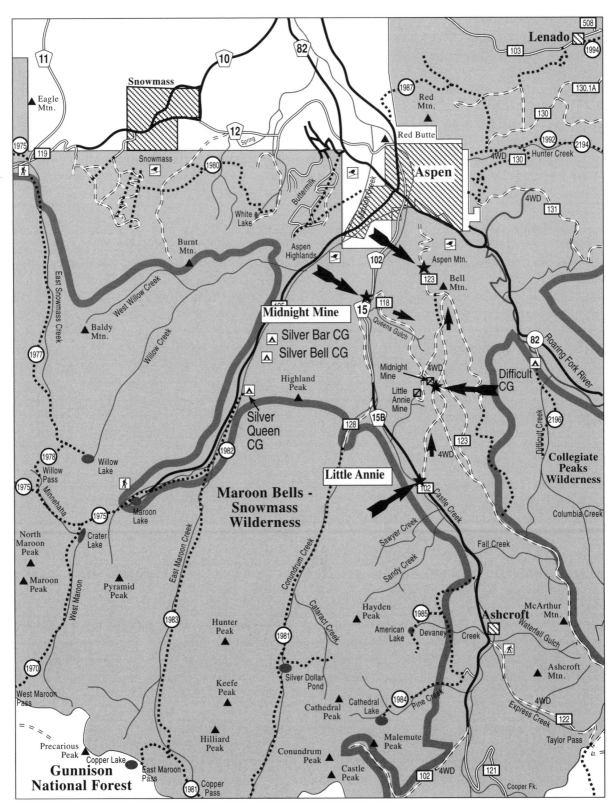

White River Map 21

Road Name	Road Number	Length Miles	Difficulty	Beginning Elevation	Ending Elev.	Usage	Ranger District
Midnight Mine		4.5	Difficult	9,000'	11,892'	Heavy	Aspen

USGS Maps: Highland Peak, Aspen.

This is a fairly well maintained dirt road with several steep sections. This road is not used by four-wheel drivers as much as Little Annie or Summer Roads. A loop ride can be made by going up Midnight Mine and down Little Annie or a longer route down Summer Road. The road follows Queens Gulch, passing through aspen and fir stands.

The road begins with a short descent then crosses a bridge and begins its continuous uphill climb. There are numerous private drives, please stay on the main road. The road becomes steeper with several switchbacks. In approximately 2 miles there is a cabin on the left and a large mound of mine tailings on the right. The road climbs steeply between them continuing to ascend to the junction with Little Annie Road at about the 4-mile mark. Stay left to continue to the top of Aspen Mountain and the Sundeck Restaurant. From the top you can access Richmond Hill Road (which follows the ridge behind Aspen Mountain), or Summer Road (which goes down the front of Aspen Mountain).

Directions from Aspen: Travel west from Aspen .5 mile on Highway 82 and turn left at the Maroon Creek Road turnoff, then immediately take a left onto Castle Creek Road. Travel about 2 miles on Castle Creek Road to the turn-off to Midnight Mine Road on the left. There is some parking at the start of Midnight Mine Road.

Road Name	Road Number	Length Miles	Difficulty	Beginning Elevation	Ending Elev.	Usage	Ranger District
Little Annie		7.5	Difficult	9,000'	11,212'	Heavy	Aspen

USGS Maps: Hayden Peak, Aspen.

The road is fairly well maintained. It is used heavily by 4WD's, especially on weekends. Going up Little Annie Road and down Midnight Mine Road, or a longer trip down Summer Road can make a loop ride. This is a very scenic ride with great views of the Castle Creek Valley.

The road climbs gradually with several private drives along the first few miles please stay on the main road. The road becomes steeper and climbs to the intersection with Midnight Mine Road in a little over 3 miles. Stay straight to continue to the top of Aspen Mountain. The last section climbs to the top of Aspen Mountain and the Sundeck Restaurant. Them are spectacular views in all directions. From the top you can access Richmond Hill Road (which follows the ridge behind Aspen Mountain) or Summer Road (which goes down the front of Aspen Mountain).

Directions from Aspen: Travel west from Aspen .5 mile on Highway 82 and turn left as the Maroon Creek Road turnoff. Then immediately take a left onto Castle Creek Road; travel 7 miles to Little Annie Road on the left. There is a small parking area on the right.

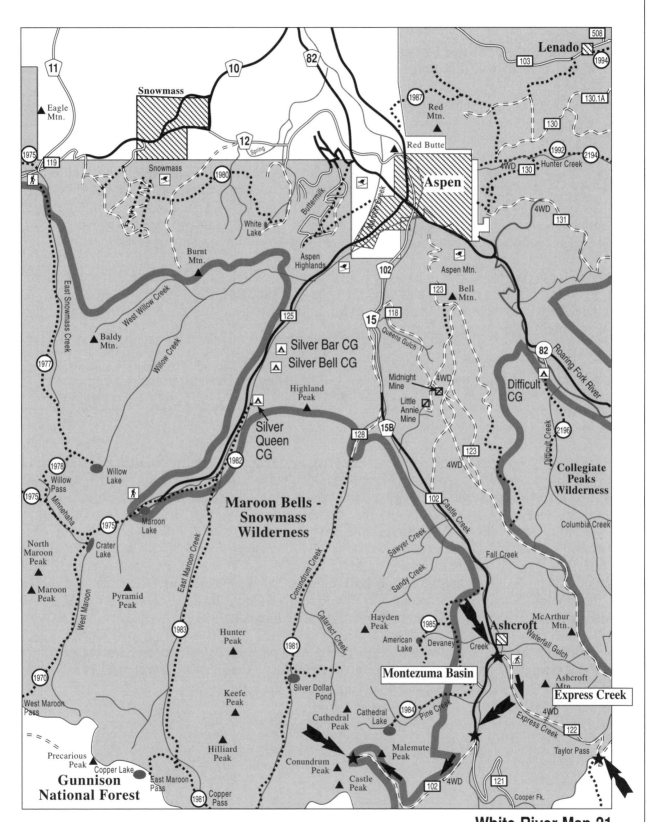

White River Map 21

Road Name	Road Number	Length Miles	Difficulty	Beginning Elevation	Ending Elev.	Usage	Ranger District
Pearl Pass	102	6	Difficult	9,728'	12,600'	Moderate	Aspen

Montezuma Basin/ Pearl Pass
Elevation Gain: 2,872 Feet.
USGS Maps: Hayden Peak, Pearl Pass.

There is often snow on the road well into July. The lower section of the road receives heavy use, especially on the weekends. This road is very rugged, and in some sections is located in a stream. It climbs well above the timberline and continues for a mile or so, through fields of rocks tinted with lichen of various colors. This road was built to serve the Montezuma Mine and debris from the operation of the mine may he seen along the way.

The first .5 mile is fairly level, then begins to climb. There are some steep uphill sections and at the 1.5 mile mark there is a footbridge. At the bridge you will need to cross the stream. The road continues to climb through spruce groves crossing a vehicle bridge and immediately becoming steeper and more rugged. Three miles up the road, the Mace cabin is passed on the right. A .25 past the cabin, the road to Pearl Pass forks steeply to the left (Refer to the Pearl Pass topographic map). At this fork bear right, the road soon climbs some steep, continuous switchbacks. The road is very narrow and rugged in some areas. The road ends at the parking area for Castle Peak

Directions from Aspen: Travel west from Aspen .5 mile on Highway 82 and turn left at the Maroon Creek Road turn-off. Immediately take a left onto Castle Creek Road, travel l3.5 miles on Castle Creek Road (2 miles past Ashcroft) to the intersection with the 4WD Pearl Pass Road FDR 102. There is a small parking area at the junction.

Road Name	Road Number	Length Miles	Difficulty	Beginning Elevation	Ending Elev.	Usage	Ranger District
Express Creek	122	5.5	Mod/Diff	9,422'	11,928'	Heavy	Aspen

Express Creek Road to Taylor Pass FDR 122.
USGS Maps: Hayden Peak.

This is a popular high-altitude 4WD route beginning at Express Creek Road. Because of the altitude snow is often present well into mid-July. From the top of Taylor Pass you can see Taylor Lake below and magnificent views of the Castle Creek Valley and surrounding peaks. Once at the pass you are offered several choices of extending your trip by making a loop back to Aspen via Richmond Hill Road or travel to Crested Butte along the Taylor River making a full day trip.

The first 1/8-mile is fairly flat; the road soon crosses a bridge and begins to climb steeply. There are several private drives along the first mile, stay on the main road. In approximately 2 miles, there is a spur to the right, again follow the main road. The road becomes a little steeper and in another 1.75 miles begins a long steep uphill climb. The road crosses a bridge and is very steep the last mile.

Directions from Aspen: Drive west on Highway 82 from Aspen .5 mile and take Maroon Creek Road on your left and immediately turn left again onto Castle Creek Road. Drive about 11 miles, just past Elk Mountain Lodge and before the ghost town of Ashcroft, on your left will be Express Creek Road.

TAYLOR PASS from Almont in Gunnison National Forest - Gunnison Ranger District.
Length: 4 Miles. Difficulty: Most Difficult. Beginning Elevation: 10,000 Feet. Ending Elevation: 11,928 Feet.
USGS Maps: New York Peak, Italian Creek.
Usage: Medium.

This route leaves the Taylor River Toad at 10,065' and climbs steadily through Aspen groves. The road can be very rough at times. After following a stream for three miles, you will reach Taylor Lake. Taylor Pass lies a short distance above the lake at 11,928 feet.

Directions from Almont: Take Taylor River Road FDR 742, east 36 miles to Taylor Pass Road (FDR 761).

Directions from Ashcroft: Take Express Creek Road west to Taylor Pass (FDR 761).

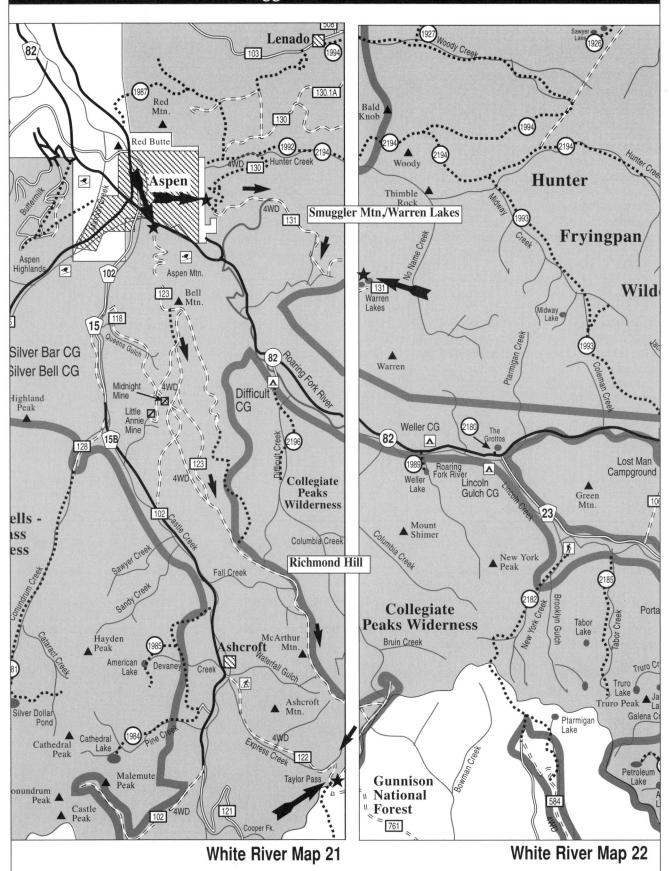

Lenado

82

Red Mtn.

Red Butte

Aspen

Aspen Highlands

Silver Bar CG
Silver Bell CG

Highland Peak

ells - ass ess

Conundrum Creek

Cataract Creek

Silver Dollar Pond

Cathedral Peak
Cathedral Lake

onundrum Peak

Castle Peak

Malemute Peak

Hayden Peak

American Lake
Devaney Creek

Midnight Mine
Little Annie Mine

Aspen Mtn.

Bell Mtn.

Queens Gulch

4WD

Difficult CG

Difficult Creek

Roaring Fork River

Collegiate Peaks Wilderness

Columbia Creek

Fall Creek

Ashcroft

McArthur Mtn.

Waterfall Gulch

Ashcroft Mtn.

Express Creek

Taylor Pass

Cooper Fk.

Smuggler Mtn./Warren Lakes

Richmond Hill

Hunter Creek

Hunter Creek

Woody Creek

Sawyer Lake

Bald Knob

Woody

Thimble Rock

Hunter

No Name Creek

Warren Lakes

Midway Creek

Fryingpan

Wild

Midway Lake

Warren

Ptarmigan Creek

Coleman Creek

82

Weller CG

2180

The Grottos

Roaring Fork River

Lincoln Gulch CG

Weller Lake

Lincoln Creek

Columbia Creek

Mount Shimer

New York Peak

Collegiate Peaks Widerness

Bruin Creek

Lost Man Campground

Green Mtn.

23

New York Creek

Brooklyn Gulch

Tabor Lake

Tabor Creek

Truro Lake

Truro Peak

Galena Cr

Ptarmigan Lake

Bowman Creek

Gunnison National Forest

Petroleum Lake

584

Road Name	Road Number	Length Miles	Difficulty	Beginning Elevation	Ending Elev.	Usage	Ranger District
Richmond Hill	123	12	Mod/Diff	11,212'	11,928'	Moderate	Aspen

USGS Maps: Hayden Peak, Aspen.

This route runs southeast from the top of Aspen Mountain to Taylor Pass. A gentle rolling route among evergreens until the open tundra-like fields beyond McArthur Mountain. It is rated difficult to moderate because of steep sections found at the beginning and end of this road and because of its exposure. The last 5 miles is above timberline and very exposed. Watch for afternoon thunderstorms. Great view of Castle Creek valley is provided.

Directions are from the top of Aspen Mountain, if starting from Taylor Pass follow the directions in reverse. Travel east behind the gondola onto Richmond Hill Road heading south. The road begins with rolling hills. In about 1.25 miles there is a fork at the bottom of a steep hill, bear left. In a short distance another fork, keep straight towards the trees. The road continues in a rolling pattern until reaching a long downhill with some steep sections at approximately 4.5 mile mark that ends with a steep climb. The last section switchbacks up then descends to the top of Taylor Pass. You can take Express Creek Road to Castle Creek Road and return to Aspen.

Directions: There are 4 options for accessing Richmond Hill Road:
Express Creek Road: Go west on Hwy 82 from Aspen .5 mile and take Maroon Creek Road on the left and immediately turn left again onto Castle Creek Road. Drive 11 miles to the intersection with Express Creek Road (signed). Follow this route about 5.5 miles to Taylor Pass.
Little Annie Road: Go west on Hwy 82 from Aspen .5 mile and take Maroon Creek Road on the left and immediately turn left again onto Castle Creek Road. Drive approximately 6.5 miles to Little Annie Road (usually signed) on the left. Follow this route about 4.5 miles up the backside of Aspen Mountain.
Midnight Mine Road: Go west on Hwy 82 from Aspen .5 mile and take Maroon Creek Road on the left and immediately turn left again onto Castle Creek Road. Drive approximately 2.5 miles to Midnight Mine Road (usually signed) on the left. Follow this road about 5.5 miles up the backside of Aspen Mountain.
Summer Road: From downtown Aspen, proceed on Durant Avenue east to Original Street and turn south. Follow Original about 1/8 mile; keep straight on the paved road as it curves behind 777 Ute. Take the dirt road up the mountain about 3 miles.

Road Name	Road Number	Length Miles	Difficulty	Beginning Elevation	Ending Elev.	Usage	Ranger District
Smuggler Mtn/Warren	131	6	Moderate	7,900'	10,700'	Heavy	Aspen

Smuggler Mountain/Warren Lakes.
USGS Maps: Aspen.

Smuggler Road is used heavily by mountain bikes, runners and hikers. Smuggler Road provides a short 1.5 mile work out with great views of Aspen which makes it very popular. The remaining portion of the road to Warren Lakes is very steep and not as heavily used.

From Smuggler Road you can access Van Horn Park. Smuggler Road is a fairly well maintained 4 WD road and immediately begins a steep ascent. The road switchbacks up Smuggler with views of Aspen below. The switchbacks get longer and in about 1.5 miles the road curves behind Smuggler Mountain. There is a short steep path on the right leading to a platform, which is good for viewing Aspen. To continue to Warren Lakes, keep straight on the main road. In a short distance the road becomes a more rugged 4WD road and continues to ascend steeply. At the 2.5 mile mark there are some communication disks on the right. The road becomes even steeper until about the 3 mile mark, and then it eases. Shortly, the road becomes level with only brief steep sections until reaching the 6 mile mark. The road continues a short distance further to the gate at Warren Lakes. Beyond the gate is private land and Wilderness, please respect this and do not trespass.

Directions from Aspen: East on Hwy 82, turn left (north) onto Mill Street. Travel 1/4 mile and turn right after the bridge onto Gibson. Follow Gibson 1/8 mile to a "Y" intersection and bear left onto South Ave. Shortly, turn right onto Park Circle and follow for 1/8 mile to the Smuggler Mountain Road on the left. There is parking on the right.

Road Name	Road Number	Length Miles	Difficulty	Beginning Elevation	Ending Elev.	Usage	Ranger District
Lincoln Creek	106	11	Moderate	9,785'	11,000'	Heavy	Aspen

USGS Maps: Independence, New York Peak.

The first 6 miles is to Grizzly reservoir is easily accessible and is heavily used on weekends. The road crosses a bridge and heads downhill past Lincoln Gulch Campground. The road rolls up and down with some steep uphill sections that level out on top. The road follows Lincoln Creek with an uphill, downhill pattern to Grizzly Reservoir at the 6-mile mark.

From Grizzly Reservoir the road is less traveled and is suitable only for hiking, mountain biking and 4WD vehicles. To continue to the ghost town of Ruby, stay on the main road that curves to the southeast of the reservoir and past Portal Campground. The road climbs easily to the ruins of an old mining cabin at the 9-mile mark. The road forks at another .5 mile, take the left fork. The ghost town of Ruby is a short distance before the road ends. Ruby consists of a few old buildings in the advanced stages of decay and is situated in an open basin with tundra like terrain. Although there is no sign of a road beyond Ruby, traces of an old wagon trail over the Continental Divide only a mile east of the ruins can be detected. Two small lakes, Anderson and Petroleum, are short hikes from the road. It is recommended you start your trip early, thunderstorms are frequent in the afternoon.

Directions from Aspen: Access to Lincoln Creek Road is located 11 miles southeast of the community of Aspen on Highway 82 and then 1.2 miles on Lincoln Creek Road within a grove of aspen trees.

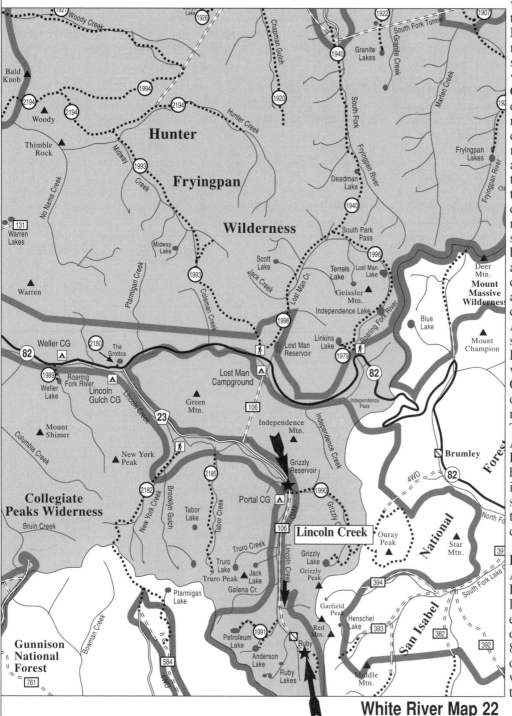

White River Map 22

GUNNISON NATIONAL FOREST

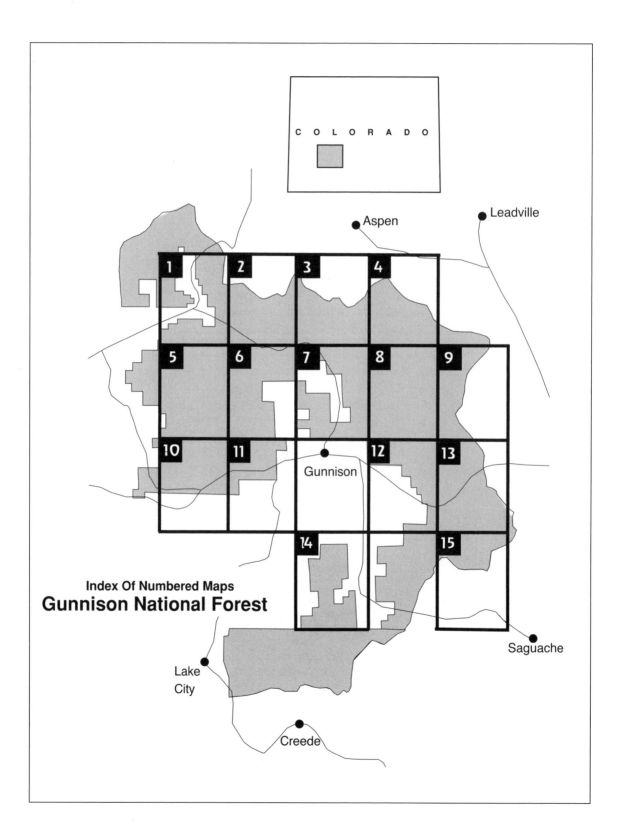

COLORADO

Leadville

Aspen

1 **2** **3** **4**

5 **6** **7** **8** **9**

10 **11** **12** **13**

Gunnison

14 **15**

Saguache

Index Of Numbered Maps
Gunnison National Forest

Lake
City

Creede

GUNNISON NATIONAL FOREST

Located north and east of Gunnison in central Colorado the present Forest includes 1.7 million acres of public land within the boundary. Outstanding mountain scenery can be found on the Forest during any season of the year. Deer and elk make the Forest a popular hunter's haven during the fall season. Fishing is good throughout the year.

The Bureau of Land Management (BLM) administers over 500,000 acres of public land in the Gunnison Basin Resource Area. These lands encompass a diversity of surrounding ranging from sagebrush plains to alpine lakes and scenic 14,000 foot peaks.

Visitors to the public lands enjoy a wide variety of recreation opportunities. Several developed campgrounds as well as many undeveloped sites can provide a base of operations for hunting, fishing, backpacking, boating, mountain climbing, jeep touring, photography, snowmobiling, skiing, and other outdoor oriented activities.

CURECANTI NATIONAL RECREATION AREA

Curecanti National Recreation Area adjoining Gunnison National Forest was named for the Ute Chief Curicata who once hunted in this area. The U.S. Bureau of Reclamation has constructed three dams on the Gunnison River. The resulting lakes; Blue Mesa, Morrow Point, and Crystal-provide stored water for flood control, hydro-electric power, public recreation, irrigation and municipal water supplies.

Twenty mile long Blue Mesa is the largest body of water in Colorado. Several arms of the lake reach into beautiful side canyons and offer boaters secluded campsites and many areas to explore, while three broad basins surrounded by open mesa country provide large areas for sailing and windsurfing. Fishing is the number one sport on Blue Mesa Lake, anglers have the opportunity to catch rainbow, brown, and lake trout, and kokanee salmon. Hunting is allowed in season and Colorado state laws are enforced.

The awesome gorge of the Black Canyon of the Gunnison National Park provides the setting for Morrow Point Lake, accessible only by rugged trails starting at the rim. Boating on the lakes is therefore limited to hand carried craft. A summer boat tour takes passengers through the deep fjord-like canyon. This tour relives the days of the historic "Scenic Line of the World" narrow gauge railroad which traveled through this part of the canyon. Visitors can walk along part of this route by following the Pine Creek Trail which can be reached from Highway 50, 29 miles west of Gunnison. The third lake, Crystal, is also located in the Black Canyon, and boating access is limited to hand carried craft. A trip on Crystal can offer good fishing opportunities and peace of mind in the quiet isolated canyon. The lake can be reached by a short trail from Cimarron.

Road Name	Road Number	Length Miles	Difficulty	Beginning Elevation	Ending Elev.	Usage	Ranger District
Cottonwood Creek	783	8	Moderate	6,224'	6,020'	Low	Paonia

USGS Map: Paonia Reservoir, Somerset.

It starts out in heavy oak brush cover. The first mile of this road is pretty steep, once you have gone about a 1.5 miles there will be a road that takes off to the left. A little more than a mile from this turn you will be on Forest Service Land. This is a Road Closure Area and you are required to stay on the main road. About a mile further the four-wheeler has to ford Thompson Creek. In the summer there is not much water in the creek. From here it is another mile to the Forest Boundary and about 2.5 miles back down to Highway 133. The first section of the road as described is impassable with a full size vehicle.

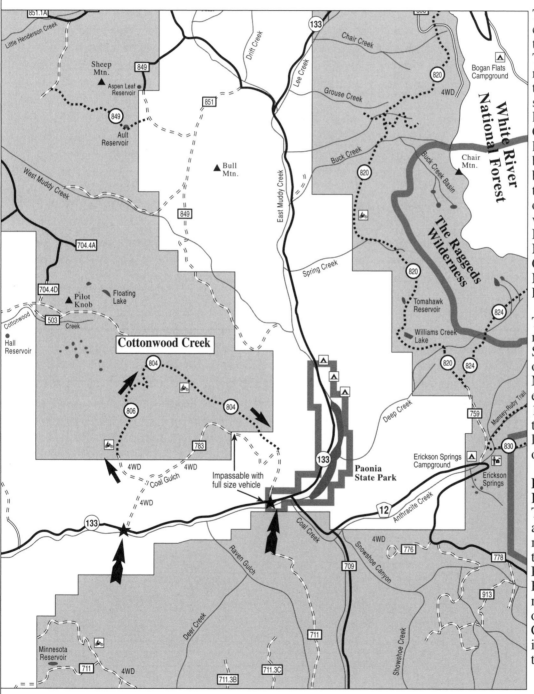

This road is difficult to find because there are no signs. This is a narrow road with few turnouts. Some switchbacks at the lower end of Coal Gulch require the long wheel drive base vehicle to back up to make the turn. This route offers a panoramic view of the Beckwith Mountains, Mount Gunnison and the Minnesota Creek Drainage.

This loop stays mainly on Forest Service and Bureau of Land Management property. There is about 1 mile of this road that is on private land at the bottom of Coal Gulch.

Directions from Kebler Pass Road: Travel west approximately 0.5 mile from the junction of Kebler Pass Road (CR 12) State Hwy 133. Turn north off highway onto cottonwood Creek Road. There is no sign marking the road entrance.

Gunnison Map 1

Road Name	Road Number	Length Miles	Difficulty	Beginning Elevation	Ending Elev.	Usage	Ranger District
Dry Fork Minnesota	711	15.1	Moderate	6,600'	8,000'	Moderate	Paonia

USGS Maps: Minnesota Pass, Somerset, Paonia Reservoir, West Beckwith Peak.

This is a narrow dirt road with few turnouts. The type of soil in this area becomes very slick when wet requiring chains on four wheel drive vehicles. Road FDR 711 provides good access to the north side of Mount Gunnison.

The road eventually ends on Raven Mesa, overlooking Paonia Reservoir and the North Fork of the Gunnison River.

There are many spur roads that take off from FDR 711. These spurs travel to places such as The Pines, a stand of ponderosa pine trees. FDR 711 will travel by the Dry Fork Wildlife Burn, the burn is approximately 700 acres. This was a coop project done by the U. S. Forest Service and the Colorado Division of Wildlife. The reason for burning is to kill the oak brush and promote new plant growth. Killing the oak brush opens the area to more sunlight which stimulates growth of grass and forbs, sprouting of the otherwise out of reach browse plants. There are also many vistas along the different routes of the surrounding areas.

Directions from Paonia: To reach FDR 711, travel east on Minnesota Creek Road, this road begins in the southeast part of town. Travel this road for approximately 7 miles. The Dry Fork of Minnesota Creek Road forks off the east side by some corrals. The first mile of FDR 711 goes through private property.

Gunnison Maps 1 & 5

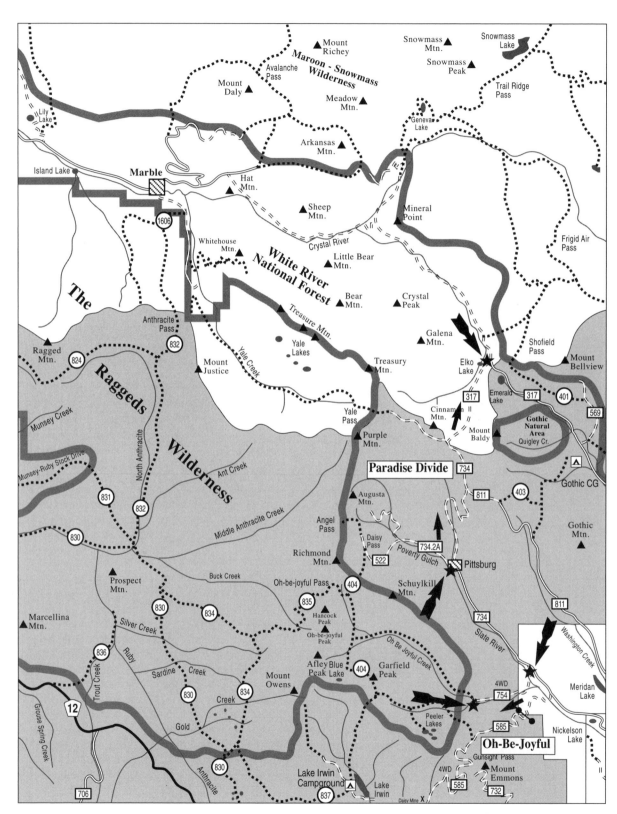

Gunnison Map 2

Road Name	Road Number	Length Miles	Difficulty	Beginning Elevation	Ending Elev.	Usage	Ranger District
Paradise Divide	734/317	4.5	Moderate	11,240'	10,707'	Heavy	Gunnison

USGS Maps: Snowmass Mtn., Oh-Be-Joyful.

Paradise Divide Road, FDR 734/317, begins at the end of Slate River Road at the top of a very steep ascent. This ascent climbs Paradise Divide and ends in Paradise Basin. This route crosses the basin and ends on Schofield Pass. It is relatively smooth 2.5 miles through the basin with a few shallow stream crossings. The scenery is breathtaking. Road can be muddy and snowy most of year.

Directions from Crested Butte: Drive 1 mile north on Hwy 135 to Slate River Road. Turn left on Slate River Road (FDR 734) and travel 9 miles to the beginning of Paradise Divide Road.

Directions from Gothic: Follow Gothic Road past Emerald Lake to Schofield Pass. Turn left on to Paradise Divide Road (FDR 317 White River NF).

Road Name	Road Number	Length Miles	Difficulty	Beginning Elevation	Ending Elev.	Usage	Ranger District
Oh-Be-Joyful	754	2	Moderate	9,050'	9,580'	Heavy	Gunnison

USGS Map: Oh-Be-Joyful.

This 4WD route leads 2 miles west from Slate River Road to the Raggeds Wilderness Area. It leaves Slate River Road at approximately at 9,000 feet and immediately descends to the Slate River and Oh-Be-Joyful Campground. From the campground the route crosses the river (there is no bridge). When the river is high 4WD and high clearance are necessary for this crossing. (This crossing is not possible until July, depending on the year.) The water in the Slate River is always cold, but crossing in sandals or bare feet is also an option for those who do not possess a 4WD vehicle. After the river crossing the road begins to ascend into the Oh-Be-Joyful Valley, following Oh-Be-Joyful Creek. This is a beautifully scenic, but short ride (approx. .5 mile) to the Raggeds Wilderness boundary. The end of the road lies at approximately 9,580 feet.

Directions from Crested Butte: Travel 0.5 mile north on Gothic Road to Slate River Road (FDR 734) and drive 3.5 miles northwest to Oh-Be-Joyful Road.

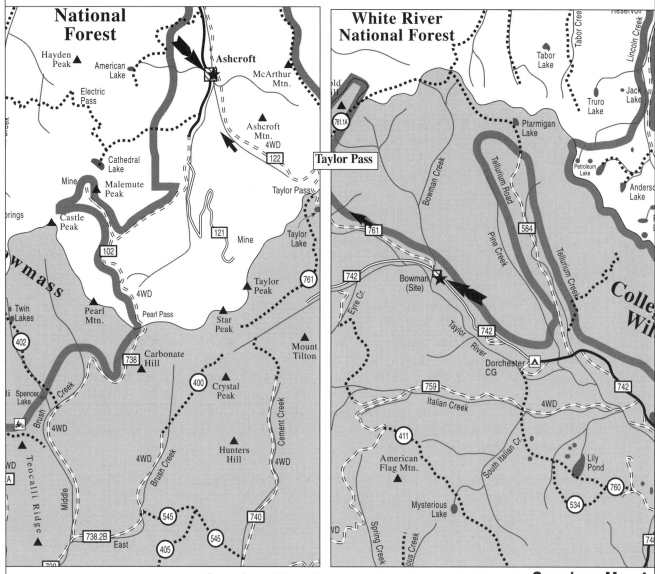

Gunnison Map 3

Gunnison Map 4

Road Name	Road Number	Length Miles	Difficulty	Beginning Elevation	Ending Elev.	Usage	Ranger District
Taylor Pass	761	4	Most Difficult	10,000'	11,000'	Heavy	Gunnison

Taylor Pass Road FDR 761 (FDR 122 White River NF).
USGS Maps: Hayden Peak, New York Peak, Italian Creek.

This road climbs from the Taylor River Valley, over Taylor Pass, to the Castle Creek Valley, near Ashcroft. The road climbs steadily through Aspen groves after leaving the Taylor River Road. After following a stream for 3 miles, you will reach Taylor Lake. Taylor Pass is reached after a short climb above the lake. (The road is slick and steep above the lake.) A very high clearance vehicle is required on the Gunnison National Forest side of pass. This road is very rough, check at District Office before using.

Directions from Aspen: Drive west on Hwy 82 0.5 mile and take Maroon Creek Road on your left and immediately turn left again onto Castle Creek Road. Drive about 11 miles to just past Elk Mountain Lodge and before the ghost town of Ashcroft, on your left will be Express Creek Road. Take Express Creek Road for approximately 6 miles. Past the first road on your right and take the next one. This is Taylor Pass Road (FDR 761/122).

Directions from Almont: Thirty six miles north of Almont on Taylor River Road (FDR 742).

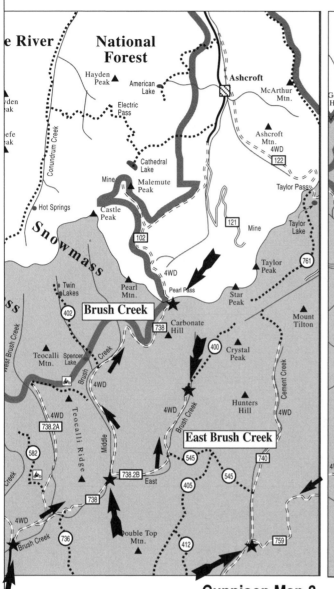

Gunnison Map 3

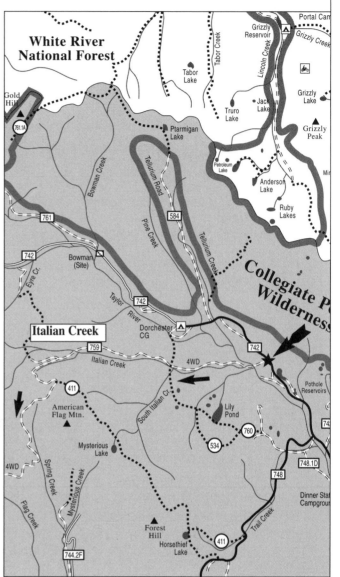

Gunnison Map 4

Gunnison

Road Name	Road Number	Length Miles	Difficulty	Beginning Elevation	Ending Elev.	Usage	Ranger District
East Brush Creek	738.2B	3.5	More Difficult	9,500'	10,800'	Moderate	Gunnison

Most Difficult about .5 mile below Block & Tackle intersection.
USGS Maps: Pearl Pass.

East Brush Creek forks from Brush Creek 8.5 miles from Highway 135. The eastern spur then continues 3.5 miles in a northeasterly direction to a parking area. The Brush Creek Trail lies at the end of East Brush Creek Road. Along the last 2 miles of East Brush Creek you will also find Block & Tackle Trail. (No trailheads,only wide spots in the road.) The road follows East Brush Creek for its entirety and is very steep with rock out-crops, high clearance vehicles only. Road becomes very slick when wet.

Directions from Crested Butte: Travel 1.5 miles south of Crested Butte on Highway 135 to Brush Creek Road (FDR 738). Turn left onto Brush Creek Road and follow it approximately 8.5 miles to East Brush Creek Road (FDR 738.2B).

Road Name	Road Number	Length Miles	Difficulty	Beginning Elevation	Ending Elev.	Usage	Ranger District
Brush Creek	738	20	Easy/Mos Diff.	8,500'	12,700'	Moderate	Gunnison

Length: 20 Miles - Pearl Pass (Continues as Castle Creek Road).
USGS Maps: Crested Butte, Gothic, and Pearl Pass.

Brush Creek leads from Highway 135, near Crested Butte, to Castle Creek Road near Aspen. A lack of signage, numerous spurs and icy conditions can make this route difficult to follow. Snowfields often block the pass throughout the year. Check at the district office for road conditions before using this route.

The first five miles from Highway 135 are passable by a two-wheel drive vehicle (unless wet). The next four miles are an easy four-wheel drive road following Brush Creek. After following Middle Brush Creek for a mile the road climbs rapidly to Pearl Pass, which culminates in a field of large, sharp and slick scree. This is a chal-lenging route for motorcyclist's, mountain bikers and four-wheelers. Road becomes very slick when wet.

Directions from Crested Butte: Travel 1.5 miles south of Crested Butte on Highway 135 to Brush Creek Road.

Directions from Aspen: Travel south from Ashcroft on Castle Creek Road, where the road splits take the left fork. This will lead you to Pearl Pass and Brush Creek Road. (See Pearl Pass Road (FDR 102) White River National Forest Section.)

Road Name	Road Number	Length Miles	Difficulty	Beginning Elevation	Ending Elev.	Usage	Ranger District
Italian Creek	759	17	More Difficult	9,822'	9,800'	Heavy	Gunnison

High Point: 12,000 Feet - Reno Divide.
USGS Maps: Pieplant, Italian Creek, and Pearl Pass.

From the Taylor River this route follows Italian Creek to Reno Divide. The road leaves the Taylor River at 9,822 feet and climbs steadily. The Lily Pond Motorized Trail intersects 3 miles from the Taylor River (10,120 feet) Road. The road continues to climb toward Reno Divide and follows Italian Creek for the next 4 miles. After passing the Star Mine and Star Trailhead (motorized) the road then climbs up over Italian Pass,then descends, then climbs up Reno Divide (12,000 ft). From this point it begins to switchback and descends into the Cement Creek drainage.

Directions from Almont: Travel 31 miles north on the Taylor River Road (FDR 742). Less than 1 mile past the Pot Hole Lakes is the junction with Italian Creek Road (FDR 759).

Directions from Crested Butte: Travel 8 miles south on Highway 135. Turn on to Cement Creek Road (FDR 740) and travel east for 7 miles to the junction with Italian Creek Road.

Road Name	Road Number	Length Miles	Difficulty	Beginning Elevation	Ending Elev.	Usage	Ranger District
Cement Creek	740	17	Easy/Diff.	8,603'	11,703'	Heavy	Gunnison

Easy to Difficult.
Length: 17 Miles to dead end.
USGS Maps: Pearl Pass, Cement Mountain, Crested Butte.

Cement Creek Road leads northeast from Highway 135, 17 miles to a mine on the southwestern flank of Mount Tilton. Travel restrictions due to private property may be in effect in this area, please check with the Gunnison Ranger District for current conditions. This road is passable by two wheel drive vehicles to the fork with Italian Creek Road (FDR 759). There are several local hiking and mountain biking opportunities available from this road. 4WD is recommended past Italian Creek Road, especially when wet.

Directions from Crested Butte: Travel 6 miles south on Highway 135. **Directions from Taylor River Road:** Seventeen miles west on Italian Creek Road (FDR 759).

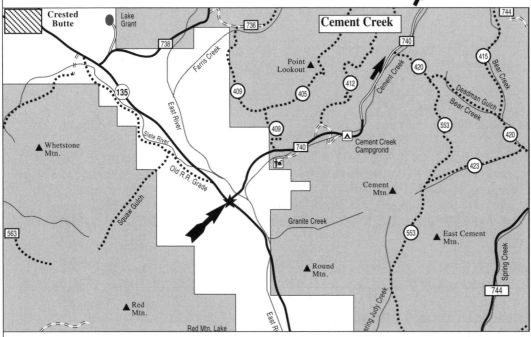

Gunnison Map 3

Gunnison Map 7

Road Name	Road Number	Length Miles	Difficulty	Beginning Elevation	Ending Elev.	Usage	Ranger District
Tellurium	584	9.5	More Difficult	9,866'	12,900'	Moderate	Gunnison

Length: 9.5 Miles - to Wilderness boundary.
USGS Maps: New York Peak, Italian Creek.

This road is bordered on both sides by wilderness. All motor vehicles must stay on the road. To access Tellurium Road travel 32 miles from Almont on the Taylor River Road. Two and one third miles past the second pothole lake, Tellurium Road leaves Taylor River Road (at 9,866') heading north.

The road follows a creek for 1 mile until you reach a road junction. The right road will dead-end in about 1.5 miles. Taking the left road, you cross a ridge and then follow Tellurium Creek to the wilderness boundary, approx. 2 miles from Ptarmigan Lake. The road goes around a ridge and climbs via switchbacks to the top of the ridge. The upper portion of this may be impassable due to rockslides. This is a good 4WD road for fishing and wilderness access.

Directions from Almont: Travel 32 miles northeast of Taylor River Road (FDR 742) to Tellurium Road, which leads north.

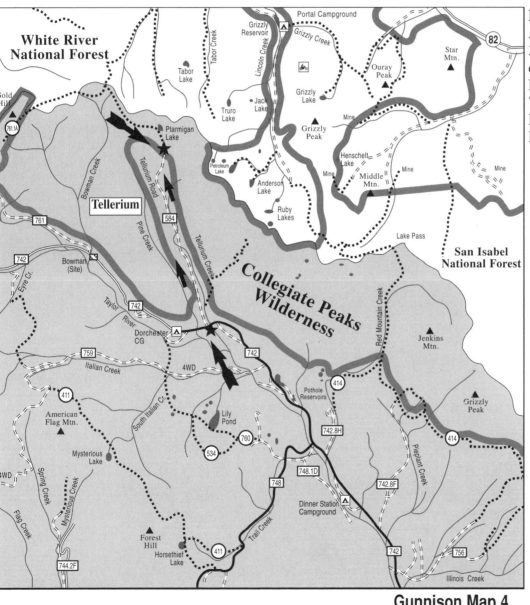

Gunnison Map 4

Road Name	Road Number	Length Miles	Difficulty	Beginning Elevation	Ending Elev.	Usage	Ranger District
Mysterious Lake	744.2F	4	Easy/Mod.	10,000'	11,600'	Moderate	Gunnison

Length: 4 Miles - To a dead end at Dark Gulch.
USGS Maps: Italian Creek, Matchless.

The road follows Mysterious Creek for the first few miles. The road then climbs above the creek going along a side hill until you reach Dark Gulch. You then climb to the summit of a small ridge to the dead end. The traveler will find two roads branching off near the end that dead end after a short distance. A trail leads from the dead end to Mysterious Lake in approximately 2.5 miles.

Directions from Almont: Travel 6 miles northeast on Taylor River Road (FDR 742) to Spring Creek Road. Then left on to Spring Creek Road and travel 11 miles passing the reservoir. Once past the reservoir continue north, you are on Forest Road 744.2F, Mysterious Lake Road.

Road Name	Road Number	Length Miles	Difficulty	Beginning Elevation	Ending Elev.	Usage	Ranger District
Red Mountain Creek	742.8H	1.8	Easy	9,700'	9,840'	Light	Gunnison

USGS Map: Pieplant.

Red Mountain Road is only about 3.6 miles long round trip. It leads to the northern terminus of the Timberline Trail. A parking lot at the cul-de-sac provides trailhead parking. The first mile of the road that leads to a group of summer homes is usually passable by two-wheel drive vehicles. The road generally follows Red Mountain Creek for the remaining distance.

Directions from Almont: Travel 29 miles northeast on Taylor River Road (FDR 742) past Dinner Station Campground to Red Mountain Road (FDR 742.8H).

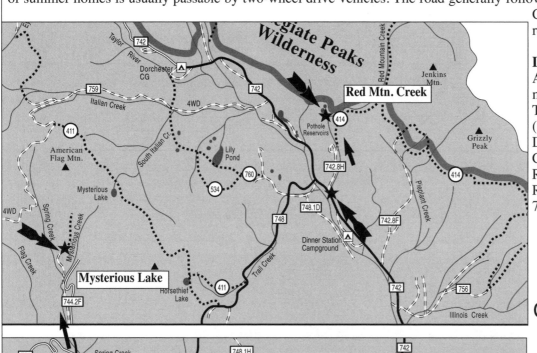

Gunnison Map 4

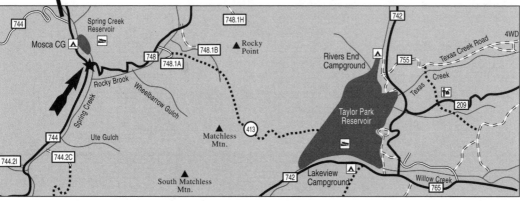

Gunnison Map 8

Road Name	Road Number	Length Miles	Difficulty	Beginning Elevation	Ending Elev.	Usage	Ranger District
Soap Creek	721	17	Easy/Mod	7,900'	8,600'	Heavy	Gunnison

More Difficult above Commissary Campground.
USGS Maps: Little Soap Park, Big Soap Creek.

The first 11 miles of the Soap Creek between Hwy 92 and Commissary Campground is passable by two-wheel drive vehicles. A 4WD vehicle is required above Commissary Campground. The entire length of the road can be very slippery during wet weather. The road leaves Commissary Campground heading north parallel to Soap Creek. After driving 1 mile you will climb a very steep, scary hill, (not recommended when wet) and then drive through a narrow canyon. About 2 miles from the campground, the road goes through Little Soap Park. Four miles further the road will bring you to Big Soap Park. East Curecanti Trail (FDT 454), leaves the road and heads west as you enter the park. About 1 mile further Trail FDT 456 leaves the road and enters the West Elk Wilderness within 2 miles. Soap Creek Road continues approximately .5 miles beyond Trail FDR 456 to the Soap Creek parking area.

Directions from Gunnison: Travel 26 miles west on Hwy 50 to the intersection with Hwy 92. Travel 1 mile north on Hwy 92 to Soap Creek Road (FDR 721).

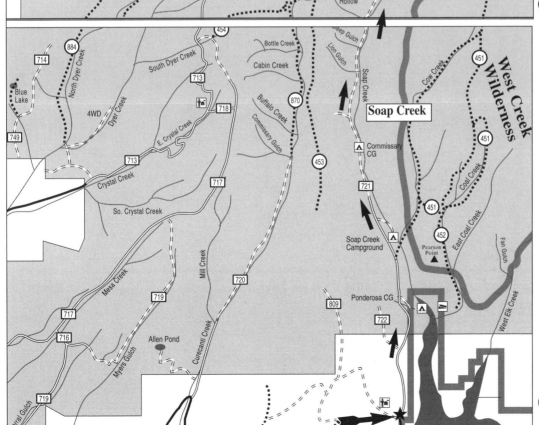

Gunnison Map 5

Gunnison Map 10

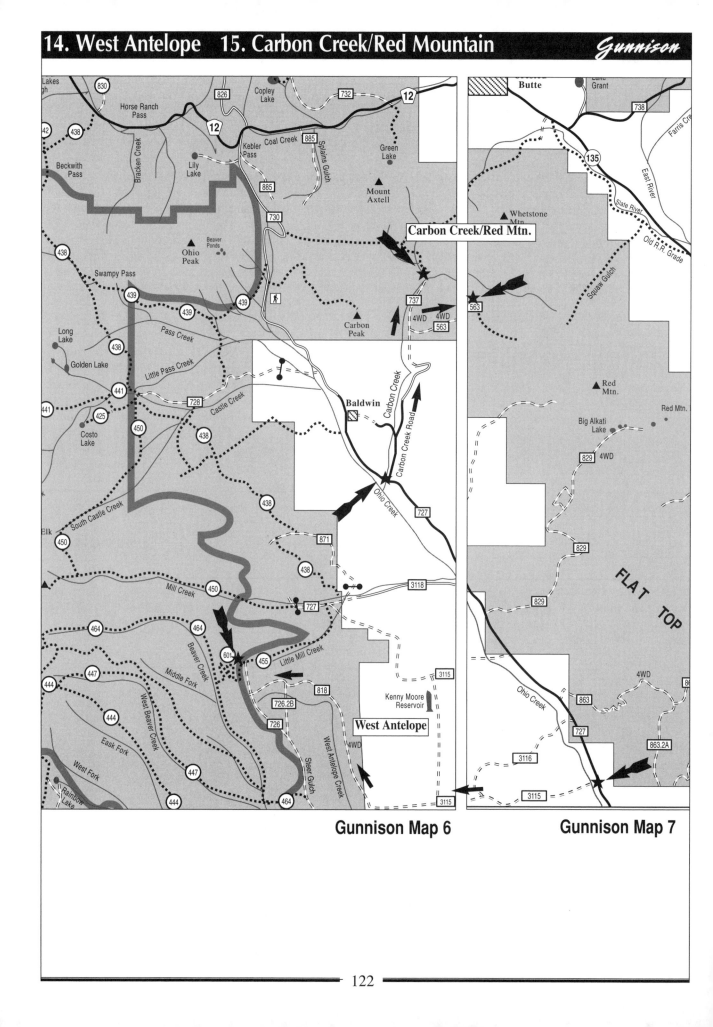

Gunnison Map 6

Gunnison Map 7

Road Name	Road Number	Length Miles	Difficulty	Beginning Elevation	Ending Elev.	Usage	Ranger District
West Antelope	818	12	Moderate	7,900'	11,127'	Moderate	Gunnison & BLM

Ending Elevation: 11,127 Feet junction with Steers Road.
USGS Maps: Gunnison, McIntosh Mtn, Squirrel Creek.

West Antelope Road leaves Ohio Creek Road as BLM Road 3115. From Ohio Creek Road you will drive through 8 miles of private land before reaching the National Forest boundary. The first 4 miles on BLM 3115 are passable by two-wheel drive vehicles; the remainder of the trip requires a high-clearance vehicle. A mile past the fork with BLM 3116 is the turn-off for West Antelope Road. It leads westward after a very sharp turn. This part of the road follows Deep Gulch around the north side of an 8,860 foot peak. At the next fork follow the right side and continue climbing. After a short distance the road comes to a T; turn right here. Almost immediately after the T is another fork; take the right side at this junction. The wilderness boundary is 2 miles from this junction. The road follows a ridge 5 miles past this junction to the next fork in the road. At this point follow the right side of the road to the junction with Steers Gulch Road (FDR 726). The last mile has many four-wheel drive roads that branch off and are all dead ends.

Directions from Steers Gulch Road: Drive 11 miles north on the Steers Gulch Road (FDR 726). West Antelope Road leads east just south of the wilderness boundary.

Directions from Gunnison: Travel north 2.5 miles on Hwy 135. Drive 2 miles north on Ohio Creek Road and turn west onto West Antelope Road (BLM Rd 3115)/FDR 818.

Road Name	Road Number	Length Miles	Difficulty	Beginning Elevation	Ending Elev.	Usage	Ranger District
Carbon Creek/Red Mtn.	737/563	7	Easy/Mod.	8,400'	9,200'	Moderate	Gunnison

High point FDR 563 - 10,300 Feet.
USGS Maps: Mt. Axtell, Crested Butte, Squirrel Creek.

Carbon Creek Road is usually passable by two-wheel drive vehicles and follows Carbon Creek for the entire distance.

Red Mountain Road (FDR 563) 3.0 miles on the right climbs gradually through aspen groves until it forks. The total mileage for this route is approximately 7 miles. This road ends at private land. 4WD vehicle required, very slick when wet.

Directions from Gunnison: Travel 2 miles north on Highway 135 to Ohio Creek Road. Turn right and travel 10 miles north on Ohio Creek Road to Carbon Creek Road. Carbon Creek Road leads to the right of Ohio Creek Road.

Gunnison

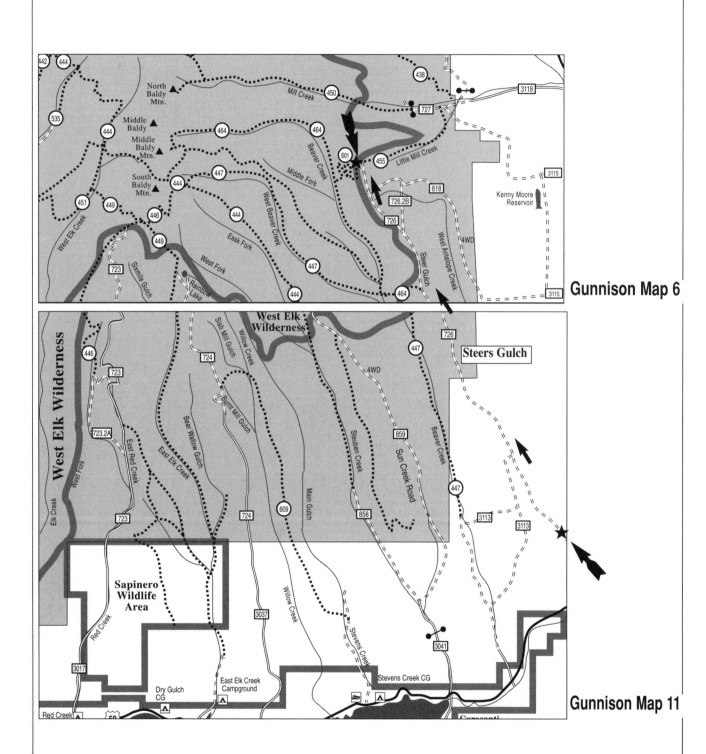

Gunnison Map 6

Gunnison Map 11

Road Name	Road Number	Length Miles	Difficulty	Beginning Elevation	Ending Elev.	Usage	Ranger District
Steers Gulch	726	12	Moderate	7,700'	11,240'	Moderate	Gunnison &BLM

Length: 12 Miles. - Junction with Beaver Creek Trail (FDT 464).
USGS Maps: Gunnison, McIntosh Mtn, Squirrel Creek.

Steers Gulch Road begins as BLM Road 3113 a few miles west of Gunnison on Hwy 50. The road follows Steers Gulch almost to the forest boundary. After entering the forest the road climbs gradually and follows the eastern boundary of the West Elk Wilderness. After passing the junction with West antelope Road, Steers Road continues about 1 mile to the wilderness boundary, where it intersects with Little Mill Creek (FDT 455) and Zig Zag (601) Trails. Zig Zag Trail drops into Beaver Creek wilderness trail. West Elk Wilderness is closed to all mechanized and motorized vehicles.

Directions from Gunnison: Travel west approximately two miles on Hwy 50. Turn north on to BLM Road 3113, which is Steers Gulch Road.

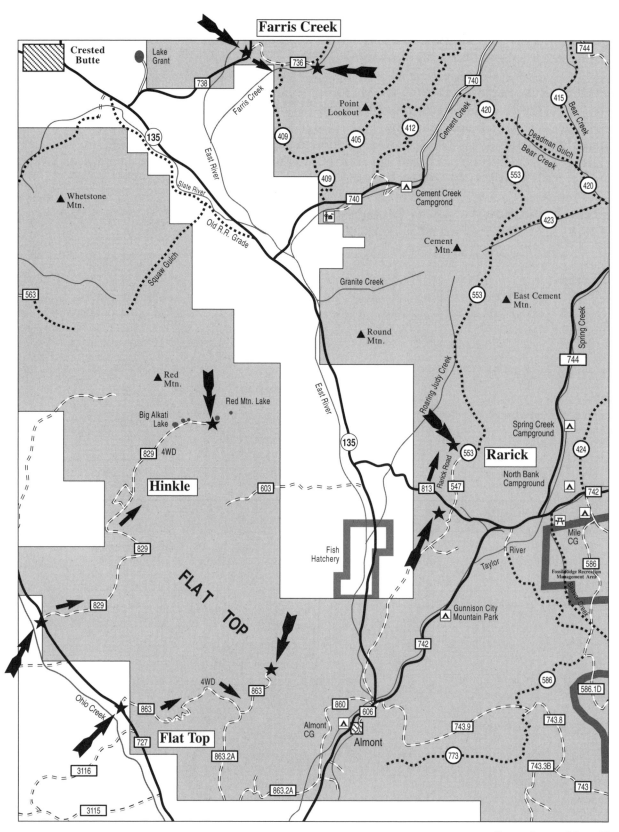

Gunnison Map 7

Road Name	Road Number	Length Miles	Difficulty	Beginning Elevation	Ending Elev.	Usage	Ranger District
Rarick	547	1.5	More Difficult	8,760'	11,600'	Light	Gunnison

USGS Maps: Almont, Cement Mountain.

Lack of signs may make this route difficult to follow. The road leaves the junction with Jack's Cabin Cutoff and leads along a side hill, climbing gradually for the first mile. After the first mile the road becomes too narrow for 4 WD vehicles and barely wide enough for ATV's. Road ends at beginning of FDT 553.

Directions from Almont: Travel 5 miles northeast on Taylor River Road to Jack's Cabin Cutoff Road. Turn left on to Jack's Cabin Cut-off and travel approximately 2 miles to the junction with Rarick and Triangle Roads. Turn right on to Rarick Road.

Road Name	Road Number	Length Miles	Difficulty	Beginning Elevation	Ending Elev.	Usage	Ranger District
Hinkle	829	7.5	Most Difficult	8,160'	10,300'	Heavy	Gunnison & BLM

Length: 7.5 Miles to a dead end at Red Mountain Lake.
USGS Maps: Flat Top, Crested Butte.

Hinkle Road leaves Ohio Creek Road climbing steadily for 12 miles to a junction overlooking Alkali Basin. Hinkle Road turns left at this junction and descends gradually 1 mile to a fence (the road to the right ends in 1 mile). Turn right at the fence to stay on Hinkle Road. The road then climbs gradually, leads north along Alkali Basin and passes south of Red Mountain Lake. It ends within a mile of Red Mountain Lake at 10,360 feet. This road has many washouts and is extremely rough in places. Vehicle restrictions may be in effect on parts of this road, please check the current travel information at the Gunnison Ranger District. This road is impassable when wet.

Directions from Gunnison: Travel north 2.5 miles on Highway 135 to Ohio Creek Road. Turn left on to Ohio Creek Road and drive 7 miles to Forest Road 829, Hinkle Road.

Road Name	Road Number	Length Miles	Difficulty	Beginning Elevation	Ending Elev.	Usage	Ranger District
Farris Creek	736	3	Easy/Mod	9,000'	9,800'	Moderate	Gunnison

Length: 3 Miles - To a dead end. May need 4WD when wet.
USGS Maps: Crested Butte, Cement Mountain, and Pearl Pass.

The Farris Creek Road leaves Brush Creek Road and gaining elevation traveling east. After climbing for 1.2 miles, the road descends into the Farris Creek drainage. Users can gain access to Strand Hill and Farris Creek and mountain biking trails from this road.

Directions from Crested Butte: Travel 1.5 miles south on Highway 135 to Brush Creek Road. Turn left onto Brush Creek Road and drive 3 miles to Farris Creek Road.

Road Name	Road Number	Length Miles	Difficulty	Beginning Elevation	Ending Elev.	Usage	Ranger District
Flat Top	863	7.5	Moderate	8,061'	9,900'	Moderate	Gunnison

Length: 7.5 Miles - To a dead end.
USGS Maps: Flat Top, Almont.

Flat Top Road begins on private land but enters National Forest land .5 mile from Ohio Creek Road. The road then climbs steadily and passes several forks in the path. Forest Road FDR 863 leads to the left at the second fork. FDR 863.2A heads to the right. There are many roads, a few listed above, that lead to dead ends in this area. Be sure to bring a map of the area so as not to experience difficulty. There is no access to this area from Highway 135.

Directions from Gunnison: Travel 2.5 miles north on Highway 135 to Ohio Creek Road. Turn left and drive 4.5 miles north on Ohio Creek Road. Flat Top Road leads toward the east.

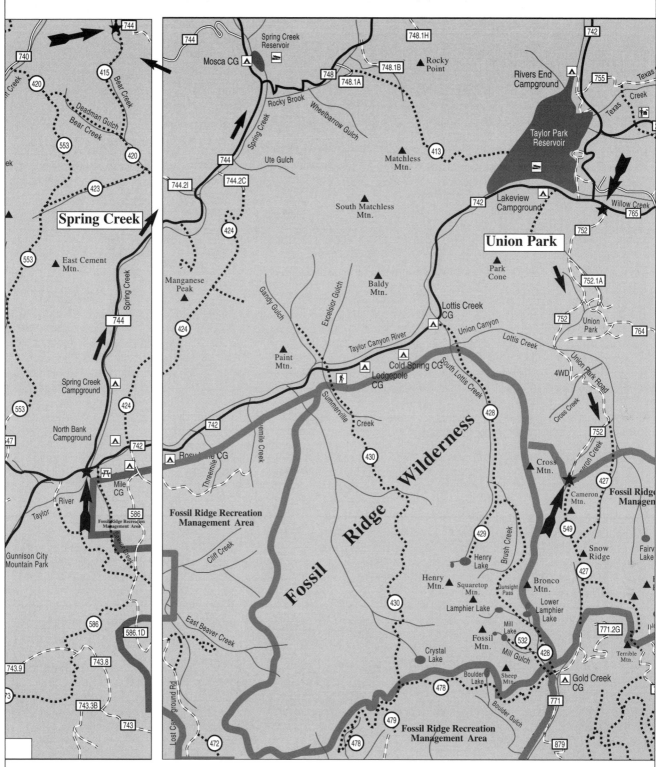

Gunnison Map 7

Gunnison Map 8

Road Name	Road Number	Length Miles	Difficulty	Beginning Elevation	Ending Elev.	Usage	Ranger District
Spring Creek	744	20.5	Easy	9,700'	11,050'	Heavy	Gunnison

USGS Maps: Pearl Pass, Cement Mountain, Matchless Mountain, Italian Creek.

Spring Creek Road, FDR 744, begins from the paved Taylor River Road. The pavement lasts approximately 2 miles until the road enters a canyon with steep walls. Here, the road changes to improved dirt. The road follows Spring Creek through the varied terrain carved by the stream over thousands of years.

After approximately 6.5 miles Manganese Peak Trail leads east (right) from Spring Creek Road. In another 1.5 miles Spring Creek Road intersects with Deadman Road (FDR 741.21). In another mile Doctor Park Road FDR 744.2C) leads east from Spring Creek Road. The road continues to Spring Creek Reservoir, where boating, fishing and camping opportunities abound. One half mile past the reservoir is a fork. The Spring Creek Road follows the left road. The road gradually ascends going along side hills until you reach a dead end.

Directions from Almont: Travel 6 miles northeast on the Taylor River Road, FDR 742, to Spring Creek Road, FDR 744.

Road Name	Road Number	Length Miles	Difficulty	Beginning Elevation	Ending Elev.	Usage	Ranger District
Union Park	752	11	Easy/Mod.	9,413'	11,800'	Heavy	Gunnison

USGS Maps: Fairview Peak, Taylor Park Reservoir.

The first 1.5 miles of this road is usually passable by two wheel drive vehicles. There are numerous roads branching off the main road, all except Slaughterhouse Gulch (FDR 764) are dead ends. Union Park Road leaves Cumberland Pass Road, at an elevation of 9,413 feet leading southward and climbing. In 1.5 miles, the road reaches a high point of 10,076 feet before dropping into Union Park. Within Union Park a few roads intersect with Union Park Road. At the third fork in the road follow Union Park Road to the right, Slaughterhouse Gulch Road leads to the left. On the south side of the park, the road heads southeast along a hillside for 2 miles. The road then joins Lottis Creek and follows it for 2 miles before climbing a ridge to a dead end at the Fossil Ridge Wilderness boundary.

Directions from Almont: Travel 21 miles east on the Taylor River Road (FDR 742) to Cumberland Pass Road (FDR 765). Turn right on to FDR 765 and drive less then 1 mile east to Union Park Road (FDR 752) on the south side of the road.

Taylor Park Reservoir
From Cottonwood Pass

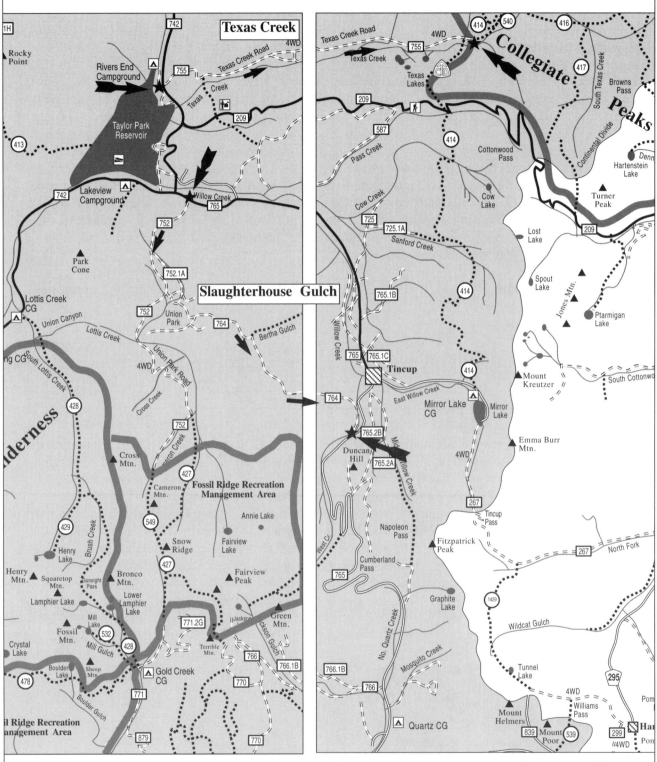

Gunnison Map 8

Gunnison Map 9

Road Name	Road Number	Length Miles	Difficulty	Beginning Elevation	Ending Elev.	Usage	Ranger District
Texas Creek	755	9	Easy/Mod.	9,350'	9,940'	Heavy	Gunnison

Easy/Moderate/Difficult.
Length: 9 Miles - Collegiate Peaks Wilderness boundary.
USGS Maps: Mt. Harvard, Taylor Peak Reservoir.

Texas Creek Road leaves Taylor Canyon Road approximately one mile north of Cottonwood Pass (FDR 209). The road junction lies at 9,350' and Texas Creek Road climbs slowly from that elevation. After the first mile, the road joins the Texas Creek and generally follows the creek the remainder of the distance. The first 3 miles are usually passable by two-wheel drive vehicles. The upper portion of Texas Creek Road to Texas Lakes is not passable by 2WD vehicles. High clearance vehicles are recommended after the first 3 miles. Texas Lakes provide excellent opportunities for fishing. The road ends at the Collegiate Peaks Wilderness boundary (9,945'). Use of mechanized and motorized vehicles or equipment is not allowed within the wilderness. Travel restrictions may be in effect in this area, please check the current travel map.

Directions from Almont: Travel 25 miles northeast on the Taylor River Road FDR 742, to Texas Creek Road.

Road Name	Road Number	Length Miles	Difficulty	Beginning Elevation	Ending Elev.	Usage	Ranger District
Slaughterhouse Gulch	764	8	Easy/Diff.	10,200'	9,700'	Moderate	Gunnison

USGS Maps: Taylor Park Reservoir, Fairview, Garfield.

There are numerous roads branching off the Slaughterhouse Gulch Road on the west end in Union Park that are all dead ends except for the Union Park Road. The first 3 miles are usually passable by two-wheel drive vehicles.

The first 2 miles follows the creek. The road then climbs over a small pass and descends to another creek, following the creek until the end of the road.

Directions from Almont: Twenty one miles east of Almont on the Taylor River Road (FDR 742). Seven miles east on the Cumberland Pass Road (FDR 765).

Access 2: Twenty one miles east of Almont on the Taylor River Road (FDR 742). One half mile east on the Willow Creek Road, 2.5 miles south on the Union Park Road (FDR 752).

Road Name	Road Number	Length Miles	Difficulty	Beginning Elevation	Ending Elev.	Usage	Ranger District
Willow Creek	882	5.5	Moderate	8,500'	11,200'	Moderate	Gunnison

USGS Map: Parlin.

This road is adequate for 2WD vehicles for the first 4 miles. Vehicles should be pickups or the like with sufficient ground clearance. A high clearance 4WD vehicle is required the last mile of this road. Camping is discouraged in the Fossil Ridge Recreation Management Area next to Willow Creek. Respect Forest Service information signs.

Directions from Gunnison: Take Highway 50 to Parlin and turn left towards Ohio City and Pitkin. About one mile before Ohio City, Willow Creek Road turns to the left. From there, it is about 6 miles to where the road ends at the Fossil Ridge Trail (FDT 478).

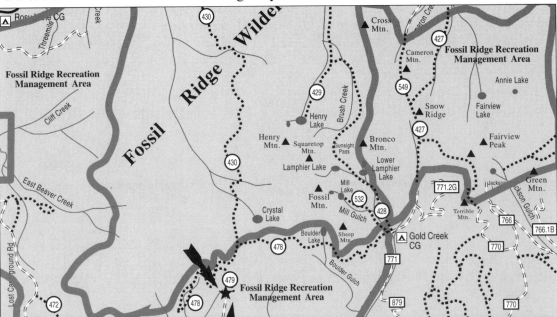

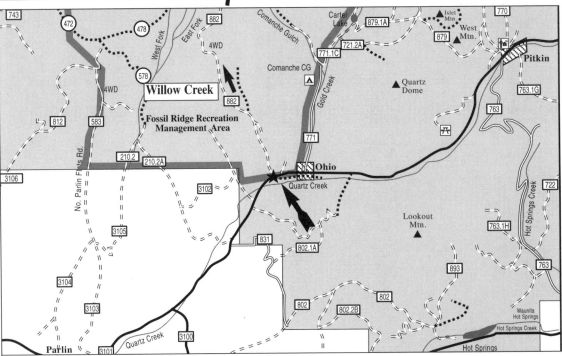

Gunnison Maps 8 & 12

Road Name	Road Number	Length Miles	Difficulty	Beginning Elevation	Ending Elev.	Usage	Ranger District
Mirror Lake	267	7	Easy/More Diff.	10,200'	12,150'	Heavy	Gunnison

Mirror Lake Road FDR 267 (Tincup Pass).
Length: 7 Miles - Tincup Pass (Road continues as North Fork Chalk Creek Road San Isabel National Forest).
USGS Maps: Mt Harvard, Garfield.

The first 4 miles of this road, from Tincup to Mirror Lake are usually passable by two-wheel drive vehicles. Beyond the lake the road becomes a lesser used four-wheel drive road with high-clearance recommended. After the lake the road follows East Willow Creek for a mile then climbs rapidly to the pass. The condition of the road near the pass is variable so check with the Gunnison Ranger District office before using it.

Directions from St Elmo: Travel 6 miles west on the North Chalk Creek Road to the junction of Mirror Lake and Chalk Creek Roads.

Directions from Almont: Travel 21 miles east on the Taylor River Road. Then go 7 miles south to Tincup on the Cumberland Pass Road. Mirror Lake Road (FDR 267) leads east from Tincup.

Gunnison Map 9

Road Name	Road Number	Length Miles	Difficulty	Beginning Elevation	Ending Elev.	Usage	Ranger District
Hancock Pass	266/299	2.5	Mod/Diff.	11,450'	12,125'	Heavy	Gunnison

High Point: 12,125 Feet - Hancock Pass.
USGS Maps: Cumberland Pass, Whitepine.

Hancock Pass Road, FDR 266/County Road 299, is the one of two motorized trails (see Mirror Lake/Tincup Pass) over the Continental Divide south of Cottonwood Pass in the Sawatch Mountains. It leads north/south 2 miles from Tominchi Pass Road to Williams Pass Road. A high-clearance, four-wheel drive vehicle is necessary for this route, which is rated as moderately difficult. Hancock Pass Road should not be attempted if any snow lies on the trail.

The beginning elevation for Hancock Pass Road is 11,450 feet, (Tomichi Pass Road). Forest Road 266, Hancock Road south of Hancock Pass, stems from Tomichi Pass Road in Brittle Silver Basin. The road begins climbing north toward the Continental Divide. Within 1 mile the road reaches the Continental Divide and Hancock Pass.

On the northern side of the pass the road number changes to FDR 299. Hancock Pass Road leads northeastward while descending into the upper Chalk Creek Valley. County Road 299 ends 1.5 miles north of the pass at Forest Road 298. If you turn right at this junction the road will lead you to the abandoned town site of Hancock.

Directions from Pitkin: Drive north on Forest Road 765, 2.5 miles to the Alpine Tunnel Road, Forest Road 839. Turn right on FDR 839 and drive approximately 7.5 miles to Tomichi Pass Road (FDR 888). Travel .5 mile east on Tomichi Pass Road to Hancock Pass Road (FDR 266).

Directions from St Elmo: Travel south on County Road 295. You will pass the town site of Romley at 2.5 miles. Continue driving south on Hancock Road to the town site of Hancock, 3.5 miles. Turn right on Forest Road 298; drive almost .5 mile to County Road 299. This is Hancock Pass Road.

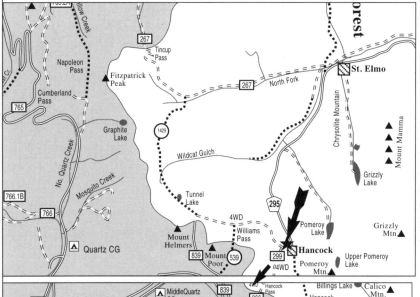

Gunnison Map 9

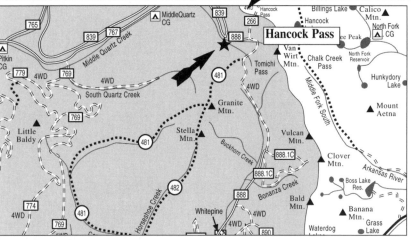

Gunnison Map 13

Road Name	Road Number	Length Miles	Difficulty	Beginning Elevation	Ending Elev.	Usage	Ranger District
West Red Creek	723.2A	3.5	Easy	9,600'	10,300'	Moderate	Gunnison

USGS: West Elk Peak SW.

This road is a loop that begins and ends on Red Creek Road. Most of the road is located in the narrow drainage of West Red Creek. When driving north on this road, you will come to a junction at about 2.5 miles. The left road will lead to the West Elk Rim Trail and the right road will bring you back to the Red Creek Road.

Directions from Gunnison: Travel 18 miles west on Hwy 50 to Red Creek Road (BLM 3017). Turn right (north) onto Red Creek Road and drive 9.5 miles to West Red Creek Road.

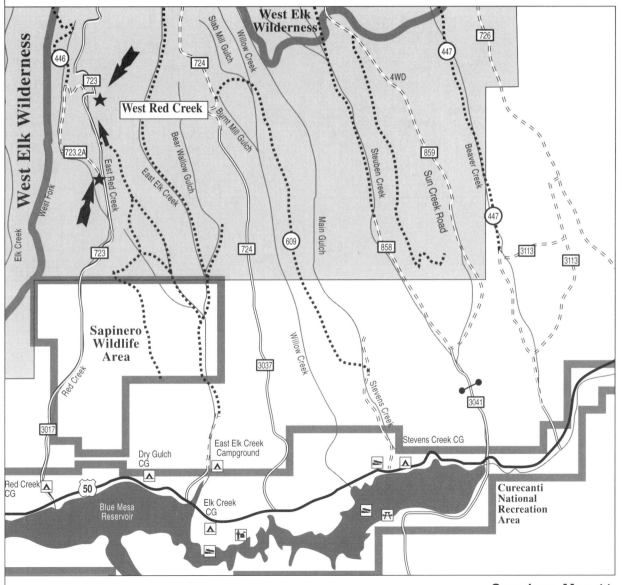

Gunnison Map 11

Road Name	Road Number	Length Miles	Difficulty	Beginning Elevation	Ending Elev.	Usage	Ranger District
Dry Gulch	812	11	Moderate	7,803'	10,423'	Moderate	Gunnison

Length: 11 Miles to a dead end.
USGS Maps: Parlin, Signal Peak.

Leaving Highway 50 this road follows Dry Gulch for the first 4 miles. It climbs from 7,813 feet at Highway 50, to 10,403 feet at the wilderness boundary. Dry Gulch Road route is approximately 8.5 miles from the highway to the wilderness boundary. The number of this road changes at the Forest boundary. It begins as BLM road 3106, but after approximately 5 miles BLM 3106 bears to the right and leads back to Highway 50. Forest Road FDR 812 begins and continues the northern traverse of the area, take the left fork to reach Cabin Creek Road.

Directions from Gunnison:
Travel east on Highway 50 seven miles to Dry Gulch Road (BLM Road 3106). Turn left onto Dry Gulch Road.

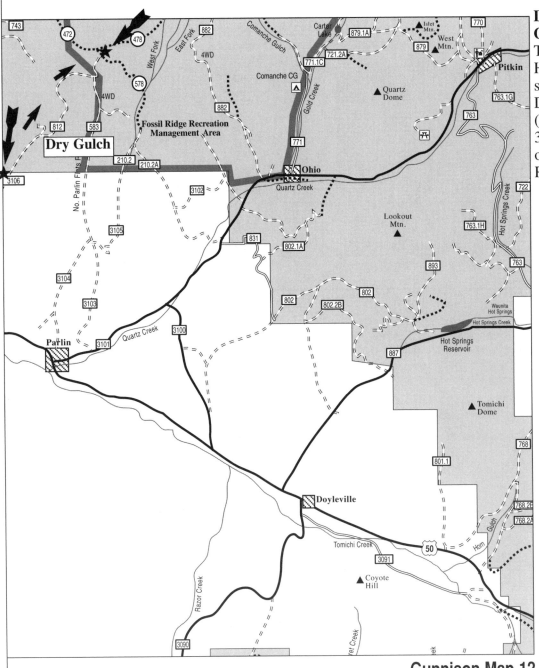

Gunnison Map 12

Road Name	Road Number	Length Miles	Difficulty	Beginning Elevation	Ending Elev.	Usage	Ranger District
Tomichi Pass	888	16	Most Difficult	8,600'	11,050'	Moderate	Gunnison

Length: 16 Miles. (From Sargents)
Beginning Elevation: Junction Hwy 50 and FDR 888. Ending Elevation: Junction with FDR 839.
USGS Maps: Garfield.

Tomichi Pass Road, FDR 888, begins a few miles north of Sargents. It branches from Hwy 50 and leads north to Snowblind Campground. Two miles north of the campground is the small cluster of summer cabins known as Whitepine. Up to this site the road may be referred to as Whitepine Road, but regardless of the name it is still FDR 888.

The road follows Tomichi Creek and climbs steadily up the valley. Two and quarter miles from Whitepine the road splits. Tomichi Pass Road follows the road to the left; FDR 888.1C leads to the right. Approximately .25 mile passed this fork in the road lie the remains of the Tomichi townsite, the cemetery. The road becomes steeper and narrower after this point. The road is tree lined for the next two miles as it begins to climb to Tomichi Pass. Approximately 0.5 mile south of the pass the road emerges from the trees. At the pass summit there is a small area to pull off the road or turn around.

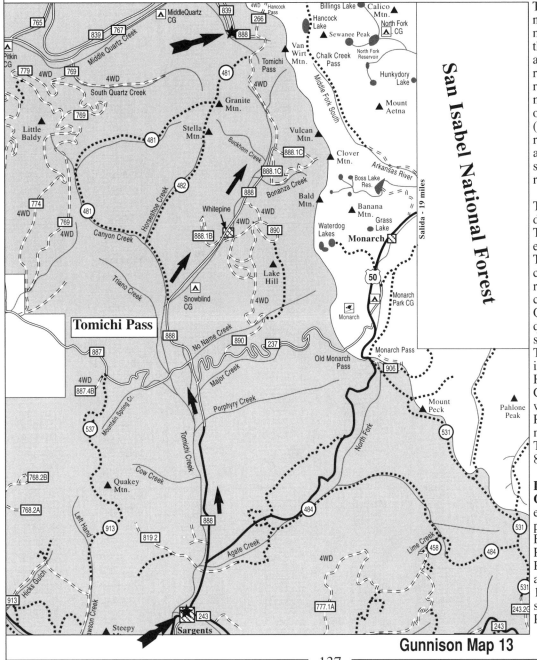

The northern side of Tomichi Pass is significantly steeper and more dangerous than the southern approach. Often talus rock slides into the roadbed and may need to be cleared in order to pass safely. (This section of the road should not be attempted if any snow exists on the road).

The first mile descending from Tomichi Pass is exposed and narrow. This is the most difficult section of the road. It ends after crossing Middle Quartz Creek. A quarter mile from the stream crossing Tomichi Pass Road intersects with Hancock Pass Road. Continuing westward, Tomichi Pass Road ends in one mile on the Alpine Tunnel Road, FDR 839.

Directions from Gunnison: Travel east on Hwy 50 passed Sargents to FDR 888 (Whitepine Road and/or Tomichi Pass Road). Turn left and follow FDR 888 10.5 miles to the summit of Tomichi Pass.

Road Name	Road Number	Length Miles	Difficulty	Beginning Elevation	Ending Elev.	Usage	Ranger District
Muddy Creek	775	Varies	Mod/Diff.	Varies		Moderate	Gunnison

Elevation Gain: 1,900 Feet.
USGS Maps: Sawtooth Mountain, Springhill Creek, Rock Creek Park, and Cold Spring Park.

The Sawtooth Mountain Loop Road incorporates Long Park - East Beaver Road (FDR 786), Lick Park - Bead Creek Road (FDR 789), Muddy Creek Road (FDR 775), Homestead Road (FDR 854) and Beaver Creek Road (FDR 806). These roads form, a loop that surrounds Sawtooth Mountain. The area is south of Highway 50 and immediately west of Cochetopa Canyon. It is lightly used during the summer months and heavily used during the fall big game seasons.

Because of resource damage many of the roads in this area - other than those mentioned here are closed. You will need to consult the Forest Travel map for timely information on travel restrictions in the Sawtooth Area.

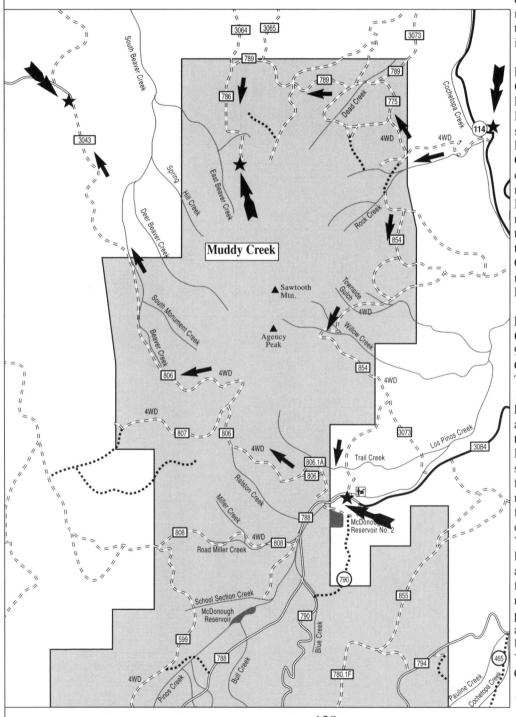

Directions from Gunnison: Long Park - Ease Beaver - Lick Park- Bead Creek Loop, drive south on the Gold Basin Road (south of the Gunnison airport). Stay on the most traveled route to the Forest Boundary. An alternate route is via Colorado 114 to the Bead Creek Road turnoff at milepost 12+. Once again, stay on the most traveled route to the Forest Boundary.

Directions from Beaver Creek Road: Drive west 9 miles from Gunnison to Colorado Highway 149. Turn left on to Highway 149 and cross Blue Mesa Reservoir. Drive 1 mile, after crossing the bridge, to a dirt toad on the left. BLM Route 3043, drive southward 2.5 miles to a fork in the road. Take the right side of the fork and follow it 9 miles to the old mining town of Vulcan. Continue to follow BLM Route 3043 another 8 miles to the forest boundary. This road will cross the lower portion of the Sawtooth area and lead to the old Ute Agency Work Center. You can return to Gunnison from there.

Gunnison Map 14

GRAND MESA & UNCOMPAHGRE NATIONAL FORESTS

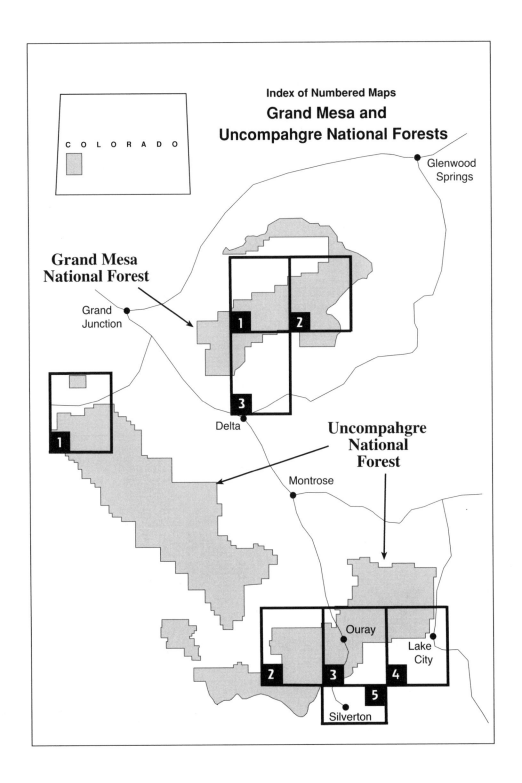

Index of Numbered Maps
**Grand Mesa and
Uncompahgre National Forests**

COLORADO

**Grand Mesa
National Forest**

Grand
Junction

Glenwood
Springs

1   2

3

Delta

**Uncompahgre
National
Forest**

1

Montrose

Ouray

Lake
City

2   3   4

5

Silverton

GRAND MESA NATIONAL FOREST

Grand Mesa and Uncompahgre National Forests are located east and south of Grand Junction in western Colorado. Grand Mesa's average elevation of 10,000 feet is the worlds largest flat-top mountain. The product of several hundred million years of geologic processes including volcanic action, glaciation, uplift deposition and erosion. Varied terrain, magnificent scenery and vast reaches of wild country await outdoor visitors in Grand Mesa National Forest.

The10 mile circular Crag Crest National Recreation Trail and the 7.5 mile Crag Crest National Recreation Ski Trail provide scenic views from an elevation of more than 11,000 feet. The many trails crisscrossing the mesa are your guide to scenery, wildlife viewing, fishing and backcountry camping. Elk, deer and many smaller mammals roam the forest. Wild flowers are abundant during the summer.

The Grand Mesa National Forest offers excellent fishing, hiking, camping and other winter and summer recreation opportunities. Some 300 stream fed lakes, sixteen developed campgrounds and four picnic grounds are open from early July when the snow melts until late September. Excellent fishing, hiking and camping can be enjoyed along this byway. The 300 hundred lakes scattered across the Grand Mesa provide superb opportunities for anglers. Golden aspen shimmering in the fall provide an unequaled panoramic view.

UNCOMPAHGRE NATIONAL FOREST

The Uncompahgre National Forest includes the Uncompahgre Plateau that rises to about 10,000 feet with its sides cut by gorges.

The San Juan Mountain Range with four peaks over 14,000 feet and another 100 peaks over 13,000 feet in elevation, and the Uncompahgre, Mount Sneffels, and Lizard Head Wilderness Areas.

The 4.2 mile Bear Creek National Recreation Trail traverses along steep narrow rocky ledges. Some of the best 4-wheel drive opportunities on primitive mining roads are located in these areas. Ouray is well known as the "Jeep Capital of the World" and the "Switzerland of America". Telluride Ski Area provides world-class skiing near the town of Telluride, Colorado.

The San Juan Skyway, Colorado's first designated scenic byway, winds for 232 miles through the San Juan and Uncompahgre National Forests offering views of spectacular, rugged, and primitive country as well as cultural and historical sites. There are some wonderful places for backcountry enthusiasts to get away and enjoy a wilderness adventure.

Road Name	Road Number	Length Miles	Difficulty	Beginning Elevation	Ending Elev.	Usage	Ranger District
Granby Access	115	4.5	Moderate	10,300'	10,000'	Moderate	Grand Junction

USGS Maps: Skyway, Hells Kitchen.
Usage: Moderate.

Granby Trail is a relatively short but challenging four-wheel drive trail with narrow corridors, large rocks, and numerous mud holes.

The trail begins at the parking area for Island Lake Campground leading southwest past Rimrock Lake. Rocks and mud holes line the path until reaching Granby-Battlement Reservoir chain, where fishing for rainbow and brook trout is at its finest. The road ends at the dam of Big Battlement Reservoir with a short hike to Little Battlement Reservoir.

Directions from Cedaredge: Travel north on Hwy 65 to FDR 116.1 and 1-mile west on FDR 116.1 to a campground. Enter the campground and follow the Island Lake campground road to the fisherman parking lot at the rear of the campground. The area is marked.

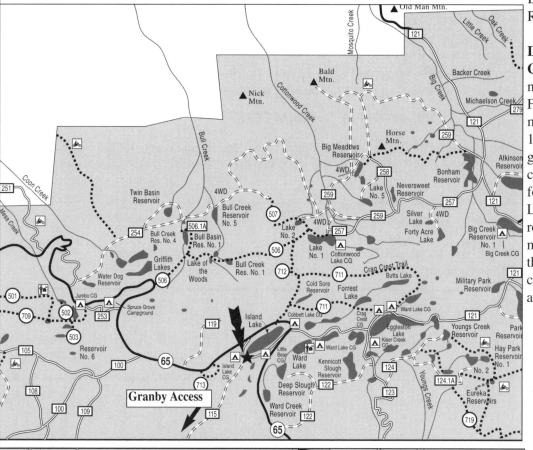

Grand Mesa Map 1

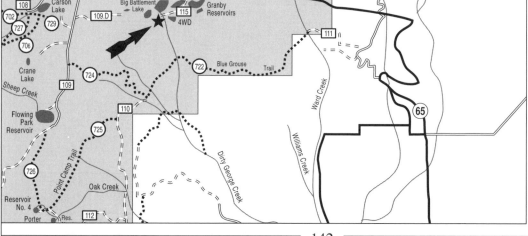

Grand Mesa Map 3

Road Name	Road Number	Length Miles	Difficulty	Beginning Elevation	Ending Elev.	Usage	Ranger District
Leon Lake	127	8	Moderate	8,640'	10,400'	Moderate	Grand Junction

USGS Maps: Leon Peak.

Not all of the 8 miles is rough four-wheeling. The more difficult area comes after reaching Marcott Reservoir, although there are still challenging creeks that you must ford. Many people enjoy traveling this road due to access extending past the District Boundary eventually arriving at the Vega Reservoir east of Collbran.

Directions from Cedaredge: Travel 3.5 miles on Hwy 65 north to County Road U50/25. Go six miles east and north to Forest Boundary. Marcott Road access is east of the road beyond the corral.

Grand Mesa Map 2

Grand Mesa National Forest
Collbran District 4WD Road Summary

Road Name	Road No.	Miles

Sunnyside Area
Sunnyside Road ....FDR 274 ....3.1

Battlement Area
Kimball Creek Road ......FDR 575 ....6.1
Hawxhurst Creek Road ..FDR 273 ....0.5
Brush Creek Road ....FDR 272 ....2.2
Silt Road ....FDR 270 ....3.8
Mudd Hill Road ....FDR 271 ....5.0
Raven Trail ....FDR 533 ....1.0

Buzzard Area
Road Gulch Road ....FDR 270 ....1.0
Hightower Creek Road ....FDR 269 ....2.0
Sheep Creek Road ....FDR 281 ....2.0
Porter Flat Road ....FDR 266 ....6.5
Owens Creek Road ....FDR 268 ....7.0
Willow Creek Road ....FDR 263 ....6.0
The Burn Road ....FDR 277 .... 5.0
Log Pile Flat Road ....FDR 277 ....1.5

Leon Area
Park Creek Road ....FDR 262 ....4.5
Park Creek Spur ....FDR 262 .... 0.7
Leon Lake Road ....FDR 127 ....4.5
Hunter Reservoir Road ..FDR 280 ....2.7

Cottonwood & Big Creek Area
Lambert Road ....FDR 260 .... 6.0
Sheep Flats Road ....FDR 279 .... 6.0
Englehart Road ....FDR 276 .... 4.0
Silver Lake Road ....FDR 257 .... 8.0
Park View Road ....FDR 258............ 8.0
Cottonwood Lake #5 Road FDR 258 ....6.0
Cottonwood Lake #4 Road FDR 257 ....1.1
Bureau Pipeline Road ....FDR 259 ....11.0
Atkinson Reservoir Road FDR 114 .... 5.0

Mesa Lakes Area
Easter Seal Road ....FDR 251 ....3.5
Long Slough Road 6.0

Road Name	Road Number	Length Miles	Difficulty	Beginning Elevation	Ending Elev.	Usage	Ranger District
Basin Trail	603	5.3	Moderate	6,200'	9,127'	Moderate	Grand Junction

USGS Maps: Casto Reservoir and Pine Mountain.

The trail is being utilized as a four-wheel drive road during hunting season. The trail can be used as a loop with the Cabin Trail to extend the mileage to approximately 12 miles. Although, the trail is used by four-wheel drive vehicles. No closures are established. Attractions, including wildlife and vegetation, are best identified when hiking or horseback riding.

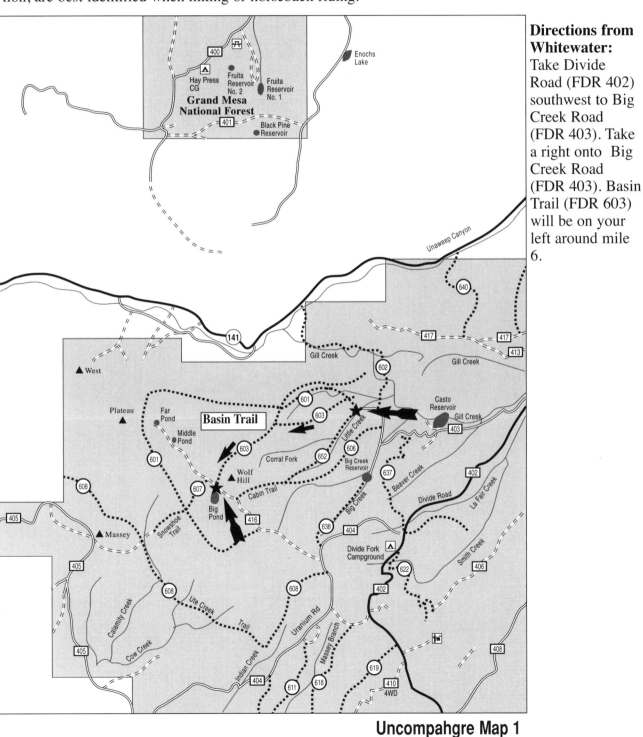

Directions from Whitewater:
Take Divide Road (FDR 402) southwest to Big Creek Road (FDR 403). Take a right onto Big Creek Road (FDR 403). Basin Trail (FDR 603) will be on your left around mile 6.

Uncompahgre Map 1

Road Name	Road Number	Length Miles	Difficulty	Beginning Elevation	Ending Elev.	Usage	Ranger District
Cabin Trail	606	5	Moderate	8,200'	9,042'	Moderate	Grand Junction

USGS Maps: Casto Reservoir, Pine Mountain.

The trail is being utilized as a four-wheel drive road during hunting season. The trail can be used as a loop trail with Basin Trail to extend the mileage to approximately 12 miles.

Directions from Whitewater: Take Divide Road (FDR 402) southwest to Uranium Road, Take a right onto Big Creek Road (FDR 403). Drive 5 miles to the lowest termini of Cabin Trail.

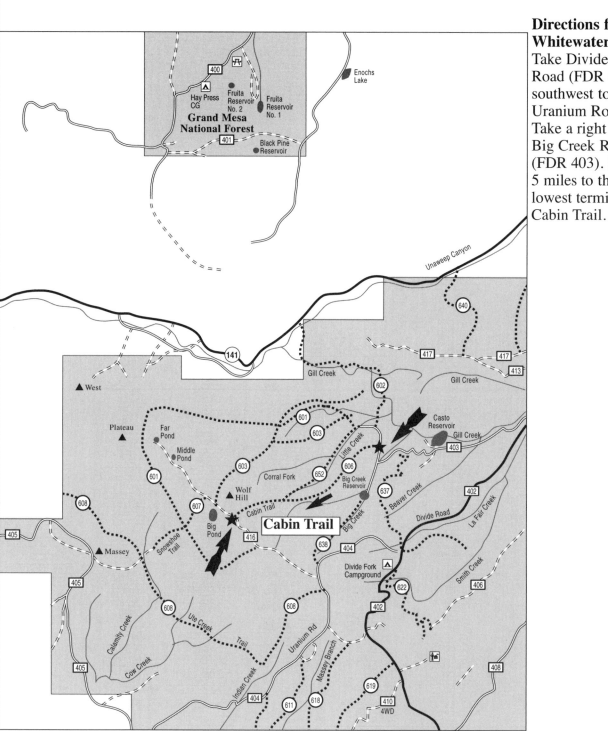

Uncompahgre Map 1

Road Name	Road Number	Length Miles	Difficulty	Beginning Elevation	Ending Elev.	Usage	Ranger District
Black Bear	648	3.6	Most Difficult	12,840'	10,320'	Moderate	Norwood

USGS Maps: Ironton and Telluride.

The Black Bear Road is a challenge to any four-wheeler or biker. It is widely known as the grand daddy of all jeep roads. Due to sharp switchbacks, steep grades and narrow tread with no room to pass, it has been designated as a one- way road. Travel it from east to west so the direction of travel is downhill over the worst sections.

This scenic route goes from Red Mountain Pass to Telluride via Black Bear Road. The road is named after the Black Bear Mine located in the north branch of Ingram Creek in Ingram Basin. The road from Red Mountain Pass to the summit to Ingram Creek crossing is all in slide rock but not terribly steep. The road is one-way from Ingram down to the Bridal Veil Road. The steepest section is just above Ingram Falls at the Old Ingram mill site. The road crosses Ingram Creek on solid rock just at the top of the Falls.

The section from the falls to Bridal Veil Road is very steep and most vehicles have to back up to get around the switchbacks. In past years when miners from Telluride used to go to work in Ingram Basin, they traveled this road in jeeps. Signs on each end directed traffic to go up for thirty minutes, then down traffic had thirty minutes thus avoiding meeting on the steep grade.

It is suggested that anyone using this road use extreme caution. Travel slowly and keep your vehicle in control at all times.

Directions from Red Mountain Pass: Turn west from Highway 550 on to Black Bear Road at the summit of Red Mountain Pass.

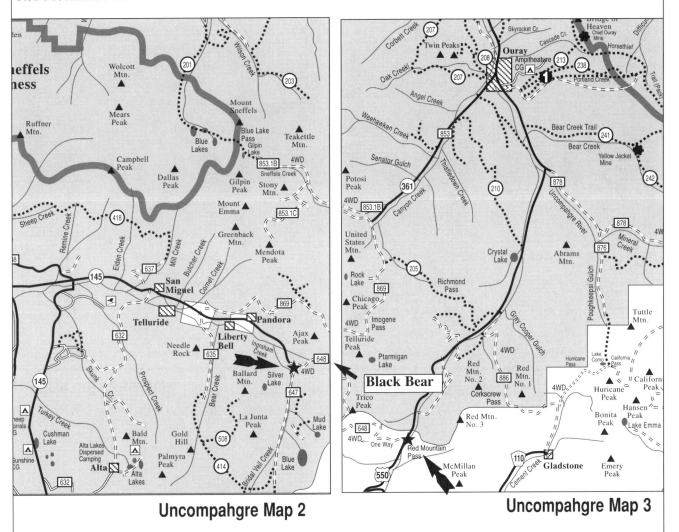

Uncompahgre Map 2

Uncompahgre Map 3

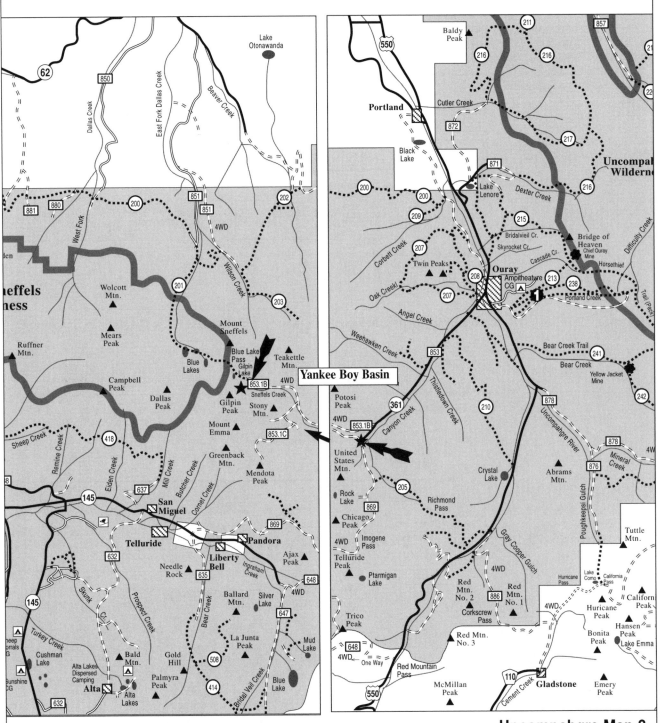

Yankee Boy Basin

Uncompahgre Map 2

Uncompahgre Map 3

Road Name	Road Number	Length Miles	Difficulty	Beginning Elevation	Ending Elev.	Usage	Ranger District
Yankee Boy Basin	853.1B	4.2	Easy	9,692'	12,200'	Heavy	Ouray

Length: 4.2 miles to Gilpin Lake.
USGS Maps: Ironton, Telluride.

Yankee Boy Basin (FDR 853) is an extension of the Canyon Creek Road past the Camp Bird Mine. Spectacular mountain scenery, alpine flowers, waterfalls and many active and abandoned mines may be seen along the route.

The condition of the road is good. Traffic by ore trucks and recreational vehicles is very heavy. All vehicles must stay on developed roads.

For "flat landers" visiting the Ouray area, the Yankee Boy Basin Road offers a superb combination of scenery, mining history, and relatively easy four-wheel driving.

Where the Camp Bird Mine entrance road turns to the left, keep right to continue up into Yankee Boy Basin. From the intersection, the road makes a sharp right turn in .25 mile. At this point the road was constructed on a ledge and widened by blasting. A cliff overhangs the road for a few hundred feet. Vehicles may only pass in one direction at a time through this section. Check the road ahead before starting.

A good road continues for over 2 miles past the old Sneffels town site, where the road forks, turn right to follow into Yankee boy Basin. The road to the left leads to Governor Basin. From this point, the road gets rockier and much rougher.

In about 1.25 miles the road climbs to an open basin. Beyond the basin the road continues about .75 miles to Gilpin Lake. The last section of road is not located on rock like the lower portion. If the ground is wet, steep grades will prevent you from driving this section without damage to the road and alpine soils.

Throughout the trip are superb views of rugged mountain scenery and unusual rock formations, characteristic of the San Juan Mountains. Potosi Peak and Teakettle Mountain may be seen north of the road. On the south side are United States Mountain, Gilpin Peak and Stony Mountain. Although Mount Sneffels lies just northwest of Gilpin Lake, the top of that peak cannot be seen.

July and early August are favorite times for many to view alpine flowers, which brighten the hillsides and open meadows. Entire fields of blue Colorado Columbines, red Indian Paintbrush and yellow Buttercups are common.

The road and mines up Canyon Creek past Camp Bird into the Sneffels mining District exemplifies the ingenuity, desires, and abilities of early day miners to extract minerals under extremes of nature's conditions.

Camp Bird Mine was one of the largest and most productive gold mines in Colorado. An estimated $40 to $50 million has been removed since its beginnings in the mid-1890's. Supplies and ore were hauled over the narrow, steep winding Canyon Creek Road by six horse teams. A boarding house with two men per room and a recreation building were built. Accommodations were considered good at Camp Bird compared with other mining camps. The first mill site buildings and mine were destroyed by avalanches. The current mine is located to avoid snow slides.

Just beyond the junction to Imogene Pass is the town site of Sneffels and the Revenue Mine. A mill, boarding house, store, post office, powerhouse and other buildings once stood at this location. For over twenty years the Revenue Mine was the largest shipper of ore from the county. Sneffels began in 1881 and lasted until 1919. A total of $27 million in gold was mined from this site.

At the Governor Basin junction is the Ruby Trust Mine, 100 yards from the intersection. Originally, the mine was named the Speedwell. The name was changed to the Ruby Trust, because of beautiful ruby silver produced from the mine.

Yankee Boy receives particularly heavy traffic throughout the summer. Allow plenty of time for slow driving and plenty of picture taking.

Directions from Ouray: From Ouray take Hwy 550 south .25 mile to Canyon Creek Road (FDR 853). Turn right and continue to Camp Bird Mine. Keep right on the main road 4WD travel is recommended after the intersection.

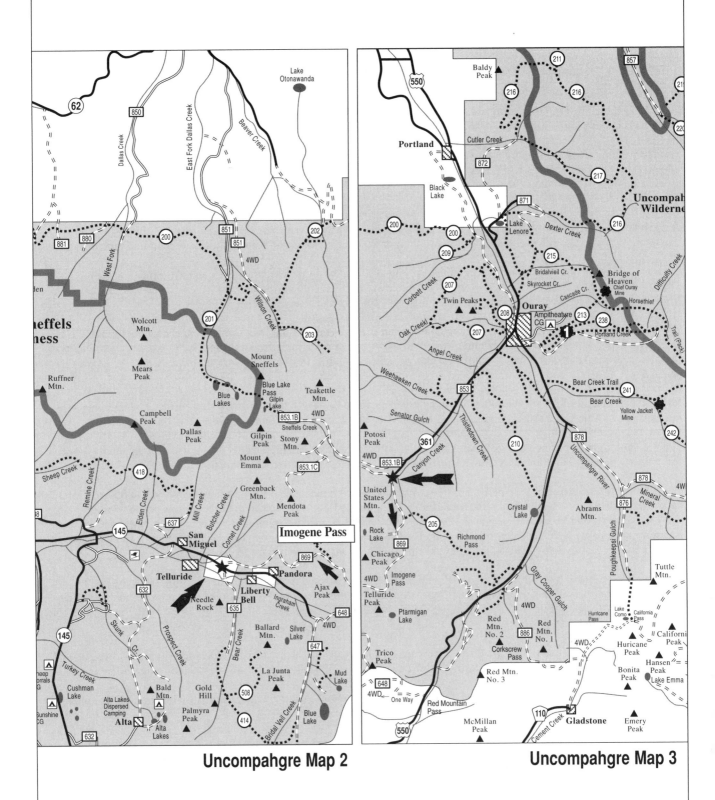

Uncompahgre Map 2

Uncompahgre Map 3

Road Name	Road Number	Length Miles	Difficulty	Beginning Elevation	Ending Elev.	Usage	Ranger District
Imogene Pass	869	5	Moderate	10,576'	13,114'	Heavy	Ouray

Length: 5 Miles to the Summit of Imogene Pass.
USGS Map: Ironton.

Imogene Pass is the highest and most spectacular of the four-wheel drive passes in the Ouray District. Deep late season snowdrifts frequently prevent opening beyond upper Camp Bird until mid July. From the Yankee Boy Road to upper Camp Bird the road it rough and slow, but not difficult. Steep switchbacks above the Upper Camp Bird require careful driving.

Imogene Pass offers a more challenging route to four-wheelers than most of the popular "jeep" trips in the Ouray District.

Beginning near the town site of Sneffels, the Imogene Road fords Sneffels Creek. In about 1.5 miles the road joins a second road leading from Camp Bird. This is a private road to the mine and not open for public use. Along this first section are breathtaking views looking down almost vertically 450 feet into the Camp Bird mill and mine facilities.

Continue up the Imogene Road .75 mile keep left and cross the creek past the old Yellow Rose Mine. This section is narrow. In about .33 mile the road crosses Imogene Creek to your right. The mine buildings in the basin above are the portals and workings of the Upper Camp Bird. Over 25 miles of tunnels were carved out tying together the different "levels" of the Camp Bird Mine.

Keep left as you reach Upper Camp Bird to continue up the pass. Narrow steep switchbacks make this the most difficult section of the Imogene Road. On the Ironton Quadrangle map the road from Upper Camp Bird is shown as a pack trail.

From the 13,114 foot summit is a superb view of Red Mountain and the surrounding San Juan's. Ptarmigan Lake lies in the nearby basin below. Allow plenty of time to enjoy and photograph the scenery.

Across Imogene Pass is a good road that drops into Savage Basin and the extensive ruins of the Tom Boy Mine. Before reaching Telluride you drop over 4,000 feet in elevation.

Directions from Ouray: Take Hwy 550 south .25 mile to Canyon Creek Road (FDR 853) and turn right. Continue past Camp Bird Mine on Yankee Boy Basin Road 2 miles. Turn left and cross Sneffels Creek .25 mile before Sneffels town site.

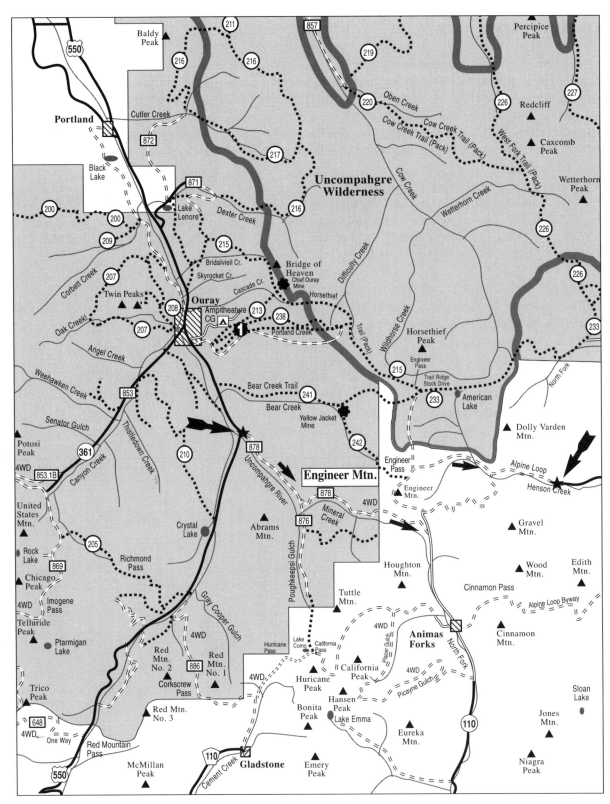

Uncompahgre Map 3

8. Engineer Mountain

Road Name	Road Number	Length Miles	Difficulty	Beginning Elevation	Ending Elev.	Usage	Ranger District
Engineer Mountain	878	5.6	Easy	8,854'	12,840'	Heavy	Ouray

Length: 5.6 Miles to Engineer Pass.
Elevation Gain: 3,946 Feet.
USGS Maps: Handies Peak and Ironton Park.

Engineer Mountain is a relatively easy four-wheel drive route. Many trip combinations may be taken using old interconnecting mine roads crossing the alpine country between Lake City, Silverton and Ouray.

Engineer Mountain is a popular and scenic route for "four-wheelers" to the Ouray area. The road begins from the Million-Dollar Highway 4 miles south of Ouray.

From the highway to the Michael Breen Mine is 1.3 miles, the condition of the road is good. About .6 miles past the mine the road begins to get narrower and rougher. To your right is a large avalanche path in a rock chute that begins near the top of Mount Abrams. Snow deposited in the canyon below lasts well into the summer.

In about .5 miles is the junction to Poughkeepsie Gulch. Little is left of the "Biggest Little Camp in the San Juan's". In the late 1870's or early 1880's, Poughkeepsie Gulch had as many as 250 residents. The town had stores, restaurants, a saloon, and a post office. The most famous mine in the gulch was the Old Lout Mine located 1.5 miles from the junction.

Keep left at Poughkeepsie Gulch to continue up Engineer Mountain. Steep sharp switchbacks climb 2 miles to Mineral Creek and a small group of old mines buildings. The National Forest Boundary is crossed another mile past the buildings.

Continuing up the Engineer Mountain Road .7 mile is an area that is called Mineral Point. A town began here in 1873 and lasted until the early 1890's. During its peak years as many as 1,000 people lived in the town which had a hotel, several restaurants, a post office, saloons, and even a Justice of the Peace. Ruins of the San Juan Chief Mill still exist and are a particularly scenic photo stop for travelers.

From the mill, keep left to continue up Engineer Mountain. In just over 1 mile the road crosses an alpine meadow. At the far end is a road junction. The right fork parallels the North Fork of the Animas River and eventually brings you out to Silverton. It is also the direction to turn if you decide try Cinnamon Pass. Keep left to continue up Engineer Mountain.

The next portion of road is steep and narrow in spots and requires careful driving. From the junction to Engineer Pass is over 2 miles.

The road down the east side of Engineer Mountain is well developed and may be driven on two-wheel drive. Total driving distance from U.S. 550 to Lake City is 31 miles.

From the top of the pass are excellent views of the high peaks of the San Juan Mountains. In the basin just to the east is the Engineer City where in 1875 as many as 400 prospectors developed a town. The wide open alpine country northeast of Engineer Mountain is referred to as Americans flats.

Directions from Ouray: Take Hwy 550 south 3.5 miles to the junction with Engineer Mountain Road.

Directions from Lake City: Take Henson Creek west eighteen miles to the top of the pass.

Road Name	Road Number	Length Miles	Difficulty	Beginning Elevation	Ending Elev.	Usage	Ranger District
Corkscrew Pass	866	4.5	Moderate	9,800'	12,600'	Moderate	Ouray

Length: 4.5 Miles - from US 550.
USGS Maps: Ironton.

This is a moderate trail from US 550 proceeding up steep inclines and sharp, narrow switchbacks, be aware for oncoming traffic. Road can be rough in spots. During heavy rain the lower third of the trail can be very slippery. Proceeding up through the spruce forest you will pass cabins once occupied by the miners of the Midnight, Earl and Carbonate King mines. Corkscrew Pass lies between Red Mountain 1 and 2 and presents some of the most unusual vistas of the San Juans. The color of the Red Mountain alone is astonishing. This trail gives access to Hurricane Pass. From the Gladstone approach the drive is relatively easy however the road is very narrow in spots.

Directions from Ouray: Out of Ouray proceed 7.7 miles south on US 550 and turn left at large Idarado mining dump site and cross over small wooden bridge. Follow signs to Corkscrew Pass.

Directions from Silverton: Proceed approximately 15 miles north on US 550 to County Road 110 to Gladstone approximately 6.5 miles. Turn left up County Road 110 approximately 1.5 miles. Turn sharp left a junction of trails then 1.25 miles up to Corkscrew Pass.

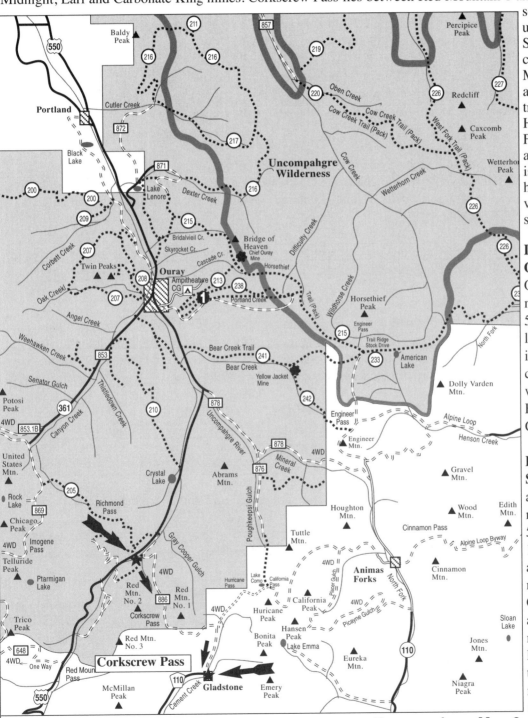

Uncompahgre Map 3

Road Name	Road Number	Length Miles	Difficulty	Beginning Elevation	Ending Elev.	Usage	Ranger District
Treasure Mountain Loop		30.5	Moderate	9,200'	12,000'	Heavy	Ouray

USGS Maps: Handies Peak, Ironton.

This drive is very rich in mining history and has numerous mining ruins. Placer Gulch is lined with mining operations including the Gold Prince, Mastodon, Silver Queen, South Democrat and Hidden Treasure to name but a few. Remains of tramways, boarding houses, power houses, portals and mills are abundant throughout. Proceeding up the back of the gulch above the Sunnyside Mine extension you will make your way into the Picayne Basin. As you descend back into the forested area you will pass by the remains of the Treasure Mountain Mining Company on the right. The road joins back with Colorado 110 to Silverton.

Directions from Silverton: The preferred way to drive this loop in from the Placer Gulch side because the Picayne side is so steep and narrow on the lower third. From Silverton take Colorado 110 right out of town towards Animas Forks approximately 12.5 miles. Take the left hand road out of Animas Forks towards California Pass. Go approximately 1.5 miles to turn off up Placer Gulch. Road on top can be very muddy and treacherous after rains or spring thaw.

Uncompahgre Map 3

Road Name	Road Number	Length Miles	Difficulty	Beginning Elevation	Ending Elev.	Usage	Ranger District
Hurricane/California Pass		9.8	Moderate	9,200'	12,407'	Moderate	Ouray

Length: 9.8 - 10.5 Miles.
USGS Maps: Handies Peak, Ironton.

Accessing the passes on County Road 110 from Gladstone the road is ledge-like and narrow. This canyon, called Ross Basin, was dominated by the Mogul Mine and Mill. The mine itself is on the right hand side as you proceed past the Corkscrew turnoff. The upper canyon is stark but ruggedly beautiful. At Hurricane Pass you are overlooking Lake Como to the north, the headwaters for the Uncompahgre River. Proceeding along the road you will drop sharply down to an intersection with the Poughkeepsie Trail. Keep right up to California Pass at 12,930 feet. The drive from California Pass to Animas Forks is easy passing through a number of mining areas. This route is moderate drive with spectacular views.

Directions from Silverton: The preferred way to drive this loop is from the Placer Gulch side because the Picayne side is so steep and narrow on the lower third. From Silverton take Colorado 110 right out of town towards Animas Forks approximately 12.5 miles. Take the left hand road out of Animas Forks towards California Pass. Go approximately 1.5 miles to turn off up Placer Gulch. Road on top can be very muddy and treacherous after rains or spring thaw.

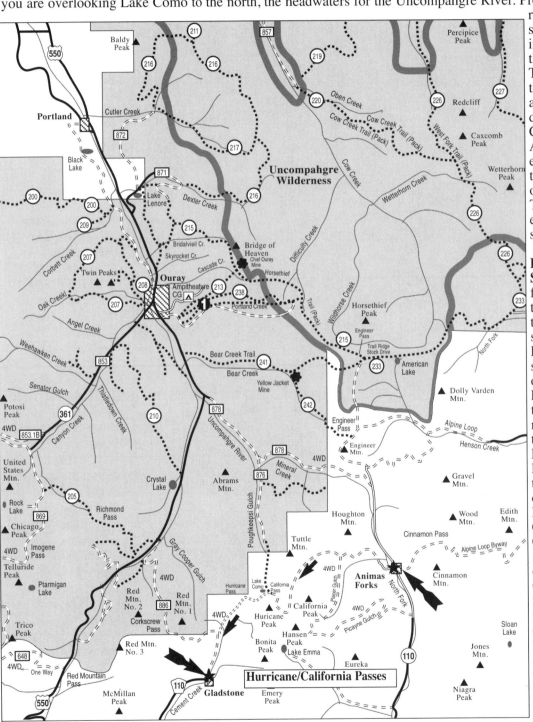

Uncompahgre Map 3

Road Name	Road Number	Length Miles	Difficulty	Beginning Elevation	Ending Elev.	Usage	Ranger District
Nellie Creek	877	4	Moderate	9,300'	11,600'	Heavy	Ouray

USGS Map: Uncompahgre Peak.

Nellie Creek Road (FDR 877) leads 4 miles north from Engineer Pass Road following the path of Nellie Creek. The beginning of the road is narrow and fairly steep, this is the most difficult part of the drive. One of the attractions of this drive is a waterfall located approximately .8 mile on your left. There are several shallow stream crossings, that can be difficult to cross during spring run off. The road leads to a large parking area that is Uncompahgre Peak Trailhead on the Uncompahgre Wilderness boundary, one of the access routes to Uncompahgre Peak.

Directions from Lake City: Take Engineer Pass Road along Henson Creek about 5.5 miles to Nellie Creek Road (FDR 877). A sign will direct you. From the Engineer Pass Road, drive north on Nellie Creek Road 1.75 miles. Here the road forks bear left as the right fork is closed to motorized vehicles.

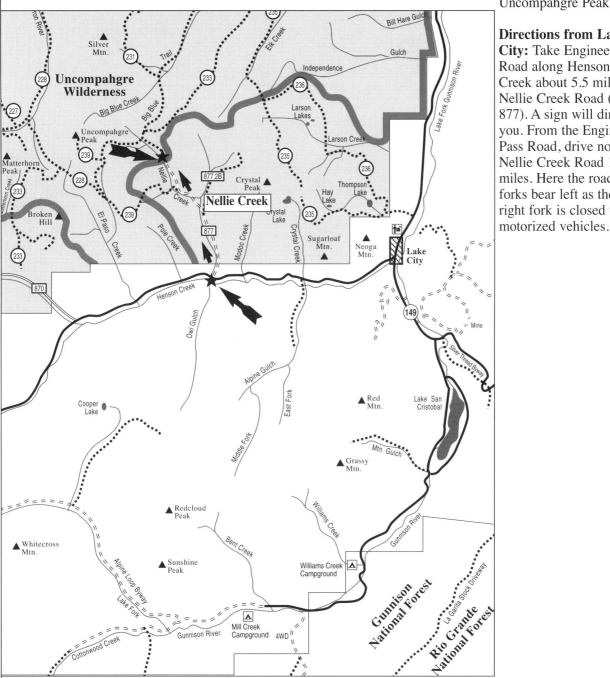

Uncompahgre Map 4

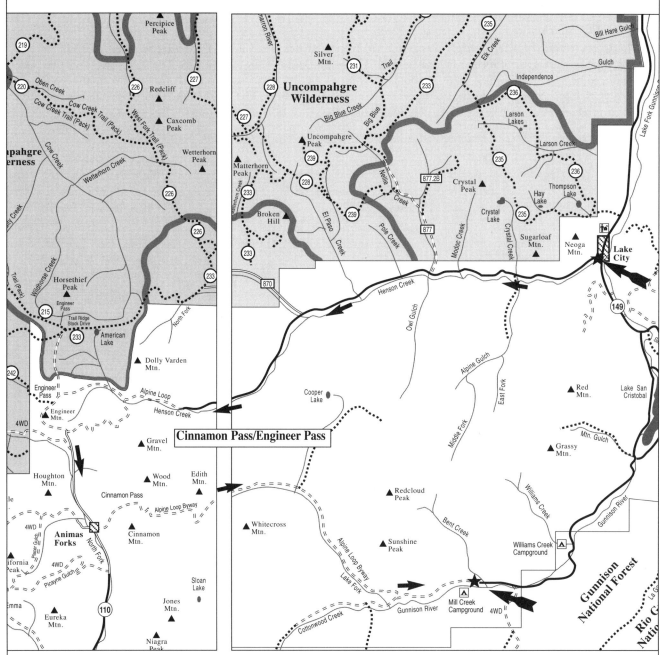

Uncompahgre Map 3

Uncompahgre Map 4

Road Name	Road Number	Length Miles	Difficulty	Beginning Elevation	Ending Elev.	Usage	Ranger District
Cinnamon/Engineer	176		Moderate	9,200'	8,670'	Heavy	Ouray

Cinnamon Pass - Engineer Pass Road
Length: 15.3 to 43 Miles.
Difficulty: Moderate to Difficult.
Beginning Elevation: 9,200 Feet, Silverton.
Ending Elevation: 8,670 Feet, Lake City.
High Point: 13,218 Feet, Engineer Pass.

USGS Maps: Lake City, Lake San Cristobol, Redcloud Peak, Handies Peak and Uncompahgre Peak.

The route that connects Cinnamon Pass and Engineer Pass is part of the Alpine Loop Scenic Byway. This four-wheel drive loop passes through the rugged mining territory of the San Juan Mountains. Silver and gold miners first created many of the roads and trails accessible from this route during the nineteenth century.

From the Silverton side there is much to see. Animas Forks is one of the best preserved ghost towns in the area. Many buildings are still standing and historical markers explain much of how the town was. The road from Animas Forks is not difficult and climbs steadily to the pass. Coming from the Lake City side you will pass the beautiful San Cristobal Lake. At approximately 11 miles you will pass the turn off to the ghost town of Carson and at 14 miles the turn off to the town site of Sherman. As you near the top you will pass by the remains of the famous Tabasco mine and mill. During the fall the Lake City side provides spectacular fall foliage colors with grove after grove of Aspens.

From the Lake City side follow Colorado Highway 149 south from Lake City for two miles. Turn onto the road that leads to Lake San Cristobal (State Highway 3). Continue traveling on this road past Williams Creek and Mill Creek Campgrounds. 1.5 miles past Mill Creek Campground, there is a fork in the road, bear right at the fork. (You will be following the Alpine Loop Scenic Byway.) About 8 miles northwest on this road is another fork, the left road goes to the American Basin Trailhead. Take the right fork to go to Cinnamon Pass. Once you reach Cinnamon Pass (elevation 12,600 feet) follow the road down to Animas Forks. Turn, right at Animas Forks and follow FDR 876 past Denver Lake, on your left, to a fork in the road. Follow the right side of the fork as it ascends via switchbacks. Stay on this road to Engineer Pass (elevation 13,218 feet). The road descending from Engineer Pass is the Henson Creek Road. Follow it back to Lake City (about 15 miles).

Directions from Lake City: Follow Highway 149 south from town to begin. State Highway 3, Cinnamon Flats Road, Forest Road (FDR 176) and Engineer Pass Road form the loop. Follow Alpine Loop signs. It is 24 miles from Lake City to Cinnamon Pass.

Directions from Silverton: Take Colorado 110 to Animas Forks approximately 12.4 miles. Take the Cinnamon Pass turn off to the right and proceed 2.87 miles to the Pass.

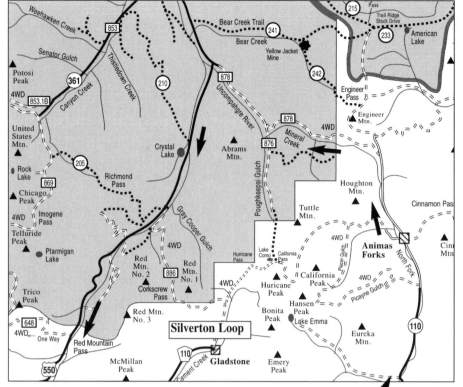

Uncompahgre Map 3

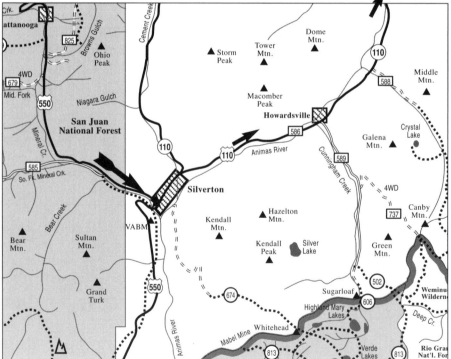

Uncompahgre Map 5

Road Name	Road Number	Length Miles	Difficulty	Beginning Elevation	Ending Elev.	Usage	Ranger District
Silverton Loop		34.5	Moderate	9,380'	9,380'	Heavy	Ouray

Beginning & Ending Elev: 9,380 feet at Silverton.
USGS Maps: Silverton, Howardsville, Handies Peak, Ironton.

Silverton to Arrastra Gulch 2.1 miles.
North of the road at that point is the old Shenandoah Mill or Mayflower Mill. The train line overhead served to transport men and supplies to and ore from the Mayflower Mine which is visible on the eastern side of the gulch. The saddle at the end of the gulch is the gateway to a large upper basin consisting of Silver Lake, a once bustling area surrounded by three mines; the Silver Lake, the Iowa and the Royal Tiger.

3.8 miles Stony Pass (Turn right at Howardsville).
The pass was opened in 1878 over a 12,000 foot pass in the Continental Divide and provided Silverton with regular passenger and freight service. (A short side trip to the top of Stony Pass at this point in the tour would give the traveler a beautiful panoramic view of the southern San Juans.)

4.0 miles Howardsville.
The oldest of the camps in the San Juans, Howardsville is located at the junction of Cunningham Gulch. Major mines of the Howardsville area during years past included the Pride of the West, the Green Mountain, the Highland Mary, the Little Nation and the Old Hundred, which is directly below its portal boarding house, clinging to the side of Galena Mountain at an elevation of 12,300 feet. The elevation at Howardsville is 9,644 feet.

7.5 miles Eureka (Go straight at Howardsville).
A settlement was started in earnest in the early 1870's with the location of the Sunnyside to the north. When the Sunnyside shut down in 1931 for the first time, Eureka faltered, and when the operation was last worked in 1938, it was the end of Eureka.

10.5 miles Animas Forks.
Animas Forks was transformed from a tent city into a town of structures and substance in 1877 and although it was never incorporated, it had its own post office, newspaper, and grade school. It is located where the wagon roads now know as Engineer Pass and Cinnamon Pass converged on the routes between Ouray, Silverton and Lake City.

13.5 miles Mineral Point.
The high Mineral Point Valley at the base of Engineer Pass was once (late 1870's and 1880's) one of the busiest areas of activity in the area. Reached mainly from Silverton, the valley contains many prospects and a few mines that were once quite productive. By the 1890's however, it was on its way toward becoming a ghost camp.

18 miles Million Dollar Highway (Turn left at asphalt).
Hundreds of men blasted a passage out of sheer cliffs from 1881 to 1883. The grade was too steep for a railroad. Early day tolls were $5 for a team and wagon, $1 for a horse and rider.

21.7 miles Ironton.
Tour proceeds to Ironton, a ghost town with several buildings, which once claimed 1,000 persons as a major transportation junction between Ouray and Silverton. Coaches and freighters from Ouray met the Silverton Railroad at Ironton.

23.7 miles Idarado Mine.
This mine is a vast complex of once rich mines including Liberty Bell, Smuggler Union, Tomboy, Black Bear and others and has more than 90 miles of tunnels going through the mountain to Pandora at Telluride.

24.5 miles Red Mountain.
The first community, just east of Red Mountain Pass, was called Congress, with 300 year 'round inhabitants. The city once had three newspapers, a municipal waterworks, depot, school, stores and a jail and 60 buildings in all. Much of the town burned in 1892. The 11.2 mile Silverton Railroad passed through the town, hauling coal up from Silverton and ore back beginning in 1889.

34.5 miles Silverton.
In 1860 an expedition led by Captain Charles Baker arrived in the high mountain park that carries his name. Reports of seemingly inexhaustible placers brought a stampede of miners to the area in the same year. Silverton was selected in at the general election in 1874 the county seat of La Plata County.

RIO GRANDE NATIONAL FOREST

INDEX MAP

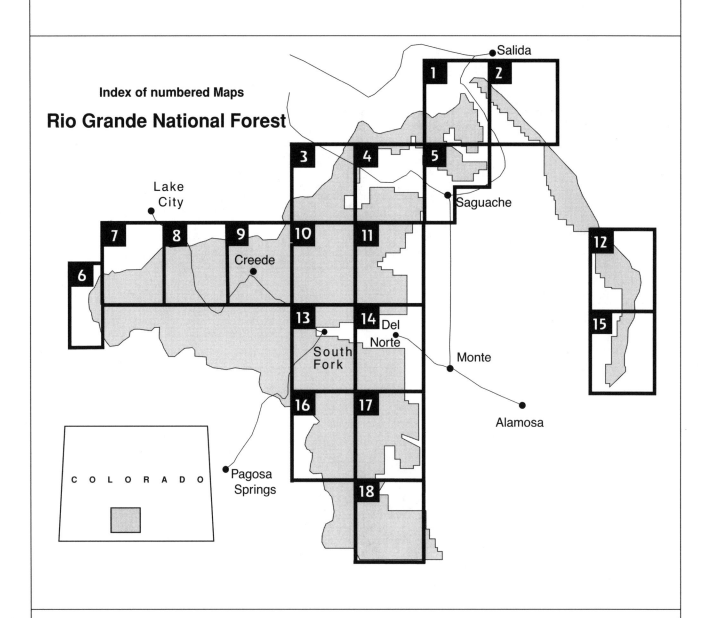

Index of numbered Maps

Rio Grande National Forest

RIO GRANDE NATIONAL FOREST

Located east of Alamosa in south central Colorado, Rio Grande National Forest includes almost two million acres of publicly owned land on the eastern slope of the Continental Divide. Parts of two spectacular mountain ranges, the San Juan and the Sangre de Cristo, are within the Forest. Also included are the headwaters of the third longest river in the United States, the Rio Grande del Norte, or "Great river of the North," as it was known by the early Spanish and Indian inhabitants of the Southwest.

Between the ranges with their 14,000 foot summits is the fertile San Luis Valley, one of several high "parks" or basins in Colorado ringed by mountains. The Communities of Alamosa, Del Norte, Monte Vista, Saguache, Antonito, and others are reminders of the area's long and colorful heritage, while names such as Bonanza, Wagon Wheel Gap, Creede, and Summitville are part of an equally colorful but more recent history.

Variety is the word describing the outdoor recreation opportunities of the Rio Grande National Forest. From the rugged and jagged peaks of the Sangre de Cristo's to the forested table lands and glacial canyons of the San Juans, the outdoor enthusiast can choose an activity suited to the day or the season.

High lakes and tumbling streams beckon the fisherman while big game and other wildlife lure the hunter or nature photographer. Hiking, backpacking, and camping amid spectacular scenery await the visitor to the Weminuche, La Garita, or South San Juan Wilderness. The trail along the Continental Divide, or the rugged Sangre de Cristo backcountry is equally exciting and challenging.

A good network of Forest highways and roads provides access for the auto traveler, with some fifty Forest Service recreation sites located in convenient spots.

Other recreation opportunities include horseback riding, skiing, snowmobiling, or nature study. History buffs may enjoy a thrilling ride on the Cumbres and Toltec Scenic Railroad, a narrow gauge steam route from Antonito, Colorado to Chama, New Mexico. Evidence of early day mining camps is scattered throughout the Forest, while Creede, Bonanza, Platoro, and Summitville are centers of continuing mineral activity. The routes of early explorer Juan Bautista de Anza, and later ones such as Zebulon Pike and John C. Fremont can he traced with a little imagination and effort. Although each season in the Rockies has a special charm, autumn on the Rio Grande is unequaled. The yellows and golds of the "quaking" or "trembling" aspen blanket the slopes and benches, the air is crisp, the sky a deep blue, and the visitor will find solitude.

The Rio Grande National Forest, and adjacent Bureau of Land Management Land, offer virtually unlimited opportunities for "Fat Tire" bike enthusiasts. All trails and roads are open for mountain biking except those trails within designated Wilderness Areas and the Wheeler Geologic Area.

1. Round Mountain

Road Name	Road Number	Length Miles	Difficulty	Beginning Elevation	Ending Elev.	Usage	Ranger District
Round Mountain	890	6	Moderate	9,400'	12,000'	Moderate	Saguache

USGS Maps: Bonanza.

The traveler can view the historical mining area in the Bonanza area. From the top of Round Mountain, the traveler has a magnificent view in all directions. Much of the area along this road is private property.

Directions: Take Hwy 285 to Villa Grove, then west on County Road 11 65 15 miles to Bonanza.

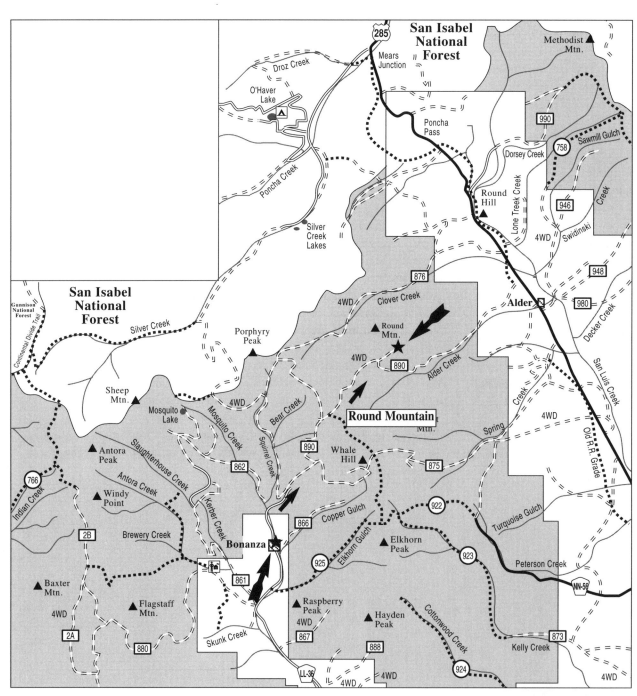

Rio Grande Map 1

Road Name	Road Number	Length Miles	Difficulty	Beginning Elevation	Ending Elev.	Usage	Ranger District
Hayden Pass	970	7.7	Difficult	8,000'	10,700'	Moderate	Saguache

Length: 7.7 Miles. (17.7 miles to Coaldale.)
Ending Elevation: 10,700 Feet - Hayden Pass in the Rio Grande National Forest.
USGS Map: Howard Quad.

The west slopes of the Sangre de Cristo Mountains are very steep. Grades up to 20 percent exist along this road. Large, loose rocks exist along lower steep slopes. The best campsite is near rise top of Hayden Pass. Water is very limited. A good view of the San Luis Valley and lower Arkansas Valley is available at Hayden Pass. The road continues down the East Side of the Sangre de Cristo Mountains in the San Isabel National Forest. You can continue east through the San Isabel National Forest an additional 10 miles to Coaldale.

Sections of the road down to Coaldale are rocky, steep and are difficult if traveled when the road is wet or frozen. Best traveled during the late summer and fall months.

Directions from Villa Grove: Villa Grove @ Highway 285, east on County Road 11 57/FDR 970, 7.7 miles to top of pass.

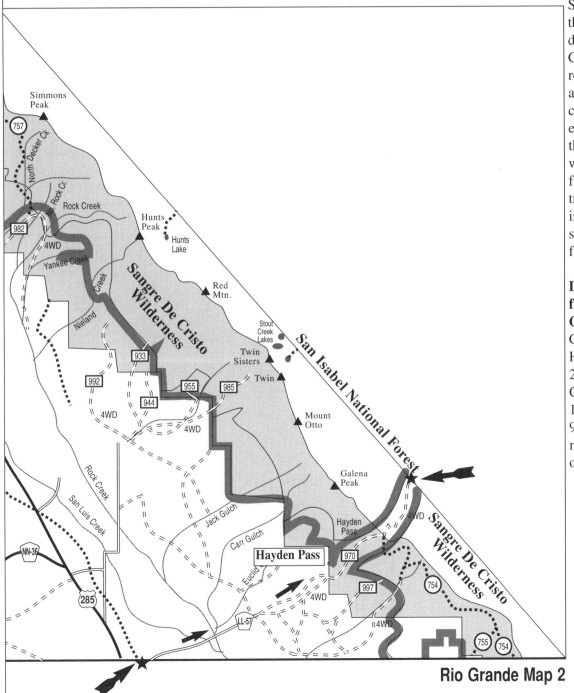

Rio Grande Map 2

Road Name	Road Number	Length Miles	Difficulty	Beginning Elevation	Ending Elev.	Usage	Ranger District
Horse Canyon/N. Fork Loop	776	14.5	Moderate	10,600'	9,600'	Light	Saguache

FDR 745/776/787.
USGS Maps: Saguache Park, Elk Park.

These two roads provided a loop jeep road on the West Side of Saguache Park. The road begins at the junction with Saguache Park Road (FDR 787) at the south end of Saguache Park and ends as intersection with Middle Fork Saguache Road (FDR 744) approximately 1.5 miles west of Stone Cellar Campground. Water is available in the North Fork of Saguache Creek. Several good campsites exist along this road. Saguache Park is a very large dry park with livestock grazing one of the major uses. Stone Cellar Campground is located near end of North Fork Road.

Directions from Saguache:
Approximately 41 miles west of Saguache along Highway 114, turn south on FDR 804 for approximately 6 miles to BLM 3083. East on BLM 3083 for 1.5 miles to the Saguache Park Road (FDR 787). Continue south on Saguache Park Road for 8 miles.

Note: Refer to a Gunnison Forest map.

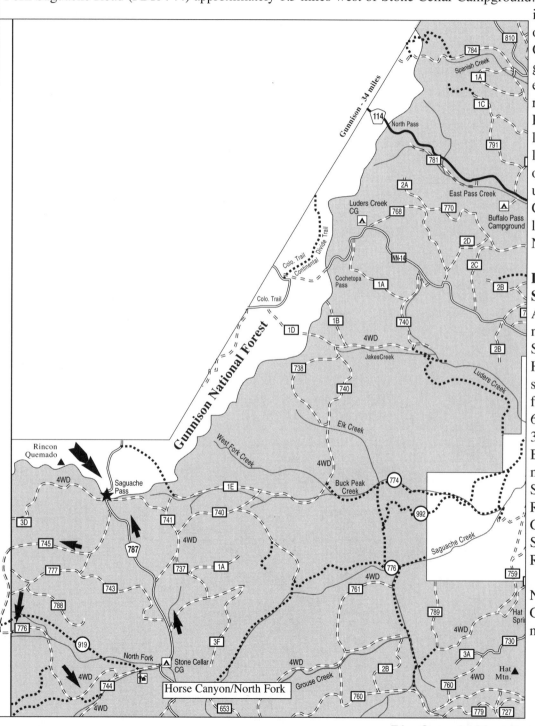

Horse Canyon/North Fork

Road Name	Road Number	Length Miles	Difficulty	Beginning Elevation	Ending Elev.	Usage	Ranger District
Four Mile	740	16	Mod/Diff.	9,600'	10,000'	Light	Saguache

Beginning Elevation: 9,600 Feet - Cochetopa Road (FDR 750) at Windy Point.
Ending Elevation: 10,000 Feet - At junction with Saguache Park Road (FDR 787).
USGS Maps: Saguache Park, Grouse Creek, and North Pass.

Road provides a jeep road between Saguache Park and the Luder Creek area. Water is available in several streams along the way. Many good campsites exist along the road's length. Saguache Park is a very large dry park with several fishable streams. Livestock grazing is one of the major uses of the park. This is a very challenging 4WD road.

Directions from Saguache:
Approximately 20 miles west of Saguache along Highway 114, turn onto Cochetopa Road. Continue west on Cochetopa Road (NN 14) for 8 miles (Windy Point).

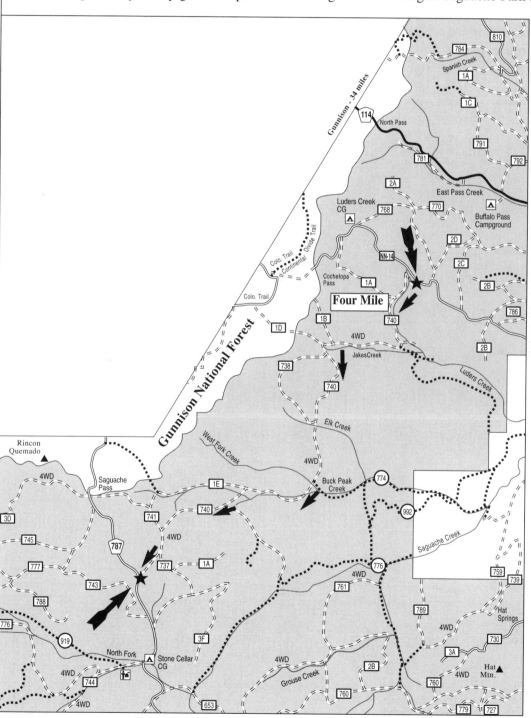

Rio Grande Map 3

Road Name	Road Number	Length Miles	Difficulty	Beginning Elevation	Ending Elev.	Usage	Ranger District
Middle Fork Saguache	744	6	Moderate	9,500'	10,200'	Moderate	Saguache

Beginning Elevation: 9,500 Feet - Stone Cellar Campground.
Ending Elevation: 10,200 Feet - Trailhead on Middle Fork of Saguache Creek.
USGS Maps: Saguache, Park and Mesa Mountain.

Middle Fork of Saguache Creek flows near this road and is a fishable stream. Road leads to Middle Park Trailhead which provides access so the La Garita Wilderness. Stone Cellar Campground is located at the beginning of this road. Saguache Park is a very large, dry park with livestock grazing one of the major uses.

Directions from Saguache: Approximately 41 miles west of Saguache along Highway 114, turn south on FDR 804 for approximately 6 miles to BLM 3083. East on BLM 3083 for 1.5 miles to the Saguache Park Road (FDR 787). Continue south on Saguache Park Road for 12 miles until you reach Stone Cellar Campground.

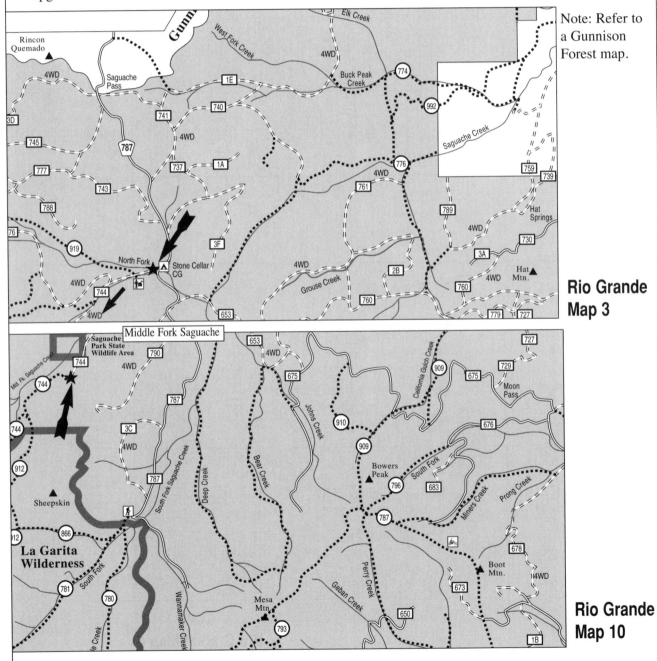

Note: Refer to a Gunnison Forest map.

Rio Grande Map 3

Rio Grande Map 10

Road Name	Road Number	Length Miles	Difficulty	Beginning Elevation	Ending Elev.	Usage	Ranger District
Fullerton Park/Laughlin G.	620/706	15	Moderate	8,500'	9,900'	Light	Saguache

Beginning Elevation: 8,500 Feet - Junction with Laughlin Gulch County Road.
Ending Elevation: 9,900 Feet - Junction with Carnero Road.
USGS Maps: Laughlin Gulch, Lake Mountain.

These roads provide access to Fullerton Park area. This area is managed for livestock grazing. The traveler may observe deer and elk along the way. Camping sites exist along the length of this tour. Water is available along Mill Creek and at Big Springs. Very scenic in the fall of the year when aspen change color.

Directions from Saguache: Take Houghland Hill Road (County Road 36CC) approximately 10 miles west of Saguache.

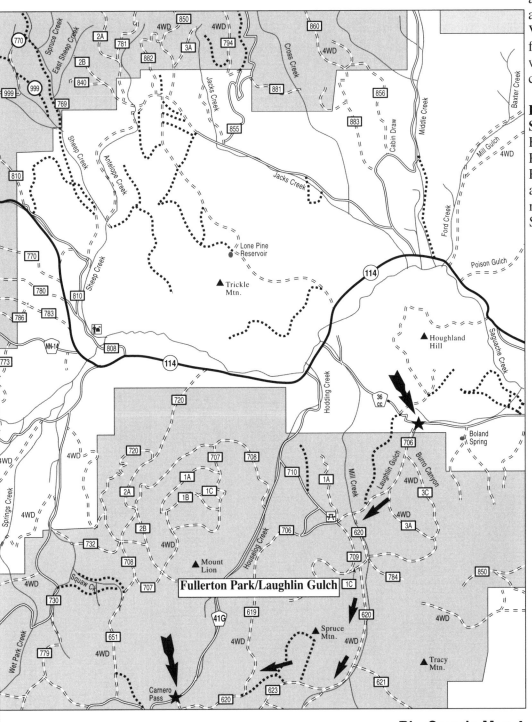

Rio Grande Map 4

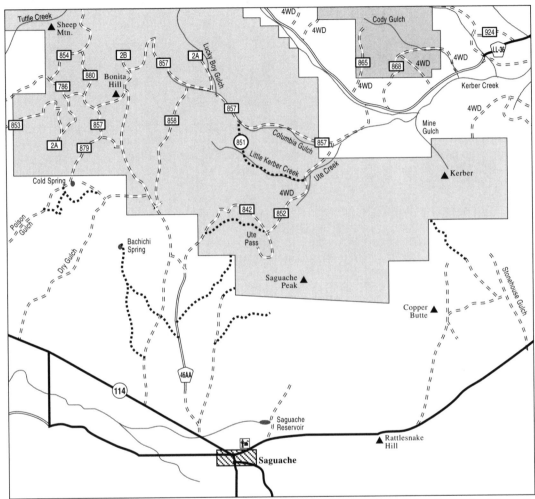

Rio Grande Map 5

Road Name	Road Number	Length Miles	Difficulty	Beginning Elevation	Ending Elev.	Usage	Ranger District
Ute Pass Loop	842	17.2	More Difficult	9,944'	9,944'	Heavy	Saguache

USGS Maps: Klondike Mine, Graveyard Gulch.

Begin at the parking area and head south. Turn left on the road with old cabin and follow to Country Rd 46AA. Turn left on 46AA, take this road to the top of Ute Pass (5.8 miles from parking area, 9,944 feet). Bear left at top and descend FDR 852 to Columbia Gulch. Turn left onto FDR 857 and follow to intersection of FDR 858. Turn left across Little Kerber Creek and proceed up Sawlog Gulch. The 0.5 mile climb leads to an open field, which then leads back down to the parking area (3.0 miles).

This primitive road is passable to 2WD vehicles with high clearance from Hwy 114 to the top of Ute Pass (FDR 842). The portion of the road north of Ute Pass (FDR 852) is narrow, winding, and boulder strewn and best suited for four-wheel drive vehicles.

The valley views while climbing Ute Pass are beautiful and the Ute Pass downhill is enjoyable (and fast!). If you choose, turn right atop Ute Pass and ride another mile uphill on a slight detour to a radio repeater site. You will be rewarded by an even more breathtaking scene of the San Luis Valley than those who proceed directly downhill will see. Once up there, however, you must turn around and ride back down to Ute Pass and follow the directions for the descent.

The cliffs and wildlife along Columbia Gulch provide a pleasant background for that leg of the trip and Little Kerber Creek provides musical accompaniment. Once atop Sawlog Gulch, the meadow and wildflowers provide an excellent resting place. Be extremely careful on the descent, it is strewn with large rocks and ruts in the trail. Trail consists of drivable roads and mostly smooth surfaces. There are long and sustained grades with a few streambeds that are easily crossed.

Directions from Saguache: Take Colorado Hwy 114 from Saguache west 1.5 miles and turn right onto County Rd 46 AA (Findley Gulch). Follow to intersection of FDR 858 (Sawlog Gulch), park at designated area. This location will access both the Ute Pass Trail and the Bonita Hill Trail.

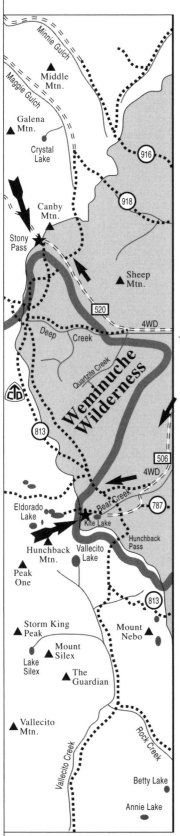

Rio Grande Map 6

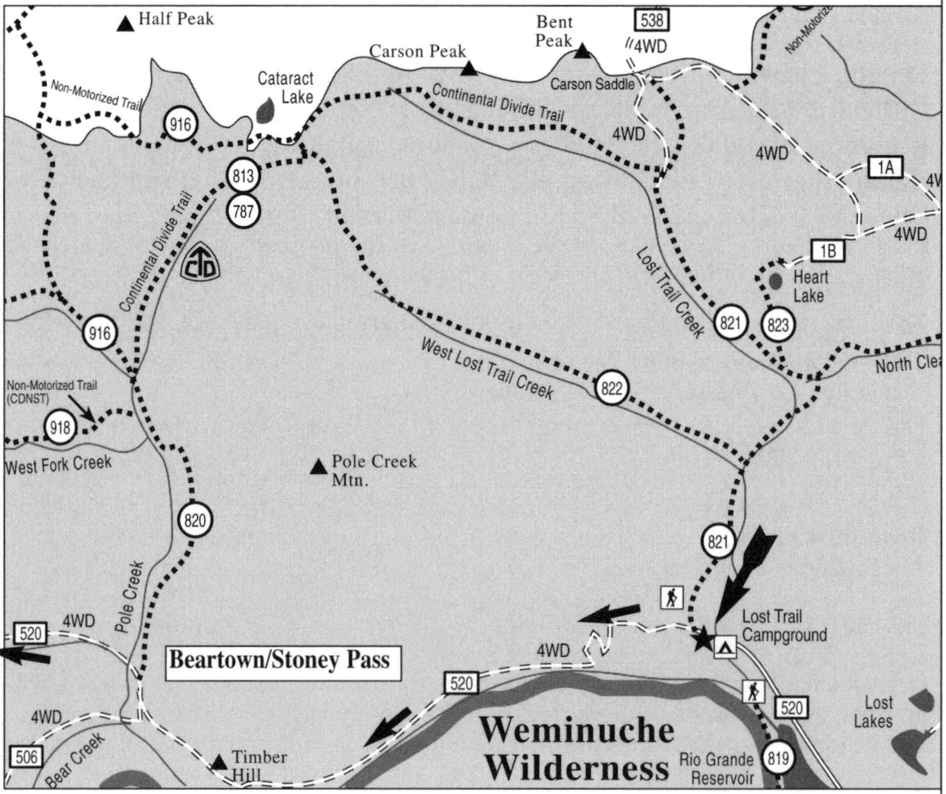

Rio Grande Map 7 (right panel)

Half Peak

Non-Motorized Trail

Carson Peak

Bent Peak

538
4WD

Carson Saddle

Continental Divide Trail

4WD

4WD

1A

4WD

Cataract Lake

916

813
787

Continental Divide Trail

CDT

916

Non-Motorized Trail (CDNST)

918

West Fork Creek

820

Pole Creek

West Lost Trail Creek

822

Lost Trail Creek

1B

Heart Lake

821
823

North Clear

Pole Creek Mtn.

821

Beartown/Stoney Pass

520

4WD

520

4WD

520

Lost Trail Campground

Weminuche Wilderness

Rio Grande Reservoir

Lost Lakes

4WD

506

Bear Creek

Timber Hill

819

520

Left panel (Map 6) labels

Minnie Gulch

Maggie Gulch

Middle Mtn.

Galena Mtn.

Crystal Lake

916

918

Canby Mtn.

Stony Pass

520

Sheep Mtn.

Deep Creek

CDT

813

506
4WD

Quartzite Creek

Weminuche Wilderness

Eldorado Lake

Bear Creek

787

Kite Lake

Hunchback Pass

Hunchback Mtn.

Vallecito Lake

Peak One

813

Storm King Peak

Mount Nebo

Mount Silex

Lake Silex

The Guardian

Vallecito Mtn.

Vallecito Creek

Rock Creek

Betty Lake

Annie Lake

Road Name	Road Number	Length Miles	Difficulty	Beginning Elevation	Ending Elev.	Usage	Ranger District
Beartown/Stoney Pass	506/520		Mod/More Diff.	10,500'	12,100'	Heavy	Divide

Length: Beartown Road 5.9 miles from FDR 520. Stoney Pass 14.6 miles.
Difficulty: Moderate to More Difficult.
Beginning Elevation: 10,500 Feet - Junction of Beartown Road 506 and Stony Pass Road 520.
Ending Elevation: 12,100 Feet - At Kite Lake, just north of Hunchback Mountain.
USGS Maps: Pole Creek Mtn., Rio Grande Pyramid, Storm King Peak.

The Beartown Road itself is the only route in the Bear Creek Drainage which is open to motorized vehicles. Most travelers include this scenic, remote and primitive road as a side trip while travelling from Creede to Silverton via Stony Pass (FDR 520).

The Beartown Road (FDR 506) leaves the Stony Pass Road (4-wheel drive) to the south, approximately 8.5 miles from Lost Trail Campground. The road then runs in a southwesterly direction for approximately 6 miles to Kite Lake located just below the Continental Divide and Hunchback Mountain and Pass, where it dead-ends.

The route generally traverses a southeast exposure throughout its length and has a well-defined double tread. With the exception of the last mile, the route is not steep but contains many rocks embedded in its tread, which makes much of the route slow going.

The road runs mostly through an open valley in which Bear Creek is located. It then climbs steeply over the last mile through high alpine country to Kite Lake (12,100 feet elevation). At its junction with the Stony Pass Road the Beartown Road drops 100 feet in .25 mile to the Rio Grande River, where it crosses the river and begins paralleling Bear Creek up the valley. This crossing generally poses no real problems except in early to mid-June if spring-off is high. Over the next 3 plus miles the road gradually climbs 400 feet in elevation. The road then climbs another 300 feet in the next .5 mile, to the lower end of the meadow in which the Beartown site is located.

Beartown is located in the upper end of this meadow. Evidence of the old mining town is nearly gone, with only telltale signs of where old cabins once stood. The structures that once stood near the old mine location are now collapsed and rapidly disappearing.

Just beyond the Beartown site, at the upper end of the meadow, the road begins to climb steeply (almost 900 feet in just over one mile) to Kite Lake. The road dead-ends at Kite Lake near an old mining shack that is still standing. Kite Lake sits in a partial bowl formed by the backbone of the Continental Divide with Hunchback Mountain and Pass just to the south. The lake is sterile, supporting no fish or other life forms.

Early to midsummer usually brings a profusion of wildflowers and breathtaking color to the mountainsides adjacent to the road, especially around and just beyond the old Beartown site. Columbines and multitudes of other species of wildflowers add color and beauty to the landscape.

Directions from Creede: Drive a little over 20 miles southwest on Highway 149 to the intersection of Highway 149 and Rio Grande Reservoir Road (FDR 520). Bear left at the junction and continue just over 18 miles west to Lost Trail Campground. Just beyond Lost Trail Campground, the road becomes Stony Pass Road (FDR 520). Continue west on this 4-wheel drive road for approximately 8.25 miles to Beartown Road (FDR 506). Turn left on the Beartown Road which runs south-southwest. With the exception of the last mile the route is not steep.

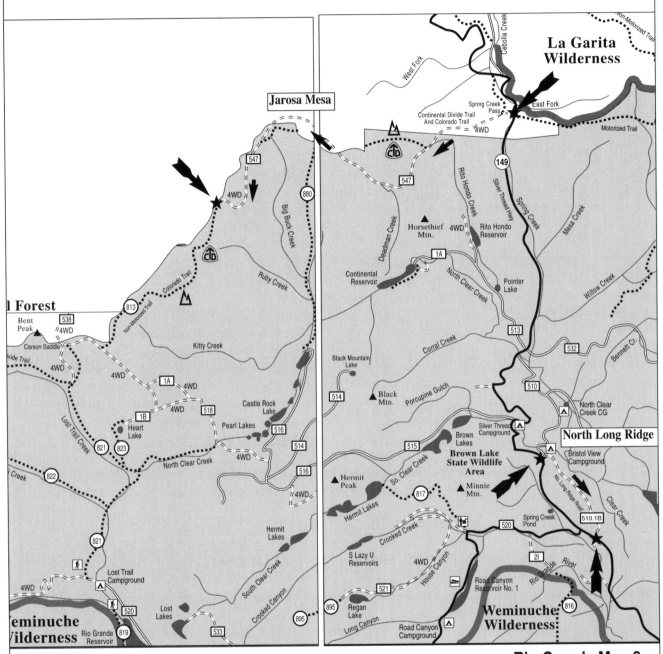

Rio Grande Map 7

Rio Grande Map 8

Road Name	Road Number	Length Miles	Difficulty	Beginning Elevation	Ending Elev.	Usage	Ranger District
Jarosa Mesa	547	8.6	Moderate	10,898'	10,500'	Moderate	Divide

USGS Maps: Slumgullion Pass and Lake San Cristobal.

This primitive road begins at Spring Creek Pass (10,898 feet elevation) within Spring Creek Pass Campground. Spring Creek Pass Campground is a low development campground that provides tables, fireplaces, and a pit toilet. No water is available in the campground.

The entire length of the Jarosa Mesa Primitive Road (approximately 8.6 miles) follows along the Continental Divide. The road climbs approximately 240 feet out of the campground in just slightly over 0.5 mile, then flattens out over the next 1.7 miles, where it runs through spruce/fir stands and open, grassy parks. From this flat the road begins to climb some 830 feet over the next 1.8 miles to an elevation of 12,054 feet. This portion of the road begins in scattered spruce/fir trees that change to willow brush as the road gains elevation.

From this point to within 0.5 mile of the end of the four-wheel drive road, the route traverses open alpine parks. The road drops 320 feet in the next 1.5 miles and then climbs 485 feet for 1.6 miles to the high point along the route (12,220 feet elevation). The final 1.4 miles of the road drops from this point approximately 700 feet to its end. Here it is marked, "No Motorized Vehicles (Snowmobilers, Scooters excepted)". Finally, the route continues to the west as the La Garita Stock Driveway Trail 787.

Except for vistas of distance mountain peaks, such as Uncompahgre Peak (14,286 feet elevation), the route offers no other real attractions other than being a high country jeep road. Except for a spring near the road, about 2.5 miles from the start, water is scarce or nonexistent along the route.

Directions from Creede: 34.5 miles west on Colorado Highway 149 to the summit of Spring Creek Pass. Turn left on FDR 547 follow the road back until you see a set of well-defined double tracks going up a hill to the west. This is the Jarosa Mesa Primitive Road.

Road Name	Road Number	Length Miles	Difficulty	Beginning Elevation	Ending Elev.	Usage	Ranger District
North Long Ridge	510.1B	3.6	Easy	9,000'	9,550'	Moderate	Divide

USGS Maps: Bristol Head, Hermit Lakes.

This is a short, 3.8 miles easy jeep road, which primarily provides fishing access to Clear Creek via two short spur roads located along it. The road begins approximately 19.2 miles southwest of Creede, on Colorado Hwy 149, at a point about midway between the lower and upper lakes at Wright's Ranch. Turn right (north) off the highway onto the dirt road which runs up the hill, and which is marked by a sign with the number 510.1B.

The North Long Ridge Primitive Road climbs approximately 680' for the first 1.7 miles through open grassland. There is a fork in the road approximately 0.8 mile from the highway. This right fork, running northeast, is a short spur road. It follows the tree line on the right for approximately 0.5-mile, where it dead-ends on a hill overlooking Clear Creek. The descent is a short but fairy steep walk down to the creek.

At this fork, the North Long Ridge Primitive Road turns to the left (northwest) and continues for another 0.9 mile to the edge of a spruce/fir stand that is interspersed with small open parks. The road drops a little and then levels out on the remainder of the trip. Approximately 0.3 mile after entering the trees another short spur road turns off to the right. (This mile-long spur drops 320 feet through the trees and down through an open park, dead-ending at a point overlooking Clear Creek. Again, it is a short but steep walk to the creek).

Except for providing fishing access to Clear Creek, or a short easy jeep trip, the route offers no other extraordinary or distinctive attractions.

Inspiring views of Bristol Head are always in the background, while the foreground give peaceful views of the open ranch land of the Upper Rio Grande River Valley.

You can make the route as short or as long as your legs or lungs can last!

Directions from Creede: Travel 19.2 miles southwest on Colorado Hwy 149 to a point approximately midway between the lower and upper lakes at Wright's Ranch. Beginning of the road is on the right (north) side of the Hwy and is marked with the number 510.1B.

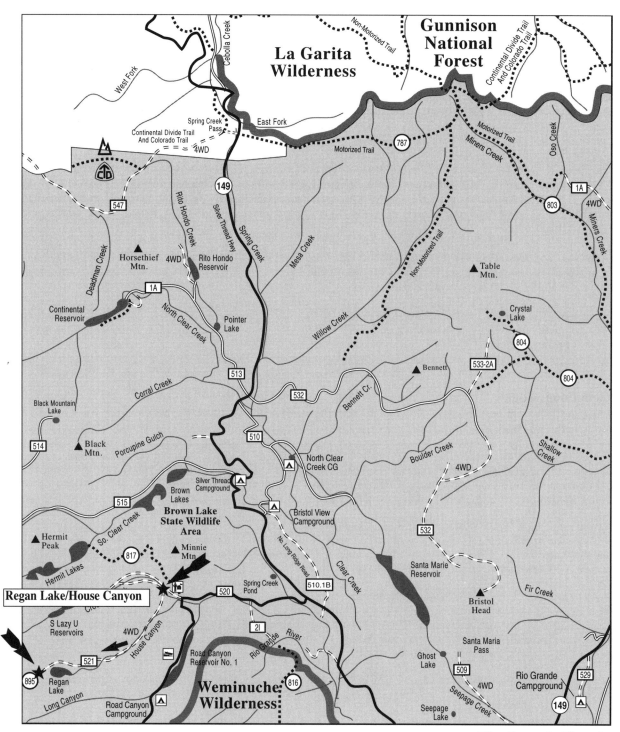

Regan Lake/House Canyon

Rio Grande Map 8

Road Name	Road Number	Length Miles	Difficulty	Beginning Elevation	Ending Elev.	Usage	Ranger District
Regan Lake/House Canyon	521	4.8	Easy	9,530'	10,080'	Heavy	Divide

USGS Maps: Hermit Lakes.

This is an easy, short (4.8 miles), dead-end jeep road which primarily provides fishing access to Regan Lake (91.5 acres). The road begins at the lower end of Wilderness Ranch reservoir. It has a well-lined double tread and runs primarily through rolling country, traversing meadow land and both open and heavy aspen and Engelmann spruce timber types. The first 2.7 miles traverses through the open meadow lands of House Canyon and is relatively level. The next 1.3 miles travels through scattered and heavy timber, climbing about 760 feet. This section has several ups and downs. The final 0.8-mile is open grassland and parallels the shoreline of Regan Reservoir. A Colorado Division of Wildlife cabin, at the west end of the reservoir, marks the end of the road.

The Colorado Division of Wildlife has two experimental windmill/aerator located on the lakeshore. One is located near the south end of the reservoir and the other at the north edge of the shoreline just off the road, about midway to the old cabin. These windmills are connected to perforated underwater pipes through which the air is pushed. The air bubbles up through the water to the surface. This keeps the ice open over a small portion of the reservoir, providing oxygen to the fish through the long cold winter, preventing winterkill of the fish population each year.

Several shorter, steep grades (10-15 percent) are encountered along the route. In the early season and wet weather, the road can become boggy in several locations.

Potential campsites exist along the route or at the reservoir.

Directions from Creede: Travel 20.1 miles southwest on Colorado Hwy 149 to the intersection of Colorado Hwy 149 and Rio Grande Reservoir Road FDR 520. Bear left at the junction. Go west on the Rio Grande Reservoir Road for 3 miles to the junction of Regan Lake (House Canyon) Road (FDR 521) (approximately 0.1 mile before reaching Bristol View Guard Station and just prior to crossing the bridge over Crooked Creek). Bear right at this junction. The road is signed, and signs for Wilderness Ranch and S-Lazy-U Ranch are also present at the junction. Continue on the Regan Lake (House Canyon) Road (FDR 521) for 1.6 miles to the lower end of Wilderness Ranch reservoir, where the Regan Lake road turns off to the left (southeast). If you come to the Wilderness Ranch building, you have gone too far.

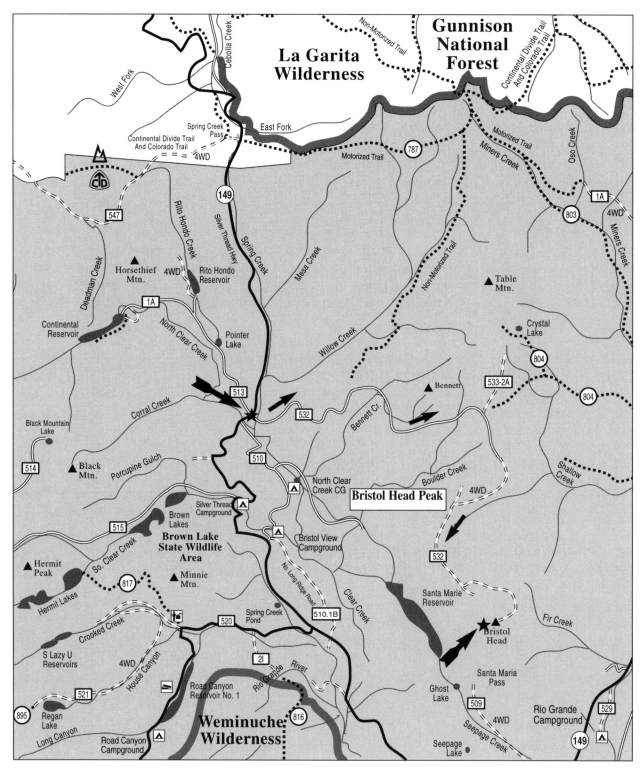

Bristol Head Peak

Rio Grande Map 8

Road Name	Road Number	Length Miles	Difficulty	Beginning Elevation	Ending Elev.	Usage	Ranger District
Bristol Head Peak	532	15.1	Easy	10,030'	12,706'	Moderate	Divide

Ending Elevation: 12,706 Feet - Top of Bristol Head Mountain.
USGS Map: Bristol Head.

The road begins by fording Spring Creek, then climbs upward through a stand of aspen and then traverses its way up through a spruce-fir timber stand until it reaches a vast, beautiful, open sub-alpine park known as Ouray Park. The road then drops downward and crosses Bennett Creek. From this point, the road flattens out and gently undulates generally following the edge of the spruce-fir timber for the next several miles.

Bennett Creek is the first of three drainages, that the road passes which drop off of Ouray Park to the south-southeast. Boulder Creek and Gooseberry Creek are the other two primary drainages to the south, across the park you will see them as you travel further along the road toward the summit of Bristol Head.

The first 6.8 miles of the road travels over a graveled timber access road, which is suitable for travel by 4-wheel drive vehicles, as well as by standard 2-wheel drive pick up trucks, when the road is dry, when wet the road is sticky mud. Because of the ford crossing at Spring Creek (just after you turn onto the Bristol Head Road) and because the last 8.3 miles of the road is rough and rocky, passenger car and van type vehicles are not recommended. They do not have adequate clearance to safely negotiate those sections of the road.

The last 8.3 miles of the road (from the end of the graveled timber road to the top of the peak) has been constructed as a 4-wheel drive road. When the road is dry standard 2-wheel drive pickup trucks or similar type vehicles can generally safely use this section. However, when this section of the road becomes wet or soft 2-wheel drive vehicles can run into traction and control problems because the road can become slick, soft, and rutted, making such use unsure and potentially unsafe.

Portions of this section, although relatively flat, are extremely bumpy and slow going, due to rock outcrops in the roadbed. The final 2 miles of road to Bristol Head Peak climbs 700 feet to the top. A Forest Service radio repeater station (radio tower, small building, and solar panels) and a microwave station are located at the top.

From the head of Bristol Head Peak, a magnificent panoramic view of the entire region exists for miles. On a clear day the San Luis Valley and the Sangre de Cristo Mountain Range almost 100 miles away to the east/northeast can be seen. In the foreground, to the northwest sits Spring Creek Pass with Uncompahgre Peak (14,309 feet) raising its rugged head majestically in the background. To the southwest, nestled directly below Bristol Head Mountain lies Santa Maria Reservoir. Twenty miles farther to the southwest, Rio Grande Pyramid stands silent vigil over the Weminuche Wilderness. Piedra, Ivy, and South River Peaks, along with Fisher, Beautiful, Copper, and Snowshoe Mountains lie to the south/southeast.

Caution should be exercised for any out-of-vehicle sightseeing or picture taking in this area due to the steep cliffs bordering the peak. Rocks and soil are extremely unstable along the edges. Also, lightning potential is intensified because of the radio tower and the openness of the peak.

Future plans for development along the road includes interpretive signing which will discuss the multiple use that takes place in the general area such as livestock grazing, timber harvesting, mineral exploration recreation, etc. Also planned are interpretive signs at the top, which will identify what one is viewing in the 360-degree panorama such as mountain peaks, drainage, and other terrain features or landmarks.

Directions from Creede: West 27.1 miles on Hwy 149 turn right onto Bristol Peak Road (FDR 513), across from the Rito Hondo/Continental Reservoir Road (FDR 532). Road passes through a gate and over cattle guard then fords Spring Creek starting its climb to Bristol Head Peak.

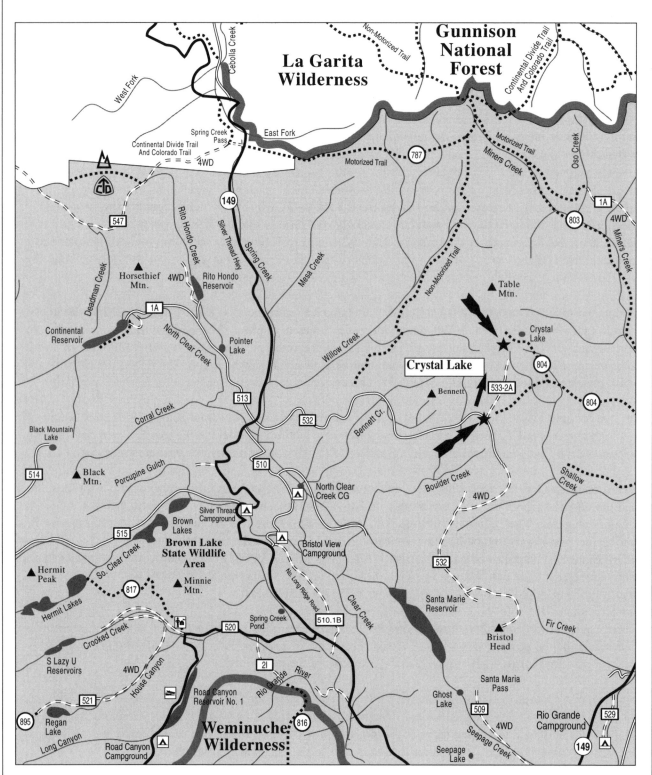

La Garita Wilderness

Gunnison National Forest

Non-Motorized Trail

Continental Divide Trail And Colorado Trail

Cebolla Creek

West Fork

Spring Creek Pass

East Fork

Continental Divide Trail And Colorado Trail

4WD

Motorized Trail

787

Motorized Trail

Motorized Trail

Miners Creek

Oso Creek

1A

803

4WD

Miners Creek

547

Rito Hondo Creek

149

Silver Thread Hwy

Spring Creek

Mesa Creek

Non-Motorized Trail

Horsethief Mtn.

4WD

Rito Hondo Reservoir

Table Mtn.

Crystal Lake

Deadman Creek

1A

North Clear Creek

Pointer Lake

Willow Creek

Crystal Lake

804

Continental Reservoir

513

Bennett

533-2A

804

Corral Creek

532

Bennett Cr.

Shallow Creek

Black Mountain Lake

510

4WD

514

Black Mtn.

Porcupine Gulch

North Clear Creek CG

Boulder Creek

Brown Lakes

Silver Thread Campground

Bristol View Campground

515

Brown Lake State Wildlife Area

532

Hermit Peak

So. Clear Creek

817

Minnie Mtn.

Santa Marie Reservoir

Fir Creek

Hermit Lakes

Crooked Creek

No. Long Ridge Road

Clear Creek

Bristol Head

S Lazy U Reservoirs

4WD

House Canyon

520

Spring Creek Pond

510.1B

Santa Maria Pass

521

2l

Rio Grande River

Road Canyon Reservoir No. 1

Ghost Lake

509

4WD

Santa Maria Pass

529

895

Regan Lake

Weminuche Wilderness

816

Rio Grande Campground

149

Long Canyon

Road Canyon Campground

Seepage Creek

Seepage Lake

Rio Grande Map 8

Road Name	Road Number	Length Miles	Difficulty	Beginning Elevation	Ending Elev.	Usage	Ranger District
Crystal Lake	533.2A	2.5	More Diff.	11,520'	12,050'	Moderate	Divide

Difficulty: More Difficult-Difficult.
Ending Elevation: 12,050 Feet, At Crystal Lake.
USGS Maps: Bristol Head, Baldy Cinco.

This is a short (2.5 miles) scenic primitive road that leads close to Crystal Lake. It is a fairly popular side trip off the main Bristol Head Peak Road (FDR 532). Crystal Lake Road 533.2A joins the Bristol Head Peak Road approximately 7 miles east from where the Bristol Head Peak Road begins directly across Colorado Highway 149 from Rito Hondo/Continental Reservoir Road (FDR 513). At the junction Crystal Lake Road continues straight ahead (northeast) just before the Boulder Creek crossing where the main Bristol Head Peak Road turns to the south.

The Crystal Lake Road usually poses no access problems unless patches of snow remain on its steeper short stretches. However, the first part of the Bristol Head Peak Road, which serves as access is extremely steep, rocky, and rough. Many of the rocks are large, making navigation difficult due to poor-to-nonexistent tread and lack of clearance. Substantial driving skill is required to successfully negotiate this section of road without damaging your vehicle.

From its junction with the Bristol Head Peak Road, the Crystal Lake Road 533.2A climbs 260 feet in the first 0.5 mile and then flattens out for 0.5 mile. Over the next 0.9 mile, the road gains 240 feet in elevation then drops 200 feet in a little over 0.1 mile where it crosses a fork of Shallow Creek. Four-wheel drive pickups with long beds may have some problems negotiating a few of the short, steep sections with tight turns. This is particularly true when the road is dry causing a spinout effect on the rocky roadbed. The final 0.9 mile of road climbs approximately 250 feet to Crystal Lake. The route travels through spruce/fir stands and small sub-alpine parks to the lake, which sits on a small open flat.

This 5 acre lake usually provides fair to good catches of rainbow, cutthroat, and brook trout to the angler. The lake is subject to winterkill. However, the Colorado Division of Wildlife periodically stocks the lake.

Directions from Creede: 27.1 miles west on Colorado Highway 149. Turn east (right) onto Bristol Head Peak Road FDR 532 (4-wheel drive) across from Rito Hondo/Continental Reservoir Road FDR 513. Road passes through a wire gate in the fence, off the east side of Colorado Highway 149, and is marked at the fence with a white arrow. Travel approximately 7 miles east on Bristol Head Peak Road 532 to where the road forks. Go straight (northeast) at the junction with Bristol Head Peak Road (FDR 532) which turns to the right (south). Follow the road 2.5 miles to Crystal Lake.

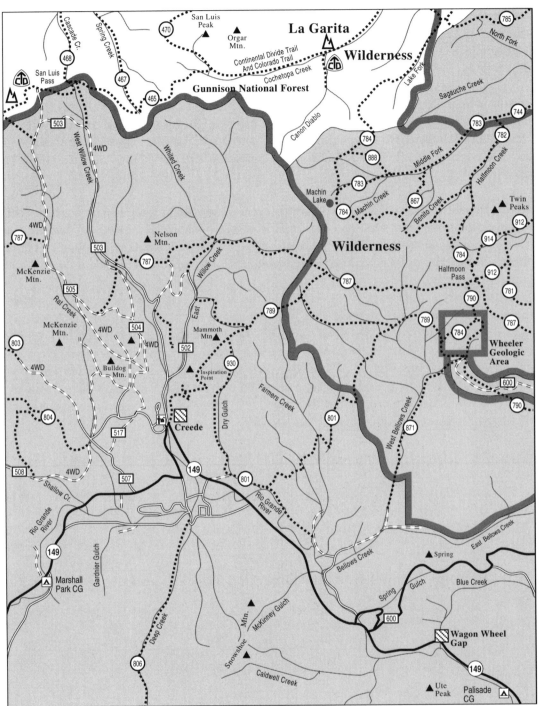

Rio Grande Map 9

Road Name	Road Number	Length Miles	Difficulty	Beginning Elevation	Ending Elev.	Usage	Ranger District
W. Willow/Bachelor Mtn.	504	21.8	More Difficult	8,825'	8,825'	Heavy	Divide

USGS Maps: Creede, San Luis Peak.

The road begins or ends at the north or south end of the town of Creede, depending on which directions this loop route is traveled.

Numerous historic mines are located along the route up West Willow Creek Road (FDR 503) from the north end of Creede to the Equity Mine. The lower portions of the West Willow Creek and Bachelor roads are also part of the "Bachelor Historic Tour" self-guided vehicle interpretive tour. "Bachelor Historic Tour" self guided tour brochures are available at the Creede Chamber of Commerce or at the Creede Forest Service office at 3rd & Creede Avenue.

Portions of the West Willow Creek Road (FDR 503) from the Equity Mine to the Continental Divide are difficult to negotiate if the road is wet or muddy. Rat Creek Road (FDR 505) can also become difficult to navigate when wet because the rocks become slick on the road and the road runs side-hill for much of its length. Patches of snow commonly block the route to vehicle travel at various locations until late June or early July. A short (0.5 mile) spur road at the head of Rat Creek runs north to the Continental Divide (12,850 feet elevation). Here alpine scenery and vegetation with an abundance of many species of small delicate alpine flowers, greets the beholder. This is approximately a three to four hour trip.

Directions from Creede: Travel to the extreme north end of town and follow the West Willow Creek Rd (FDR 503) or from Creede go to the south end of town and turn right (west) on the Bachelor Mountain Road (FDR 504) (Homestake Mine Road).

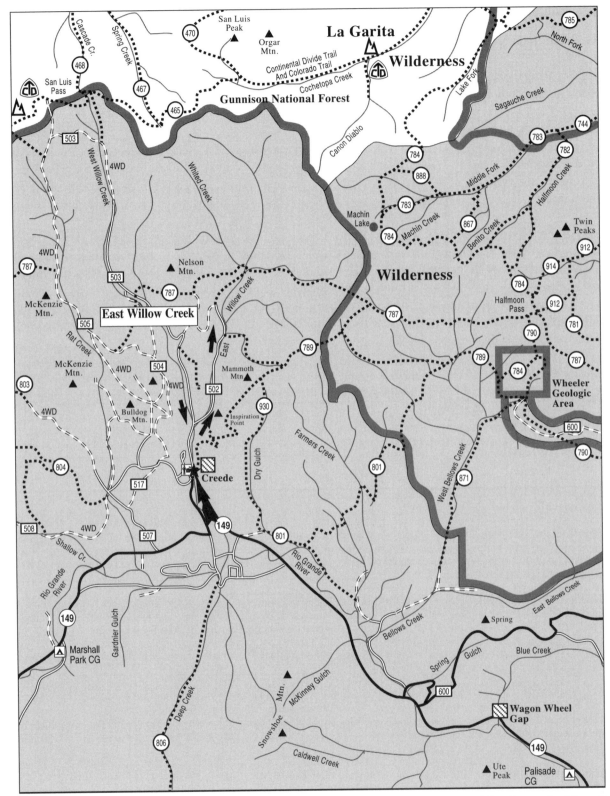

Rio Grande Map 9

Road Name	Road Number	Length Miles	Difficulty	Beginning Elevation	Ending Elev.	Usage	Ranger District
East Willow Creek	502	5.1	Mod/Diff.	8,957'	10,240'	Heavy	Divide

Length, Round Trip: 5.1 Miles. Difficulty: Moderate/More Difficult.
USGS Maps: Creede and San Luis Peak.

This is a 5.1 mile road, which begins up West Willow Creek Road 503, about 0.7 mile north of the Mineral County Courthouse in Creede and ends where it rejoins the West Willow Creek Road 503 just below the Midwest Mine (3 miles north of Creede). Much of the land along the road is private property, containing numerous abandoned mine shafts that pose a hazard to the unaware - especially children. The private property owners have requested, for your own safety and protection, that you do not leave your vehicle except to take pictures from the road. Remember, if you enter posted private property without permission, you are trespassing. The road following East Willow Creek is rough and steep and not suitable for passenger cars.

The buildings you see as you start up East Willow Creek Road (FDR 502) are part of Upper or North Creede. This was the approximate town site of Creede when the mining boom began in the late 1880's and 1890's. Several miles above the town site is where Nicholas C. Creede made his initial high-grade silver discovery. Upon striking silver, Creede shouted, Holy Moses! The fault, vein, and associated mining claims are still called the Solomon-Holy Moses.

The cinder block building on the left side of the road marks the location of the first schoolhouse. Later the site served as a hydroelectric generating plant for the Town of Creede. It is no longer used today. If you look closely at the first old building you come to on the right side of the road, you can still see bars on some of the windows; this was the Creede jail.

The first 2.8 miles of the road closely parallel and at times cross East Willow Creek. The road gains approximately 723 feet in elevation over this section. It is not really steep but extremely rough, rocky, and narrow. Precautions should be taken due to several "blind" curves along this road.

About 0.7 miles up East Willow Creek Road (FDR 502) on the right side of the road, you will notice several trestle-type structures supporting cables. One set of cables runs up the hill on the right side of the road to the Molly S Mine, which is located just below and to the left of the cliff above. Slightly to the right, or south of the Molly S, on this cliff lies the Unis Mine. These cable systems for hauling the ore down the mountain in buckets so the road was called "jig backs". A short jig back ran from the Unit to the Molly S above.

The Molly S jig back then brought the ore from both mines down to the road where you are standing. If you look directly across the road to the left (west) and high upon the cliff (just below the top), you can see wooden mine structures hanging on the cliff. This is the Monte Carlo Mine, the mine is locally known as the Kentucky Belle Mine because the Kentucky Belle Company ran it.

Approximately 0.7 mile up the road on the left side of the Solomon Mine. The Ridge Mine and the Outlet Mine are another 0.2 and 0.8 mile further up the road on the lef.t

Three miles up the road from its beginning, a jeep road/foot trail turns right into Phoenix Park and the headwaters of East Willow Creek. The East Willow Creek Road (FDR 502) continues to the left and starts to switchback up the mountain. The Phoenix Park road/trail begins just above the tailing ponds you pass on the right side of the road about 0.5 mile beyond where the road crosses East Willow Creek.

This road/trail is open to both foot and motor vehicle travel for approximately 2 miles, to just above the first beaver ponds and near an old cabin. The vehicle route ends near the cabin and is signed "No Motor Vehicles Beyond this point only foot and horse travel permitted". The beaver ponds in Phoenix Park usually provide excellent catches of trout for the angler.

The upper reaches of East Willow Creek are part of the Creede Municipal watershed. A scenic waterfall cascades down from the mountainside on the northeast side of this basin.

Returning to the East Willow Creek Road (FDR 502), from the first switchback, the road climbs steeply (920 feet) for approximately 1.4 miles. This section of road contains many switchbacks which involve some backing in order to negotiate with all but short wheel base 4x4's. From the first switchback, looking south along the mountainside, you can see the Phoenix Mine. Leading off each switchback are old mining trails and roads which lead to old diggings and mine shafts that dot the entire mountainside.

The road then drops (360 feet) from the top for 0.7 mile to the Midwest Mine and West Willow Creek Road (FDR 503). From this junction you can make hard turns to the right uphill onto the West Willow Creek Road (FDR 503) and continue on the West Willow Creek/Rat Creek/Bachelor Mountain Road Loop (18.8 miles to Creede). Or on the West Willow Creek/Bachelor Mountain Road loop (5 miles to Creede). Turning downhill to the left at this junction will bring you through the steep narrow West Willow Creek Canyon to Creede (3 miles).

Directions from Creede: The road begins 0.7 mile north of the Mineral County Courthouse in Creede. Turn right at the road junction of East Willow Creek Road and FDR 503.

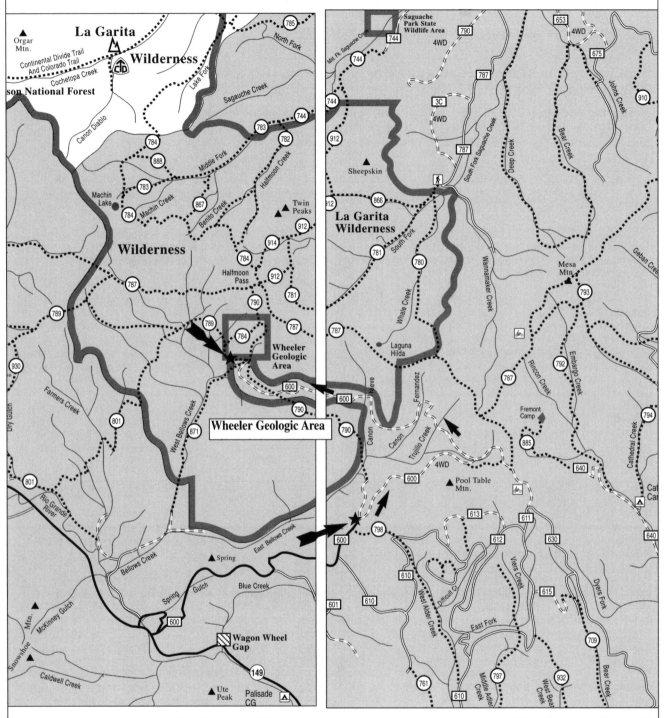

Rio Grande Map 9

Rio Grande Map 10

Road Name	Road Number	Length Miles	Difficulty	Beginning Elevation	Ending Elev.	Usage	Ranger District
Wheeler Geologic Area	600	13.7	More Difficult	10,840'	11,040'	Heavy	Divide

USGS Maps: Pool Table Mountain, Wagon Wheel Gap, and Halfmoon Pass.

This scenic and remote primitive road is a popular sub-alpine route into the Wheeler Geologic Area. While the road is relatively level (540 ft. difference between its lowest and highest points), it is rough, roundabout and very slow, with much of the roadbed made up of embedded rocks.

A round trip takes an average of 7 to 7-1/2 hours not including time to walk to and explore Wheeler Geologic Area itself. Leave early, to allow you sufficient time for the trip, and time to explore, take pictures, etc. Leaving Creede between 7 a.m. and 8 a.m. should allow you enough time, with arrival back in Creede between 6 p.m. and 7 p.m.

Wheeler Geologic Road (FDR 600) (4-wheel drive) begins at Hanson's Mill at the end of the improved graveled Pool Table Road (FDR 600). An old sawdust pile is the only remains of where the mill once stood. The area adjacent to Hanson's Mill is flat and is suitable for undeveloped camping and picnicking. The only facility provided here is a pit toilet.

From here, the 4-wheel drive road is well signed and marked. All 4-wheel drive travel is restricted to the marked road only, with the exception that you may drive off the road for up to 300 feet to gain access to suitable undeveloped campsites along the route. You should stop by any Forest Service Office and obtain a travel map if you have questions concerning travel restrictions.

The road climbs from Hanson's Mill through spruce/fir for 0.4 mile to a road junction. The left fork is not the 4-wheel drive route to Wheeler but can be driven for a little over 1 mile where it dead-ends just before East Bellows Creek. From this point, the route continues as a trail (foot, horse, and trail bike only) for 5.7 miles to the Wheeler Geologic Area. This trail is part of the old Alder Creek Stock Driveway, which today is Trail FDT 790 on your Rio Grande Forest map. There is limited parking for 3 to 4 vehicles at the end of this spur road.

If you prefer hiking, and are in good physical condition, you can probably walk to Wheeler faster than driving a 4-wheel drive vehicle the 14 miles to Wheeler via the jeep road. If you plan to drive into Wheeler, however, go straight at the road junction rather than following this left fork of the road. The junction is well signed.

From this junction, the Pool Table Road (FDR 600) travels northeast, gently climbing 360 feet in elevation over the next 3.9 miles. The first 3 miles of this section of road continues through spruce/fir and then breaks into the open to follow the tree line on the right until the road swings northwest and crosses East Bellows Creek.

From this point to within 1.5 miles of its end, the road traverses primarily through open sub-alpine country. Just up the hill from the East Bellows Creek crossing, the road turns northwest and is relatively level for the next 2.6 miles, except where the road crosses Trujillo Creek and the Canyon Fernandez drainage. From the Canyon Fernandez drainage, the road drops about 540 feet over the next 2.5 miles to the Canyon Nieve drainage. This portion of the road swings from a southwest direction to northwest. The road then continues to the west, climbs 460 feet over the next 1.2 miles, and then levels out for approximately 1.5 miles to where Trail FDT 790 joins the road.

The next mile of road/trail drops 360 feet in elevation through spruce/fir trees. This section is narrow and twists its way through the trees. The lower part of this section (which is only about 3/4 mile from the end of the road) is often muddy and rutted, making maneuverability difficult because of the tight squeeze through the trees. The slippery rutted conditions usually force vehicle wheels to follow the existing ruts. This section requires some driving skills to successfully negotiate when wet. Larger vehicles have an even more difficult time through this section.

The final half-mile of road breaks back out into a small park and dead-ends at the fence marking the end of the road and the boundary of the Geologic Area. This is as far as motor vehicles are allowed. From this point a foot and/or horse trail continues approximately 0.6 mile on to the formations.

Even though the trip is rough and slow, the sub-alpine scenery is beautiful and more than makes up for the trip. If lucky, elk and deer may be seen on occasion. Coyotes are not uncommon. Gray jays ("Camp Robbers") are plentiful, especially at the end of the road near Wheeler. If you have patience, you can usually have these friendly birds eat out of your hand.

Directions from Creede: From Creede, 7.3 miles southeast on Colorado Highway 149 to the intersection of Colorado Hwy 149 and Pool Table Road (FDR 600) (Spring Gulch). Turn left (north) at the junction and travel northeast on Pool Table Road (FDR 600) approximately ten miles to the end of the two-wheel drive road. There is a sawdust pile here which is what remains of the old Hanson Sawmill. The 4WD road begins at this point and continues for just under 14 miles to the boundary of the Wheeler Geologic Area.

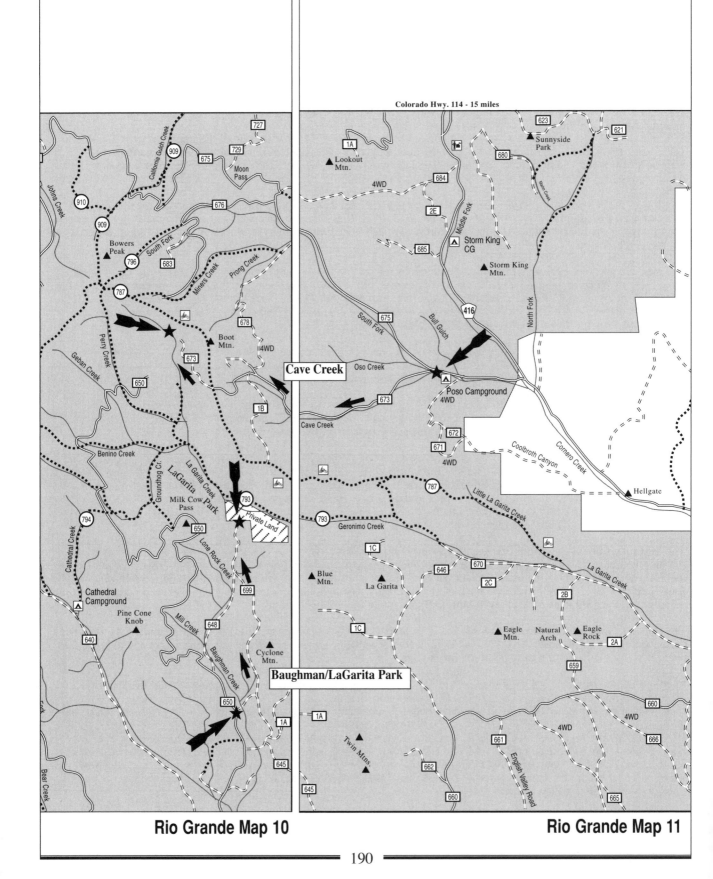

Colorado Hwy. 114 - 15 miles

Cave Creek

Baughman/LaGarita Park

Road Name	Road Number	Length Miles	Difficulty	Beginning Elevation	Ending Elev.	Usage	Ranger District
Baughman/LaGarita	648/699	9	Mod/Diff.	8,540'	10,200'	Moderate	Divide

Difficulty: Moderate to Difficult.
Beginning Elevation: Junction of FDR 650 and FDR 650.3A.
Ending Elevation: La Garita Park.
USGS Maps: Pine Cone Knob, Bowers Peak.

This road accesses La Garita Park, which has some excellent small stream fishing and ample camping spots. The road dead ends at private property line before it gets to LaGarita Park. The streams are accessed by going around the private lands. Visitors must respect private land.

Directions from Del Norte: Go west 8.5 miles on U.S. Highway 160, to the Embargo Creek Road, then north for 7.5 miles on FDR 650 to FDR 699. North on FDR 699/648, stay on this road past Shorty Spring to the end of the road at La Garita Park.

Road Name	Road Number	Length Miles	Difficulty	Beginning Elevation	Ending Elev.	Usage	Ranger District
Cave Creek	673	8	Easy/Mod.	9,000'	11,600'	Light	Divide

Difficulty: Easy/Moderate.
Beginning Elevation: Junction with South Camero Road.
Ending Elevation: On top of ridge south of Boot Mountain.
USGS Maps: Bowers Peak, Lookout Mountain.

Cave Creek is a fishable stream with several good camping sites along it. From the top of the mountain, a good view of the San Luis Valley can be seen. During the fall, the aspen are colorful along the road. This road can be followed on north to follow Prong Creek on FDR 678, but this road requires 4-wheel drive. 4-wheel drive is also required to continue west of Boot Mountain where the road dead ends.

Directions from La Garita: Travel west on the Camero Road (FDR 416) approx. 11 miles to FDR 675. West on FDR 675 0.5 mile past Poso Campground turn left on FDR 673.

Road Name	Road Number	Length Miles	Difficulty	Beginning Elevation	Ending Elev.	Usage	Ranger District
Alder/Aqua Ramon		30	Mod/Difficult	8,200'	8,200'	Heavy	Divide

Alder to Aqua Ramon Road FDR 610/611/630.
Beginning Elevation: Alder Creek Guard Station.
Ending Elevation: County Road 15 at the base of Aqua Ramon.
USGS Maps: Pool Table Mtn., Pine Cone Knob, South Fork West, South Fork East.

The first section of this loop follows the scenic Alder Creek Canyon, which offers many picture-taking opportunities. (Alder Creek Canyon is getting very rocky and rough.) The middle section of this tour leads you through several high mountain meadows, with opportunities for camping, fishing and wildlife viewing. The last leg of the tour provides some magnificent vistas of the valley. This road goes from 8,000 feet up to 12,000 feet, which takes you from the pinion juniper zone all the way to timberline.

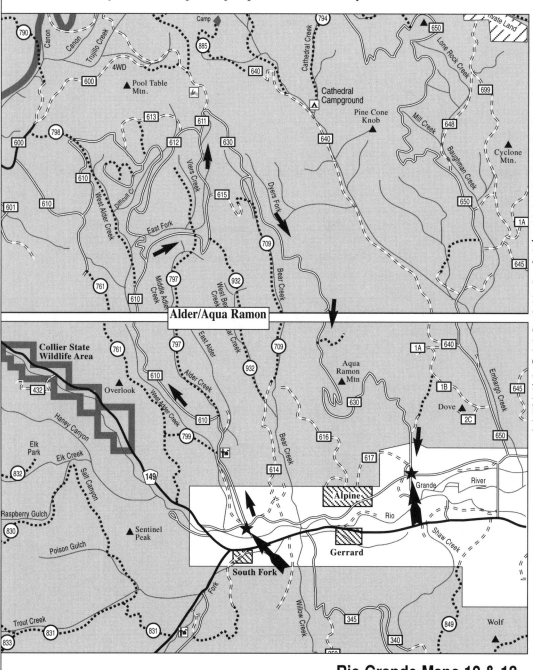

Directions from South Fork Colorado: Go northwest on Highway 149 across the Rio Grande, then right on County Road 15 (River Road) about 2 miles to FDR 610 (Alder Creek). Follow FDR 610 for about 8 miles to junction of FDR 610 and FDR 611. Take Forest Road 611 for about 6 miles to FDR 630, then follow FDR 630 to County Road 15. Once on County Road 15, you can go east to Del Norte, or west back to South Fork.

Rio Grande Maps 10 & 13

20. Animal Lovers Loop

Rio Grande

Road Name	Road Number	Length Miles	Difficulty	Beginning Elevation	Ending Elev.	Usage	Ranger District
Animals Lovers Loop	661/666	30	Easy/Mod.	7,870'	7,870'	Moderate	Divide

USGS Maps: Del Norte, Indian Head, Twin Mountain, Twin Mountain SE.

This loop is a tour called the Animal Lovers Tour, designed to provide wildlife viewing opportunities. You should see pronghorn, Bighorn Sheep and deer, as well as many varieties of birds and small animals. The best time for animal viewing is early morning or late evening.

Directions from Del Norte: From the junction of U.S. Highway 160 and Colorado 112, travel north on 112 about 1 mile. Turn left on the airport road right after crossing the Rio Grande River. Follow this across the canal and turn left on County Road 15. Go past the wrecking yard, about .25 mile, where English Valley Road leads off to the northwest, a 4WD road. Follow English Valley Road for about 7.5 miles to the intersection of FDR 660, turn east for 2.5 miles. You will first come to FDR 659 - The Natural Arch Road. Turn south on an unnumbered road .5 mile after the National Arch Road. Drive until you get to a fork in the road and stay right, you will hit a stop sign after about 9 miles, turn south here and follow County Road 33 until you hit Colorado Highway 112. Follow Colorado Highway 112 back into Del Norte.

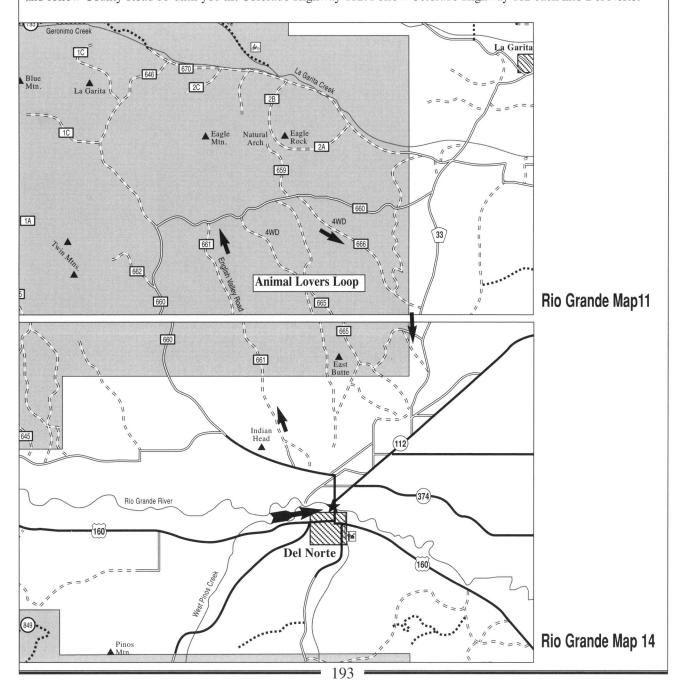

Rio Grande Map 11

Rio Grande Map 14

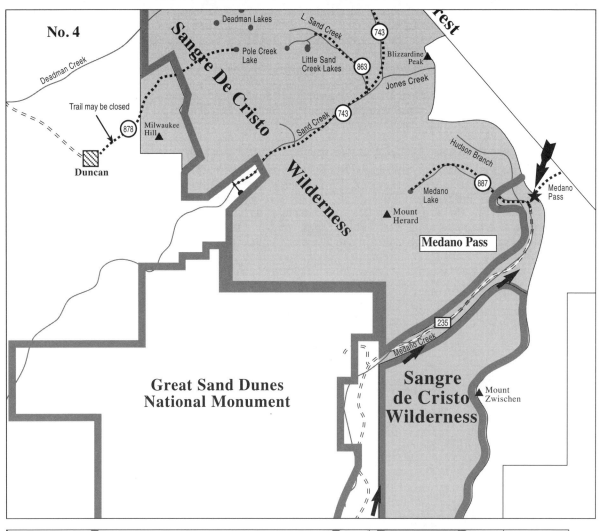

No. 4

Deadman Creek

Sangre De Cristo

Deadman Lakes

Pole Creek Lake

L. Sand Creek

(743)

Little Sand Creek Lakes

(863)

Blizzardine Peak

Jones Creek

Trail may be closed

(878)

Milwaukee Hill

Duncan

Sand Creek

(743)

Hudson Branch

(887)

Medano Lake

Mount Herard

Medano Pass

Medano Pass

(235)

Medano Creek

Wilderness

Great Sand Dunes National Monument

Sangre de Cristo Wilderness

Mount Zwischen

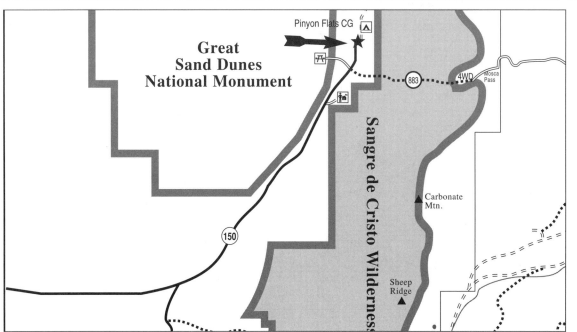

Pinyon Flats CG

Great Sand Dunes National Monument

(883)

4WD

Mosca Pass

Sangre de Cristo Wilderness

(150)

Carbonate Mtn.

Sheep Ridge

Rio Grande Maps 12 & 15

Road Name	Road Number	Length Miles	Difficulty	Beginning Elevation	Ending Elev.	Usage	Ranger District
Medano Pass	235	4	Easy/Moderate	8,200'	11,500'	Heavy	Sand Dunes N.M.

Great Sand Dunes National Monument (Rio Grande and San Isabel National Forests)
Length, One-way: 4.0 Miles to Pass.
USGS Maps: Zapata Ranch, Liberty and Medano Pass.

The Medano Pass Primitive Road is a four-wheel drive road that begins in the park and goes north to Medano Pass and the Rio Grande National Forest. Soft sand may require reducing tire pressure. Air is available at the amphitheater parking lot. This drive offers spectacular views of the dunes. Primitive picnic areas (no water, restrooms or trash containers) are located along the road.

A turn-around area and small parking area, aptly named Point of No Return, is provided for two-wheel drive vehicles and wide vehicles. It is important to heed the implied warning of Point of No Return. Losing a vehicle is no fun. Visitors that require assistance can expect to pay a towing charge.

From the top of Medano Pass, high-clearance four-wheel drive vehicles can continue northeast into the San Isabel National Forest. Eventually the road joins Highway 69.

Directions from Visitor Center: Travel north from the Great Sand Dunes Visitor Center. At the entrance to Pinyon Flats Campground the four-wheel drive road Medano Pass Road Four-Wheel Drive Road 559 continues north.

San Isabel National Forest - Eastern Approach:
The eastern approach to Medano Pass is heavily used. About 6 miles from Highway 69 is the National Forest boundary. Another short distance brings the traveler to the junction of Forest Roads FDR 559 and FDR 412. There is a huge meadow here with dispersed camping and a parking area. This is a popular place for hunters and for those with horses.

All two-wheel drive vehicles must park here. From this point on the road is rocky and hilly and should only be used by hikers and high-clearance four-wheel drive vehicles. Medano Pass is just over a mile from the meadow. The most popular activity for licensed vehicles is to continue down the other side, through the Great Sand Dunes and out to Highway 160.

Directions from, Walsenburg: Take State Hwy 69 west 36 miles, through Gardner to County Road 559. Turn west and follow the road approximately 8.5 miles to the summit of Medano Pass. The last 2.5 miles require a high-clearance four-wheel drive.

Directions from Gardner: Travel northwest from Gardner on Highway 69 until you see County Road 559 on your left. Turn here for about 6 miles you will he traveling through private property. Shortly after entering the National Forest boundary you will arrive at a parking area where Forest Road 412 and 559 meet. All two-wheel drive vehicles must stop here. High-clearance four-wheel drive vehicles may continue to Medano Pass. Licensed vehicles may drive down to the Great Sand Dunes.

Road Name	Road Number	Length Miles	Difficulty	Beginning Elevation	Ending Elev.	Usage	Ranger District
Willow Park	350	15	Easy/Diff.	9,000'	10,400'	Moderate	Divide

Difficulty: Easy to Difficult.
USGS Maps: South Fork East, Del Norte Peak, Summitville.

From Willow Park, you can go west down the Beaver Creek to South Fork, or east to Crystal Lakes and down the Pinos Creek Road. There is a good chance of seeing deer or elk along this route, especially during the early morning or late afternoon. There is a good fishing in Willow Creek along the first 4 miles of road, and ample camping spots along the entire route. The first 7.5 miles is passable with a high clearance two wheel drive vehicle, but the last 7.5 miles should be in a 4 wheel-drive.

Directions from Del Norte: Go west on US Hwy 160 for 13.5 miles to the Del Norte Peak Road (FDR 345). Go south on FDR 345 for 3 miles until you come to the junction of roads FDR 345 and FDR 350, take FDR 350. On FDR 350, it is 4 miles to Willow Park and 7.5 miles to the Cross Creek Road (FDR 359). Take FDR 359 to the south 5.5 miles to FDR 332.

Rio Grande Map 13

196

Road Name	Road Number	Length Miles	Difficulty	Beginning Elevation	Ending Elev.	Usage	Ranger District
Bear Creek	331	4	Difficult	9,780'	10,560'	Heavy	Divide

Ending Elevation: 10,560 Feet - At Ruston Park.
USGS Maps: Del Norte Peak.

Parts of this road are very rough and steep. This is heavily used during big game hunting season.

Direction from Del Norte: On the west edge of Del Norte, take County Road 14A, which turns into FDR 14 for 13.5 miles from Del Norte, to Elk Park where FDR 331 takes off. Take FDR 331 for about 4 miles to Ruston Park where the road dead-ends.

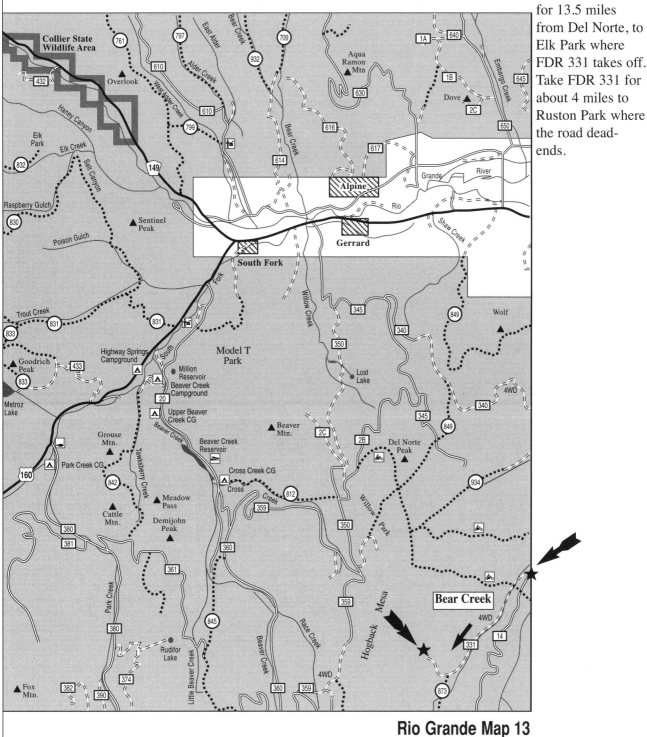

Rio Grande Map 13

24. Schrader Creek

Rio Grande

Road Name	Road Number	Length Miles	Difficulty	Beginning Elevation	Ending Elev.	Usage	Ranger District
Schrader Creek	333	7.5	Easy/Mod	8,440'	10,100'	Moderate	Divide

Beginning Elevation: Junction of the Pinos Creek Road (FDR 330) and Schrader Creek Road (FDR 333).
Ending Elevation: 7.5 miles up Schrader Creek from the Pinos Creek Road.
USGS Map: Horseshoe.

The attraction of this road is wildlife viewing and hunting access. On Schrader Creek, there are numerous camping spots.

Directions from Del Norte: Go about 7.5 miles on the Pinos Creek Road (FDR 14), (Country Road 14A) to the Schrader Creek Road (FDR 333) and turn north onto Road FDR 333.

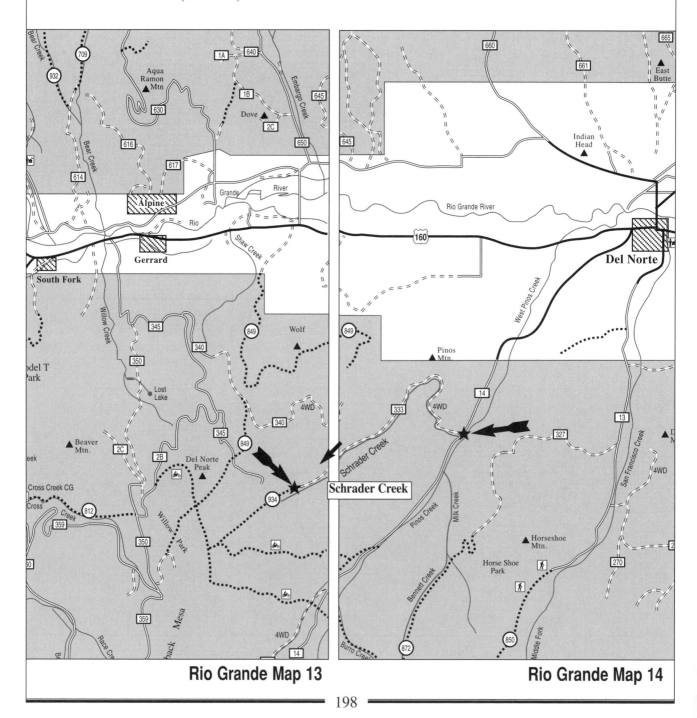

Rio Grande Map 13

Rio Grande Map 14

Road Name	Road Number	Length Miles	Difficulty	Beginning Elevation	Ending Elev.	Usage	Ranger District
Swale Lake	374	6	Easy/Mod	9,200'	9,700'	Moderate	Divide

USGS Maps: Beaver Creek Reservoir, Elwood Pass.

This road switches back and forth through the old Park Creek burn that burned 600 acres in 1960. You can see how the new young forest has established itself. Just before you get back to the Park Creek Road, you will pass Swale Lake. At this time, there are no fish in this lake. It is a pretty spot for a picnic or a camping spot.

Directions from South Fork: Go southwest on U.S. Hwy 160 for 7.5 miles to the Park Creek Road (FDR 380). Turn south on FDR 380 and go about 7 miles to FDR 374. Follow the main road (FDR 374) until it takes you back to the Park Creek Road (FDR 380).

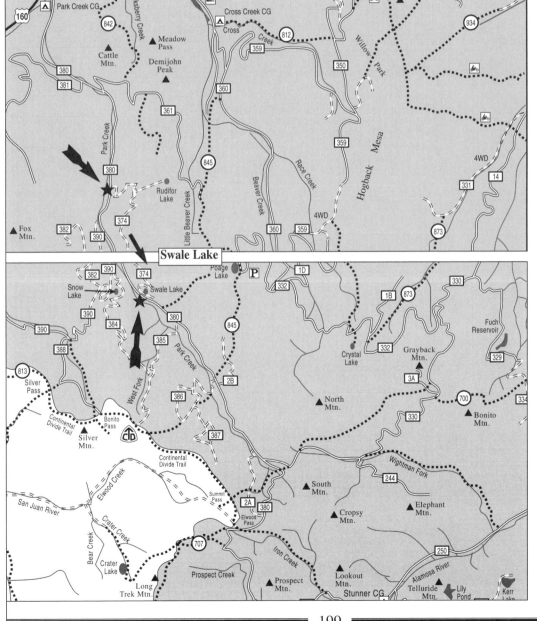

Rio Grande Map 13

Rio Grande Map 16

Road Name	Road Number	Length Miles	Difficulty	Beginning Elevation	Ending Elev.	Usage	Ranger District
Pass Creek	390	4	Mod/Diff	9,200'	10,200'	Moderate	Divide

Difficulty: Moderate to Difficult.
USGS Maps: Beaver Creek Reservoir, Elwood Pass.

This road can be very treacherous when wet and should be avoided during rainstorms or when wet. The road does not normally open until late June or early July. The main attraction of this road is the wildlife and scenic country viewing.

Directions from South Fork: Go southwest on Highway 160 for about 7.5 miles to the Park Creek Road (FDR 380). Turn south on Road FDR 380 and go about 7.5 miles to Trail Park where FDR 390 takes off to the southwest. When you come to the junction of 390 and 382, stay to the left on FDR 390. The road junctions with FDR 388 at Campo Molino. Stay on FDR 390 and go past Tucker Ponds and back to U.S. Highway 160. FDR 388 dead ends at Bonita Pass. There is a trailhead that takes you to the Continental Divide.

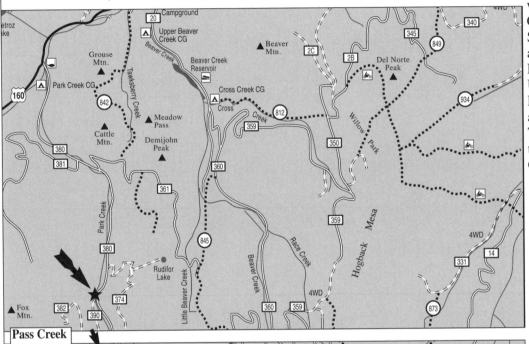

**Rio Grande
Map 13**

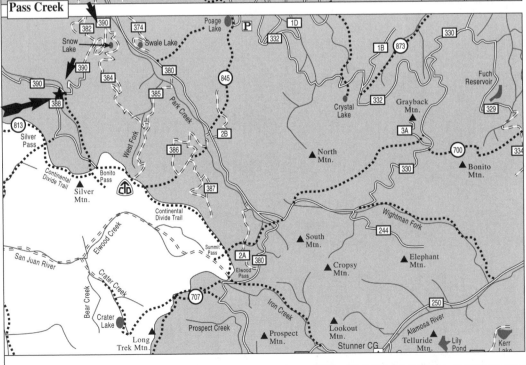

**Rio Grande
Map 16**

Road Name	Road Number	Length Miles	Difficulty	Beginning Elevation	Ending Elev.	Usage	Ranger District
Cedar Springs	327	7	Easy/Mod.	8,640'	9,850'	Moderate	Divide

Difficulty: Easy-Moderate.
Beginning Elevation: At the junction of FDR 320 and FDR 327.
Ending Elevation: Below Horseshoe Park in the aspen.
USGS Maps: Horseshoe Mountain, Dog Mountain.

The first 1.5 miles of Forest Road 327 is through a private land subdivision. Please be sure to close the gates. There is a herd of antelope and lots of deer in this low Pinion Juniper country.

Directions from Del Norte: Take the San Francisco Creek Road (County Road 13) south to the Forest boundary where the road becomes FDR 13. It is about 2.5 miles on FDR 13 to the junction of FDR 327, turn west on FDR 327, the road dead ends about 7 miles ahead. The first 1.5 miles of FDR 327 is through private a subdivision be sure to close the gates.

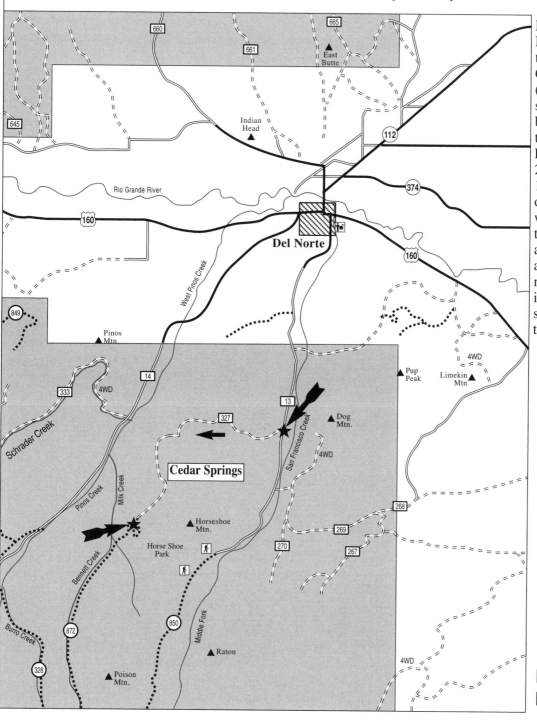

**Rio Grande
Map 14**

Road Name	Road Number	Length Miles	Difficulty	Beginning Elevation	Ending Elev.	Usage	Ranger District
Kerr Lake	257	3.6	Easy	10,541'	11,400'	Moderate	Conejos Peak

Beginning Elevation: Summit of Stunner Pass on Alamosa River Road 250.
Ending Elevation: Kerr Lake.
USGS Maps: Platoro, Summitville.

The Kerr Lake Road heads north from the summit of Stunner Pass. The road follows the side of a ridge, passing through stands of spruce/fir. After reaching the top of the ridge the road turns east and comes into an alpine meadow. From this point, Telluride Mountain can be seen to the northeast. At about the 2-mile mark Lily Pond is just north of the road. The road continues to the east, briefly passing between alpine meadows and conifer stands. There is excellent fishing (with restrictions) at Kerr Lake with good campsites available. The Kerr Lake Road offers a spectacular vista of Alamosa River Canyon and Continental Divide.

Directions from Monte Vista: Proceed south on the Gunbarrel Road, State Hwy 15, for 12 miles. Turn west onto the Alamosa River Road (FDR 250) and proceed approximately 29 miles to the junction of Kerr Lake Road (FDR 257).

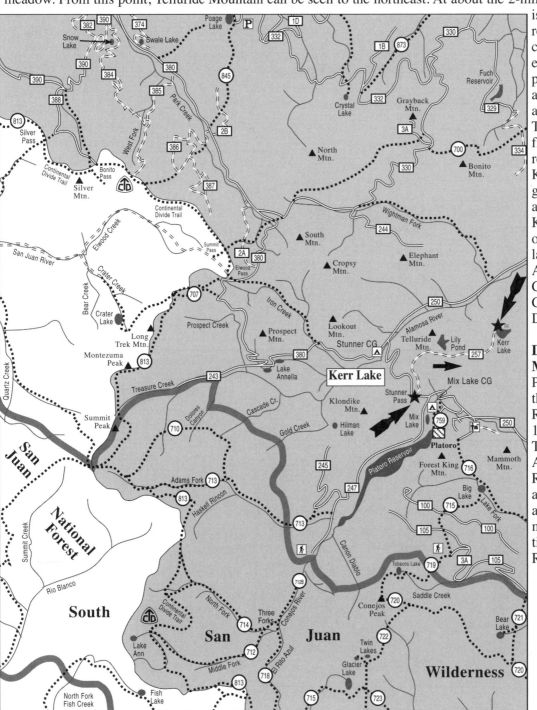

Rio Grande Map 16

Road Name	Road Number	Length Miles	Difficulty	Beginning Elevation	Ending Elev.	Usage	Ranger District
Spring Creek	280	4.3	Moderate	9,160'	11,800'	Moderate	Conejos Peak

USGS Maps: Jasper.

This fairly well traveled road begins .5 miles west of the historic mining town of Jasper. The road was once used by miners who led burro trains over the pass down Burro Creek to Los Pinos Creek and Del Norte.

A loop can be made starting from Alamosa going up the Alamosa Canyon, over Blowout Pass and returning to Alamosa by way of Del Norte.

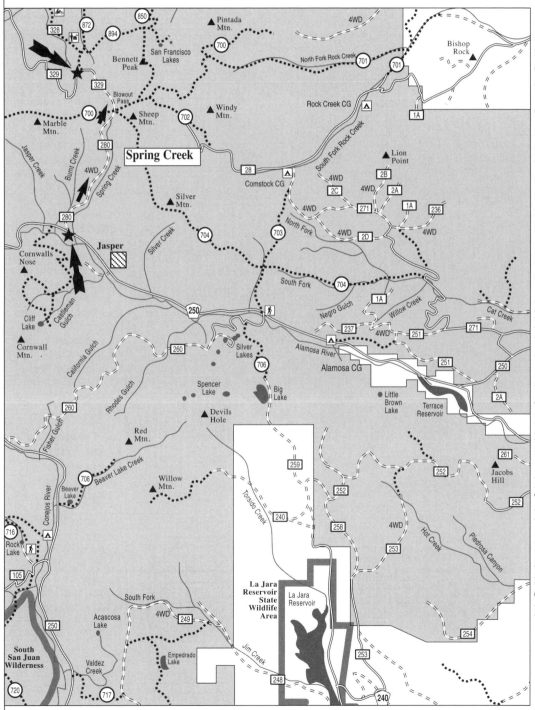

Spring Creek Road is a steep narrow road with little clearance for vehicles.

The road begins by making a very gradual climb through stands of aspen. At approximately .75 mile, the road begins climbing a steep grade and is soon traversing narrow rocky slopes.

Directions from Monte Vista: Take the Gunbarrel Road (State Road 15)south 12 miles to the Alamosa Canyon Road FDR 250. Proceed 22.5 miles west to Spring Creek Road.

From Del Norte: Take the Pinos Road (FDR 330), 18 miles to FDR 329. Proceed east approximately 12 miles to the Conejos Peak District Boundary.

Rio Grande Map 17

Road Name	Road Number	Length Miles	Difficulty	Beginning Elevation	Ending Elev.	Usage	Ranger District
Silver Lakes Toll Road	260	12.2	Easy	8,760'	9,800'	Moderate	Conejos Peak

USGS Maps: Jasper, Red Mountain.

Silver Lakes Toll Road FDR 260 is a maintained road but becomes very slick during wet periods.

Though this provides a short link between Alamosa and Platoro, due to road conditions, the time required to travel this route is the same as using FDR 250.

This toll road was originally built and used as a supply road by miners. Crossing over Cornwall Mountain, it provided access to mining camps along the Conejos River Canyon and Platoro.

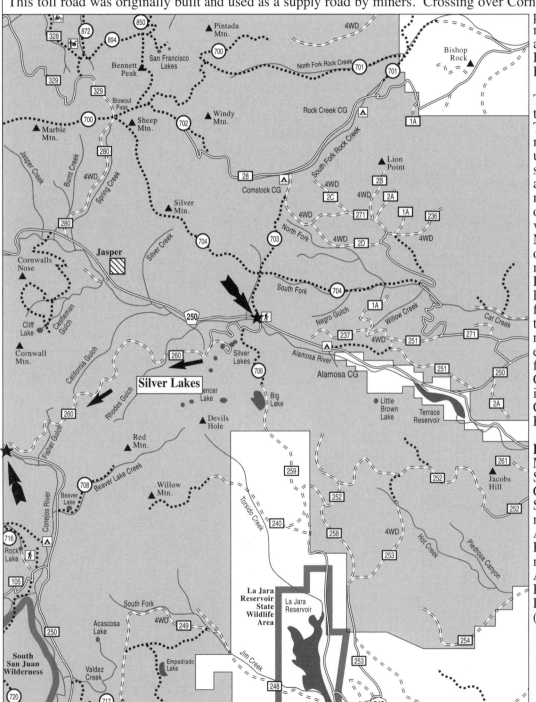

The road begins at the Alamosa River. The road begins to make a very gradual climb though spruce/fir and aspen stands and a number of meadows. Occasional views of Red Mountain are offered from the meadows. The Big Lake Trailhead is located .5 miles from the start of the road. The road reaches its highest elevation of 10,500 feet at Fisher Gulch, then begins its descent to the Conejos River.

Directions from Monte Vista: South on the Gunbarrel Road, State Hwy 15, 12 miles to the Alamosa Canyon Road. Sixteen miles west on the Alamosa Canyon Road is the Silver Lakes Toll Road (FDR 260) turnoff.

Rio Grande Map 17

Road Name	Road Number	Length Miles	Difficulty	Beginning Elevation	Ending Elev.	Usage	Ranger District
Bancos Loop	249	16.25	Easy/Diff	9,760'	9,960'	Moderate	Conejos Peak

Length, Round Trip: 16.25 Miles.
USGS Maps: La Jara Canyon, Red Mountain, and Spectacle Lake.

The Bancos Road (FDR 249) is a loop road and offers a pleasant drive through some of the districts lower foothill country. The southern section of the road is passable with a two-wheel vehicle during the dry season. The northern section should only be driven with a four-wheel drive vehicle. Caution should be exercised during the wet seasons. Numerous campsites are located along the road.

The Bancos Road leaves the southern end of La Jara Reservoir and travels southwest for .25 mile through a small stand of spruce/fir. The road then turns west and follows the northern edge of Chicago Bogs for approximately 2 miles. The Chicago Bogs are an area of large meadows bisected by Jarosa Creek with scattered potholes. At this point the road turns south and follows Jarosa Creek for approximately 3 miles. The road crosses Jarosa Creek, turns west for approximately 2 miles to the Bancos Cow Camp.

After leaving the Bancos Cow Camp, the road turns north and enters long narrow meadows surrounded by spruce/fir and aspen forests. During wet seasons the next 4.25 miles of road can be hazardous. When the road reaches the South Fork of Jim Creek it turns east. The last 3.25 miles of road should be driven only with a 4-WD vehicle because the road is narrow, steep and very rough. The road begins to follow the creek drainage down toward La Jara Meadows and comes into the meadows just below Jim Creek Cow Camp.

Directions from Centro: Take the La Jara Reservoir Road west to La Jara Reservoir, proceed to the southern end of the reservoir. The southern section of the Bancos Road intersects the La Jara Reservoir at this point. To access the northern section of the Bancos Road, continue from this intersection northwest on FDR 248 approximately 4 miles to the junction of Bancos Road (FDR 249).

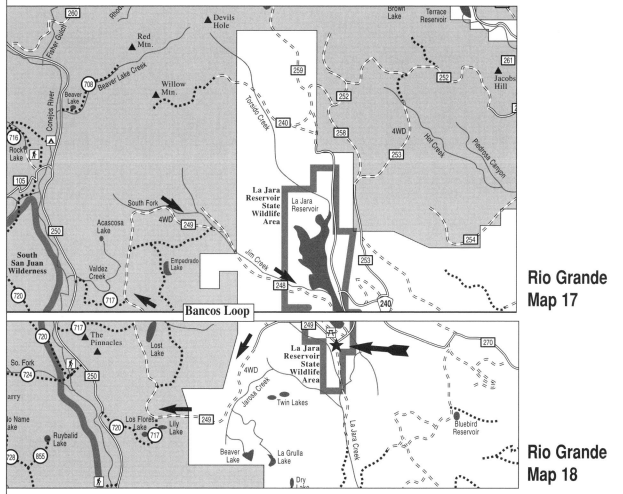

Rio Grande Map 17

Rio Grande Map 18

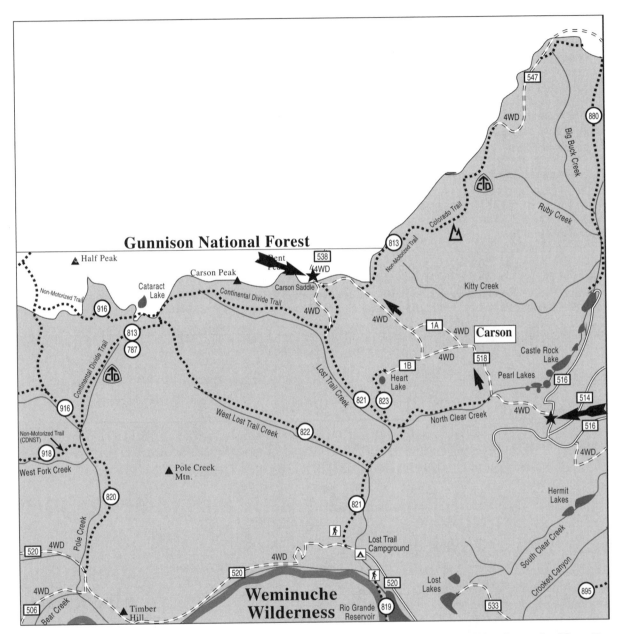

Rio Grande Map 7

Road Name	Road Number	Length Miles	Difficulty	Beginning Elevation	Ending Elev.	Usage	Ranger District
Carson	518	9.5	Moderate	10,600'	12,360'	Moderate	Divide

Ending Elevation: At Carson Saddle on the Continental Divide.
High Point: 13,l00 Feet.
USGS Map: Finger Mesa.

The Carson Road begins just above Pearl Lakes (private property) and turns off Pearl Lakes Road (FDR 516) to the west-southwest. The road weaves its way through a short stretch of timber before breaking out into the open and crossing the North Clear Creek drainage. The road then begins to climb through spruce-fir timber for about 1 mile and then breaks into the open again until its junction with a short 2.5 mile loop segment (FDR 518.1A). The road turns off the main road to the north about 3 miles from the beginning of the road. This loop segment travels north for a distance and then turns back to the southwest and rejoins the main Carson Road FDR 518 approximately 1.3 miles further up the main road from this junction.

From this junction the main Carson Road (FDR 518) continues to the west until its junction with Heart Lake Road (FDR 518.1B), a little over 4 miles from its beginning. At this junction the Carson Road runs to the north and climbs through a small stand of trees and breaks into the open above timberline following a ridge to its high point (13,100 feet) just south of Coney Peak (13,339 feet). The road affords magnificent views of distant meadows, mountains, and other terrain features.

From this high point, the road turns to the west and drops the remaining mile to the Carson Saddle. As this same point, the north and northeast, the La Garita Stock Driveway Trail (FDT 787) (which also is the Colorado Trail and the Continental Divide Trail) travels on towards Coney. This trail to Coney is a non-motorized trail, and is open for foot and horse use only.

The Carson Road generally poses no problems for vehicles when the roadbed is dry and firm. However, there are some steep and rough sections along the route. Portions of the road can become soft and slick during periods of rain or snow making travel unsure and sometimes risky.

A 1.3 mile trip over the divide down Wager Gulch Road FDR 568 (located on the Gunnison National Forest) toward Lake City to the old mining camp is certainly worth taking.

The 4-wheel drive road continues downs Wager Gulch (total distance 5 miles) until its junction with Lake Fork Road (FDR 306) which serves as vehicle access to Lake City approximately 10.8 miles to the northeast.

Directions from Creede: Approximately 23.7 miles west of Creede on Colorado Highway 149 turns west onto Hermit Lakes Road FDR 515 directly across the highway from Silver Thread Campground. Travel approximately 4 miles on the Hermit Lakes Road to the junctions of Pearl Lake Road FDR 516. At this junction, turn right (northwest) onto the Pearl Lakes Road and travel approximately 4 miles to the junction of Carson Road (FDR 518). Turn left (west-southwest) onto Carson Road (FDR 518).

SAN JUAN NATIONAL FOREST

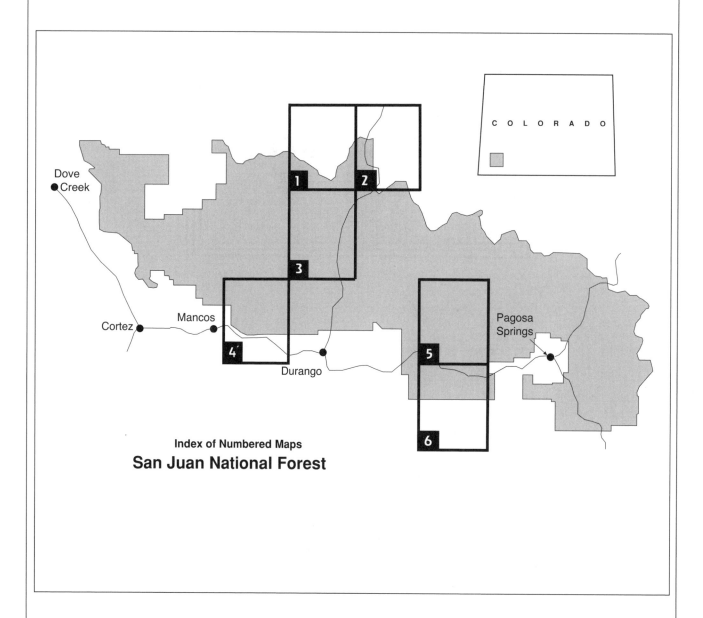

Index of Numbered Maps
San Juan National Forest

SAN JUAN NATIONAL FOREST

San Juan National Forest is located north of Durango in southwestern Colorado on the western slope of the Continental Divide. It covers an area from east to west of more than 120 miles and from north to south more than 60 miles, encompassing an area of 1,869,931 acres.

Alpine lakes, canyons, cataracts, waterfalls, unusual geologic formations, historic mines, and broad variations in elevation characterize this area. Archeological ruins of the Anasazi are preserved at Chimney Rock.

The Needle Mountains, a paradise for mountain climbers and one of the roughest ranges in the United States, lie within the Weminuche Wilderness. Three of these peaks rise to more than 14,000 feet above sea level. Within the Lizard Head Wilderness are three more peaks greater than 14,000 feet in elevation. These areas are accessible only by trail for foot or horse back use. Numerous campgrounds and picnic sites are scattered through the Forest.

Fishing for trout in high mountain lakes, swift streams, or reservoirs such as McPhee, Vallecito, Lemon and Williams Creek Lake offer the angler many challenges. Hunters stalk mule deer, elk, bear, bighorn sheep, mountain lion, grouse, turkey and ducks.

WEMINUCHE WILDERNESS

Weminuche is located in southwestern Colorado within the San Juan and Rio Grande National Forests. Scenic alpine territory, containing some of the most rugged and majestic peaks in the continental United States, lies within the Weminuche Wilderness. Encompassing nearly 460,000 acres.

Extending along the Continental Divide from the East Needle Mountains to the headwaters of the West Fork of the San Juan River, scores of peaks rise to well over 13,000 feet in elevation. Windom Peak, 14,091, Mount Eolus, 14,086, and Sunlight Peak, 14.060, are the highest in the Needle Mountains. Their remoteness and challenging climbs have made the area a mecca for mountain climbers and outdoor enthusiasts seeking primitive conditions and a degree of challenge.

Much of the area is above timberline with characteristic shallow soils. The average elevation is greater than 10,000 feet and ranges from 8,000 to more than 14,000 feet. At higher elevations in July, expect to encounter some snowbanks. However, almost all trails will be open for both horse and foot travel by the first of July. Precipitation varies from 27 to 45 inches annually, and temperatures range from highs of 80 degrees Fahrenheit to lows of minus 30 degrees Fahrenheit. Much of the area experiences continuous frost and there are numerous semi-permanent snow packs.

LIZARD HEAD WILDERNESS

The Lizard Head Wilderness, though smaller at 41,000 acres, also offers interesting and scenic trips. Within the wilderness, the San Miguel Mountains consist of two distinct clusters of peaks.

The eastern cluster, informally referred to as the Wilson Group, is the larger it contains several peaks greater than 14,000 feet. Mount Wilson, 14,245 feet; El Diente Peak, 14,159 feet; Wilson Peak, 14,017 feet; and an unnamed summit on the spur south of Mount Wilson, is known locally as South Wilson, 14,110 feet. Scarcely less imposing is Gladstone Peak, 13,913 feet. At somewhat lower elevation, about two miles east, is the spectacular landmark of Lizard Head, a nearly vertical rock spire which rises 300 feet from a conical base to 13,113 feet.

The area has short, cool summers and long, severe winters. There are several permanent snowfields, and snow patches remain in sheltered areas throughout the summer. You should be prepared for freezing weather at all times of the year.

SOUTH SAN JUAN WILDERNESS

The South San Juan Wilderness covers more than 127,000 acres of spectacular mountainous terrain in the San Juan and Rio Grande National Forests. The Wilderness straddles the Continental Divide south of the famed Wolf Creek Pass, offering high tundra, sweeping vistas, and solitude.

Elevations within the wilderness range from 8,000 feet to greater than 13,000 feet. Engelmann spruce and aspen forests cover nearly half of the area, with the rest made up of open grasslands, alpine tundra, and rocky or barren areas.

Recreation use is light in the South San Juan compared with the Weminuche. Big game hunting, hiking, horseback riding, camping, viewing the scenery, and cross-country skiing are popular. Wildlife that may be observed by visitors or hunted in season include elk, mule deer, bighorn sheep, turkey and black bear.

Road Name	Road Number	Length Miles	Difficulty	Beginning Elevation	Ending Elev.	Usage	Ranger District
South Mineral	585	3.5	Moderate	10,100'	11,789'	Moderate	Columbine

South Mineral Road FDR 585.
Length: 3.5 Miles, from Campground to dead end.
USGS Maps: Ophir, Silverton.

Provides access to trails FDT 507 which intersects the Colorado Trail.

Directions from Durango: North on Highway 550 to Silverton. South Mineral Road is located just west of Silverton is passable by two-wheel drive vehicles to South Mineral Campground. 4 WD vehicles are recommended beyond the campground.

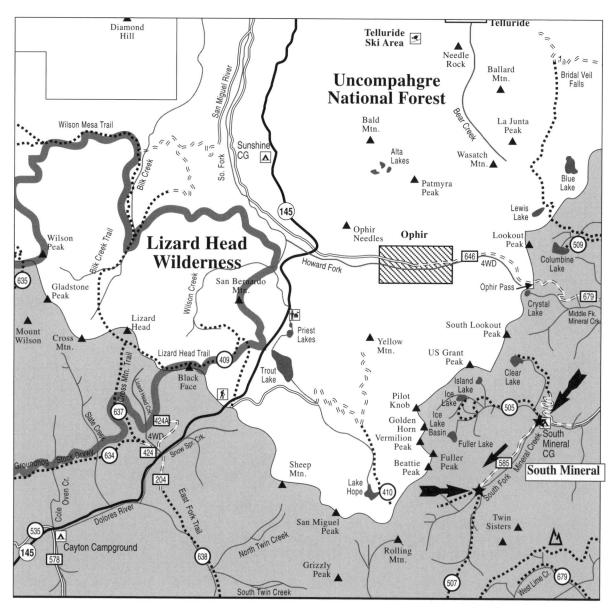

San Juan Map 1

Road Name	Road Number	Length Miles	Difficulty	Beginning Elevation	Ending Elev.	Usage	Ranger District
Ophir Pass	646/679	4	Easy	9,750'	11,789'	Heavy	

San Juan (Columbine Ranger District)/Uncompahgre National Forests (Norwood Ranger District).
Length from Ophir: 4 miles to summit, 10 miles to Highway 550.
Beginning Elevation: At the town of Ophir.
Ending Elevation: Summit of Ophir Pass, the boundary of Uncompahgre and San Juan National Forests.
USGS Maps: Ophir, Ophir Pass.

This is an easier 4-wheel drive road. The west side is mostly slide rock while the east side on the San Juan National Forest is more tundra and timber. The road is very narrow and passing is a problem. Vehicle traveling uphill has the right of way. Vehicle traveling downhill should back up or turn out at wide spots. Few streams crossings, no difficult switchbacks and decent tread makes this an enjoyable drive.

Ophir Pass is an old toll road built by Otto Mears. It was the closest route between the Telluride/Ophir area and Silverton. The pass connects Highway 145 at Ophir Loop and Highway 550 near Silverton. During summer and early fall the route is used by local people as a shortcut. It saves many miles.

Directions from Telluride: Travel south on Highway 145 approximately 10 miles to Ophir Loop. East (left) through Ophir to begin trip.

Directions from Silverton: Northeast on Hwy 110 for 9 miles. Road offers access to Cunningham Gulch, Minnie Gulch and Maggie Gulch and old mining sites. Four-Wheel drive vehicles are advisable for upper portions of these roads.

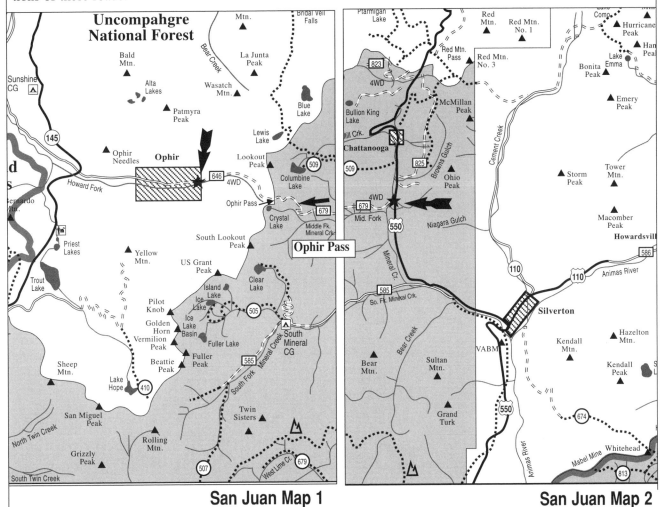

San Juan Map 1   **San Juan Map 2**

Road Name	Road Number	Length Miles	Difficulty	Beginning Elevation	Ending Elev.	Usage	Ranger District
Hermosa Park	578	22	Moderate	9,365'	11,000'	Moderate	Mancos/Dolores

Hermosa Park Road (Bolam Pass).
USGS Maps: Mount Wilson, Hermosa Peak, Engineer Mtn.

From Cayton Campground there are 4.0 miles of single lane gravel road. The road then turns steep and rocky as is climbs up the Barlow Creek drainage. Four-wheel-drive will make the climb easier on the vehicle and you. Near the top, which is called Bolam Pass, you will find outstanding scenery including an overlook of the East Fork of the Dolores River and an excellent view of Lizard Head Peak and the Lizard Head Wilderness. Incredible views of the Hermosa Peak area are also offered as the climb up the Barlow Creek is made.

The top of the East Fork trail can be located approximately .25 mile past the overlook. The Colorado Trail can be accessed near Graysill Lake. Access to the Colorado Trial is also available by hiking off of Forest Road 578. The elevation on Bolam Pass is 11,000 feet.

From Bolam Pass, you have several options, you can proceed on to Purgatory and Durango or you can go to the junction with FDR 550. The latter option will take you to Hotel Draw and a return trip to Colorado Hwy 145 via Scotch Creek Road or Roaring Fork Road. The first part of the road from Bolam Pass is narrow and has sharp, steep switchback corners which may be slick when wet. You will pass a historic marker noting the Graysill Mine.

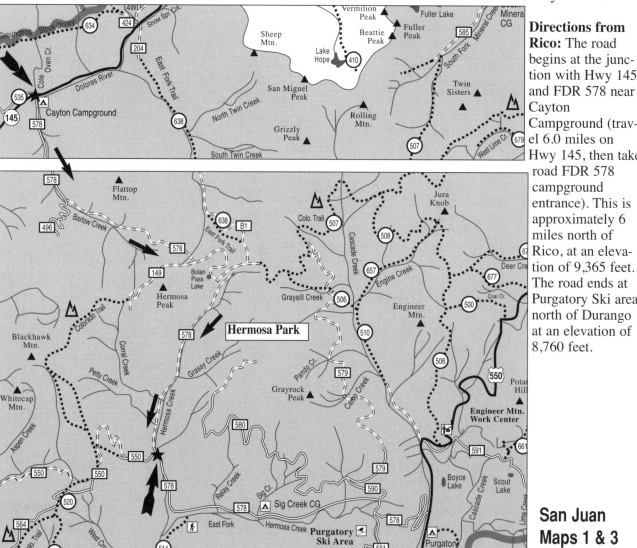

Directions from Rico: The road begins at the junction with Hwy 145 and FDR 578 near Cayton Campground (travel 6.0 miles on Hwy 145, then take road FDR 578 campground entrance). This is approximately 6 miles north of Rico, at an elevation of 9,365 feet. The road ends at Purgatory Ski area north of Durango at an elevation of 8,760 feet.

**San Juan
Maps 1 & 3**

San Juan

Road Name	Road Number	Length Miles	Difficulty	Beginning Elevation	Ending Elev.	Usage	Ranger District
Kennebec Pass	571	16	Moderate	8,600'	11,880'	Moderate	Columbine

Beginning Elevation at Forest boundary.
USGS Maps: La Plata, Heperus.

This is not a through road, you must return the way you came. The last 5 miles requires 4WD vehicle.

Colorado Trail, Highline (FDT 607) and Sharkstooth trail (FDT 607 C) can be accessed from road.

Directions from Durango: Travel west on Highway 160 to Hesperus. Turn right onto La Plata Canyon Road. The road leads to the top of Kennebec Pass.

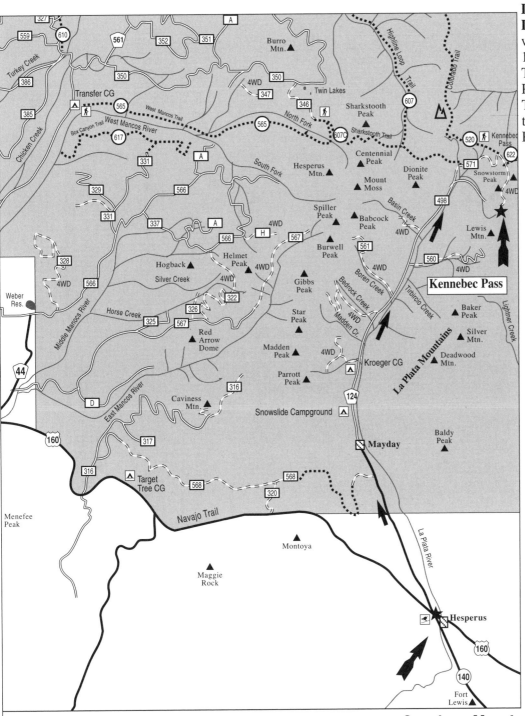

San Juan Map 4

San Juan Map 5

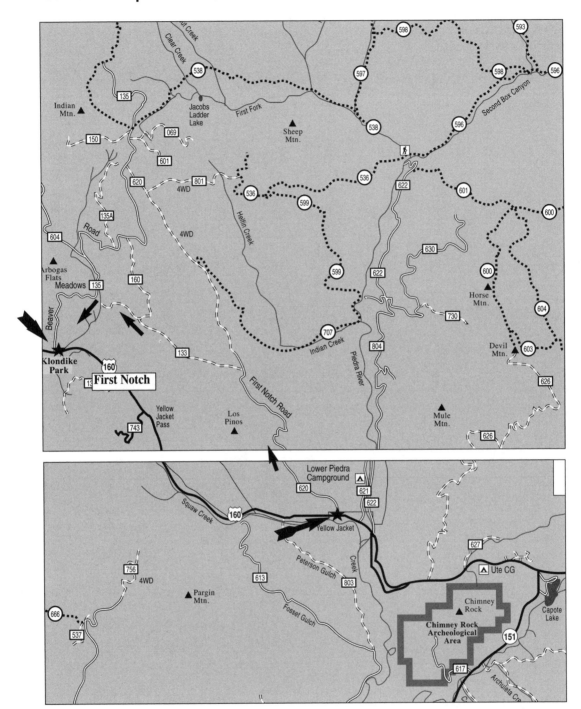

San Juan Map 6

Road Name	Road Number	Length Miles	Difficulty	Beginning Elevation	Ending Elev.	Usage	Ranger District
First Notch	620	19	Moderate	7,400'	7,400'	Moderate	Columbine

USGS Maps: Baldy Mountain, Granite Peak, Chimney Rock, Pargin Mtn.

Various four-wheel drive roads take off from First Notch Road (FDR 620) and Beaver Meadows Road (FDR 135). Please take a map or be familiar with your route. Roads closed seasonally and during poor weather conditions. Roads may be slippery when wet. Please be prepared.

Directions from Bayfield: Take U.S. Highway 160, 8 miles east to Beaver Meadows Road (FDR 135) or take U.S. Highway 160 18 miles east to First Notch Road (FDR 620).

NATIONAL FOREST	PHONE NO.

NATIONAL FOREST SERVICE WEBSITE
www.fs.fed.us

APAPAHO/ROOSEVELT NATIONAL FOREST
BOULDER RANGER DISTRICT . . . . (303) 541-2500
CANYON LAKES RANGER DISTRICT . . . . (970) 295-6600
CLEAR CREEK RANGER DISTRICT . . . . (303) 567-3000
PAWNEE RANGER DISTRICT . . . . (970) 346-5000
SULPHUR RANGER DISTRICT . . . . (970) 887-4100

GRAND MESA NATIONAL FOREST
COLLBRAN RANGER DISTRICT . . . . (970) 487-3534
GRAND JUNCTION RANGER DISTRICT . . . . (970) 242-8211

GUNNISON NATIONAL FOREST
GUNNISON RANGER DISTRICT . . . . (970) 641-0471
PAONIA RANGER DISTRICT . . . . (970) 527-4131

PIKE NATIONAL FOREST
PIKES PEAK RANGER DISTRICT . . . . (719) 636-1602
SOUTH PARK RANGER DISTRICT . . . . (719) 836-2031
SOUTH PLATTE RANGER DISTRICT . . . . (303) 275-5610

RIO GRANDE/SAN JUAN NATIONAL FOREST
CONEJOS PEAK RANGER DISTRICT . . . . (719) 274-8971
DIVIDE RANGER DISTRICT (Creede) . . . . (719) 658-2556
DIVIDE RANGER DIST. (Del Norte) . . . . (719) 657-3321
SAGUACHE RANGER DISTRICT . . . . (719) 655-2547

ROUTT NATIONAL FOREST
HAHNS PEAK/BEAR EARS RANGER DIST. . . . . (970) 879-1870
THE PARKS RANGER DISTRICT . . . . (970) 723-8204
YAMPA RANGER DISTRICT . . . . (970) 638-4516

SAN ISABEL NATIONAL FOREST
LEADVILLE RANGER DISTRICT . . . . (719) 486-0749
SALIDA RANGER DISTRICT . . . . (719) 539-3591
SAN CARLOS RANGER DISTRICT . . . . (719) 269-8500

SAN JUAN/RIO GRANDE NATIONAL FOREST
COLUMBINE EAST RANGER DIST(BAYFIELD) . (970) 884-2512
COLUMBINE WEST RANGER DIST (DURANGO) (970) 884-2512
MANCOS/DOLORES RANGER DIST. . . . . (970) 882-7296
PAGOSA RANGER DISTRICT . . . . (970) 264-2268

UNCOMPAHGRE NATIONAL FOREST
GRAND JUNCTION RANGER DISTRICT . . . . (970) 242-8211
NORWOOD RANGER DISTRICT . . . . (970) 327-4261
OURAY RANGER DISTRICT . . . . (970) 240-5300

WHITE RIVER NATIONAL FOREST
ASPEN RANGER DISTRICT . . . . (970) 925-3445
BLANCO RANGER DISTRICT . . . . (970) 878-4039
DILLON RANGER DISTRICT . . . . (970) 468-5400
EAGLE RANGER DISTRICT . . . . (970) 328-6388
HOLY CROSS RANGER DISTRICT . . . . (970) 827-5715
RIFLE RANGER DISTRICT . . . . (970) 625-2371
SOPRIS RANGER DISTRICT . . . . (970) 963-2266

REGIONAL FOREST SERVICE OFFICE
LAKEWOOD COLORADO. . . . . (303) 275-5350

AGENCY	PHONE NO.

BUREAU OF LAND MANAGEMENT
www.blm.gov
DOLORES/MANCOS FIELD OFFICE . . . . (970) 385-1207
GRAND JUNCTION FIELD OFFICE . . . . (970) 244-3000
GUNNISON FIELD OFFICE . . . . (970) 641-0471
GLENWOOD SPRINGS FIELD OFFICE . . . . (970) 947-2800
KREMMLING FIELD OFFICE . . . . (970) 724-3000
LA JARA FIELD OFFICE . . . . (719) 274-8971
LITTLE SNAKE FIELD OFFICE . . . . (970) 826-5000
SAGUACHE FIELD OFFICE. . . . . (719) 655-2547
UNCOMPAHGRE BASIN FIELD OFFICE. . . . . . . (970) 240-5300

COLORADO DIVISION OF WILDLIFE
www.wildlife.state.co.us/swa/
DOW HEADQUARTERS, DENVER. . . . . (303) 297-1192
NORTHEAST REGION, DENVER . . . . (303) 291-7227
NORTHWEST REGION, GRAND JUNCTION . . . . . (970) 255-6100
SOUTHEAST REGION, COLORADO SPRINGS . . . . (719) 227-5200
SOUTHWEST REGION, DURANGO . . . . (970) 247-0855

COLORADO STATE PARKS
www.parks.state.co.us/
DIRECTORS OFFICE, DENVER . . . . (303) 866-3437
SOUTH REGION, COLORADO SPRINGS . . . . (719) 227-5250
WEST REGION, CLIFTON . . . . (970) 434-6862

U.S. FISH AND WILDLIFE SERVICE
BROWNS PARK NATIONAL WILDLIFE REFUGE . . . . (970) 365-3613

NATIONAL PARKS SERVICE
www.nps.gov
BLACK CANYON OF THE GUNNISON . . . . (970) 641-2337
COLORADO NATIONAL MONUMENT . . . . (970) 858-3617
CURECANTI NATIONAL RECREATION AREA . . . . (970) 641-2337
DINOSAUR NATIONAL MONUMENT . . . . (970) 374-3000
GREAT SAND DUNES NATIONAL PARK. . . . . . . (719) 378-6300
MESA VERDE NATIONAL PARK . . . . (970) 529-4465
ROCKY MOUNTAIN NATIONAL PARK. . . . . (970) 586-1206

US GEOL. SURVEY MAP SALES (800) HELP MAP. . . . . (303) 202-4657

CAMPING RESERVATIONS:
NATIONAL FOREST SERVICE . . . . (877) 444-777

STATE PARKS   (From outside Metro Denver Area) . . . . (800) 678-2267
                (From inside Metro Denver Area) . . (303) 470-1144
Note: Reservation period for State Parks, April through September.

NATIONAL PARKS SERVICE. . . . . (800) 365-2267
(Rocky Mountain National Park)

Colorado Outdoor Recreation Information Phone Numbers
• U.S. Forest Service • Bureau of Land Management
• Colorado State Parks • Colorado Div. of Wildlife
• National Parks Service • Other Agencies

SOME BASIC ETHICS OF FOUR-WHEELING. TRAIL BIKE AND ATV USE
Courtesy U.S. Forest Service

- Vehicles traveling uphill have the right of way.

- Leave the land and its vegetation as you find it. Limiting travel to established roads will minimize damage to soil and plant life.

- Don't cut switchbacks or drive through meadows or across alpine tundra. Don't spin wheels unnecessarily. Avoid driving in streams or on steep hills with loose soil. Don't harass livestock or wildlife.

- Preserve America's heritage by not disturbing old mining camps, ghost towns, or other historical features. Never remove artifacts of any kind.

- Leave rocks, flowers, wood, antlers, and artifacts in their natural state for others to see and enjoy.

- Respect the rights and property of others. Miners, recreationists, ranchers, fishermen, hunters and others rely on the backcountry for enjoyment and livelihood. Get permission before you cross onto private land. Leave gates as you find them or as they may be posted.

- Take out what you brought in. Encourage others to keep a clean camp by doing more than your share to rid the backcountry of litter.

- Safety and courtesy are contagious. Spread them around!

- Brush up on the history, geology, and ecology of the area. Knowing about it makes a trip more meaningful. There are a number of good books available at your local bookstore.

- During a lightning storm, your safest place is in your rubber tired enclosed cab vehicle. Avoid open ridges, lone trees, and rock outcrops. Seek shelter in dense stands of trees, deep valleys, or at the foot of a cliff.

- Altitude sickness is caused by the lack of oxygen. The symptoms of nausea and headaches can be overcome with deep breathing, rest, and quick energy foods such as dried fruit, candy, or fruit juices. If symptoms persist, move to a lower altitude as soon as possible.

- Proper use of a winch can help reduce adverse environmental impacts on vegetation and the land. Generally, a winch should be used only for emergency situations, to overcome temporary natural barriers, such as fallen trees, landslides, and damaged stream crossings.

- Let someone know where you are going. Riding with a companion or companions adds to the enjoyment and makes good sense from a safety standpoint. Whether riding with someone or not, always let someone know where you are going and when you expect to return. If headed for back country, leave your trip plan with someone who can take action if you don't return as planned. (i.e. Forest Service Office, Sheriff's Office, local four-wheel drive or trail bike club.)

- Be prepared for emergencies --- They don't always happen to the other person. Having spare parts, tools, and adequate clothing will help. For safety sake, take a first aid kit, fire extinguisher, drinking water, flashlight, matches, blankets, and flares.

- DO NOT TRAVEL OFF THE ROAD OR TRAIL UNLESS SPECIFICALLY ALLOWED.

Index

Index

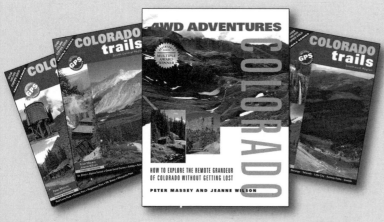

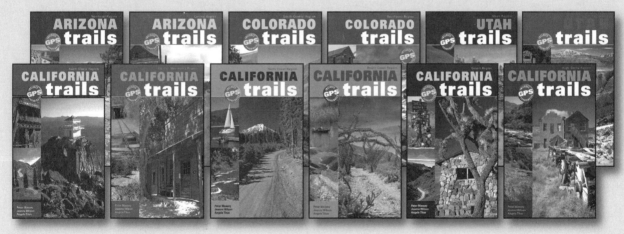